ARCHITECT

THE EVOLVING STORY OF A PROFESSION

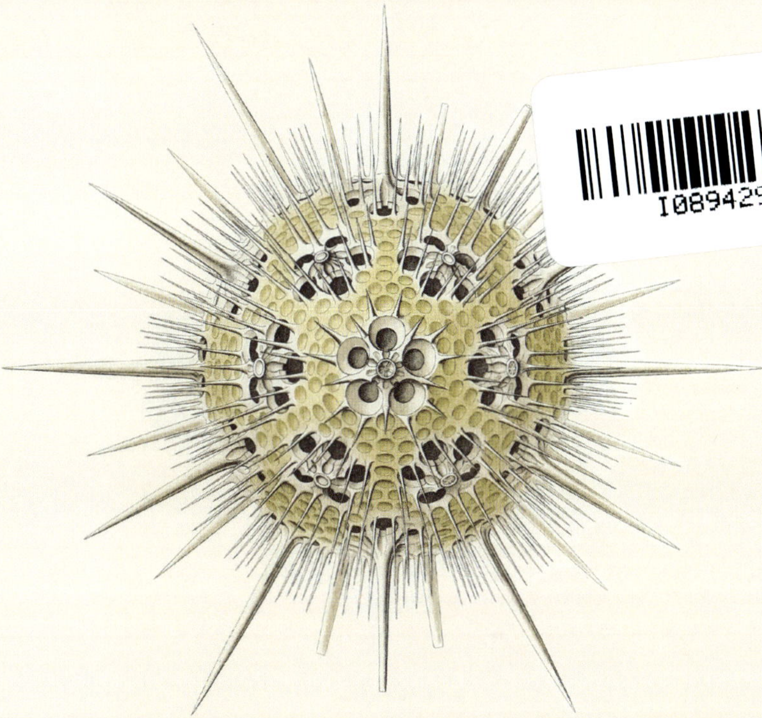

ELEANOR JOLLIFFE AND PAUL CROSBY

RIBA Publishing

Published by RIBA Publishing, 66 Portland Place, London, W1B 1AD

ISBN 978 1 91412 485 3

British Library Cataloguing-in-Publication Data
A catalogue record for this book is available from the British Library.

COMMISSIONING EDITOR: Liz Webster

PRODUCTION: Marie Doinne

DESIGNED AND TYPESET BY mercerdesign.com, London

PRINTED AND BOUND BY Page Bros, Norwich

COVER IMAGE: Ernst Haeckel's original sketches and watercolours engraved by lithographer Adolf Giltsch and published by Bibliographisches Institut between 1899 and 1904. Credit: Private Collection / AF Fotografie

www.ribapublishing.com

Contents

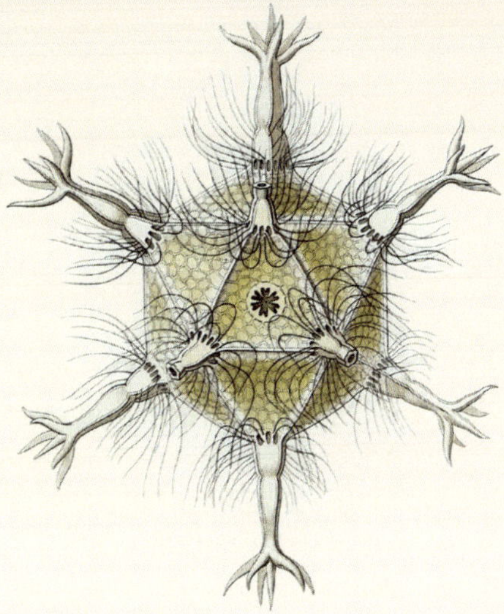

About the Authors

ELEANOR is a practising architect, an Associate at Allies and Morrison and a freelance writer with Master's degrees in engineering and architecture. She has a regular and long-running column in *Building Design* with further published work in the *Architects' Journal, Architectural Review, Dezeen, Unherd* and the Saturated Space research group at the Architectural Association. She was awarded the 2023 Rome Scholarship in Architecture.

Her written work is wide ranging but tends towards the exploration of the intersection between politics, society, history and architectural practice. Her architectural work includes experience in the UK, the Gulf and China with projects ranging in scale from masterplanning and city wide architectural guidelines, to the delivery of new homes and interior joinery design.

PAUL is a full-time academic having joined the Architectural Association in 2017 as Head of Professional Practice Part 3. His role includes advising and supporting all students on their career and professional development.

Prior to joining the AA, Paul was course leader for the MArch and a studio tutor in the BArch at Nottingham Trent University. Paul currently teaches and examines at a number of schools of architecture including the University of Bath, Cardiff University, the University of Westminster and the RIBA.

Paul has over 30 years' experience in practice and has held senior positions in the offices of Fitzroy Robinson Partnership, David Chipperfield Architects, Zaha Hadid Architects and Martha Schwartz Partners. Throughout his career he has mostly worked on international projects in America, China, Italy, Spain, the Middle East and elsewhere. In the mid-1990s he spent two years setting up and running a branch office in Leipzig, Germany.

He has contributed to a number of publications including *The Competition Grid* (RIBA Publishing, 2017), a review of competition practice. In 2018, he was a member of the consultative group of the RIBA Ethics and Sustainable Commission. He is an advocate of fostering closer relationships between academia and practice and has a research interest in the management and ethos of design studios.

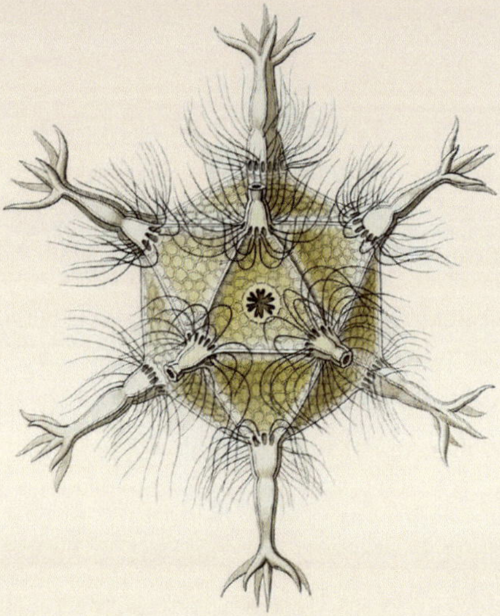

Introduction

From the very first moments of humanity we have had a need for shelter, and have sought to create it where it does not naturally occur. Arguably, the first archaeological evidence of built shelter predates modern humans – the 1.8-million-year-old stone circle structure in the Olduvai Gorge in Tanzania has been proposed as a windbreak or the supports of a crude shelter.[1] By around 400,000 BCE, however, archaeologists are fairly certain that early humans were creating shelter deliberately – with evidence of hearths and post holes at Terra Amata in France.[2]

It does not seem unrealistic to suppose that no matter how early our first forays into construction there was a human or humans who designed them. Someone – let us refer to them as the architect – saw pieces of wood and skin and propped and stretched them into a shelter. We don't know if they sketched their idea in the dust on the ground, if it was a group design or if it was an iterative process of trial and error. However, for a shelter to have been built in the first place the architect had to have imagined it. At its very essence that is what an architect is – someone who imagines built space in response to a need, and guides the process that turns that idea into a built reality.

In this book we have sought to chart the evolution of the architect in the Western world from these very first steps through to the present day in Britain. We glimpse ancient Egyptian architects in the almost religious act of laying foundation stones, then jump across the Mediterranean Sea to discover the quasi-military organisation of Roman architects, and the philosophical yet highly pragmatic practices of the ancient Greek architects. Later, the master masons of medieval Europe amaze us with their skill and breadth of knowledge, and the fiery characters of Italy's Renaissance years awe us with their guile and polymath skills. From here the organisation of French royal architects and the amateur architects of Tudor England give us glimpses of the emergence of a modern profession that crystallised in the fires of Britain's Industrial Revolution. We grapple with comprehending the role of architects in Britain's Empire, and follow them through the horror of two world wars, seeing society ripped apart and reformed. For all of this time, architects continued to imagine and to build, shaping their practice to their circumstances.

Following the world wars we see a 'golden era' of architects given scope to impose their utopian visions as Britain attempted to reinvent itself after the horrors of decades of war and recovery. A backlash against this imposed 'utopia' followed, ushering in our most recent decades of quicksilver technological change and advancement, almost exponential legislative growth and a growing crisis of position. It is tempting, at the beginning of the 2020s, to imagine we are at a watershed moment, a crisis point for the architectural profession. Many now speak of 'lost territory', and some wonder whether the profession in Britain is still viable. But to believe architects are lost is surely to believe that a profession that has been a part of society in some form since the dawn of humanity could be wiped out by a territorial spat with a quantity surveyor.

From the scope of this book – the fact that you can lift it in a single hand – it must be clear that this is not an exhaustive analysis of the profession's evolution. This book is a guide. It will signpost sources and hint at fascinating tangents we could not follow, and that we fervently hope you will. We have sought to narrate this evolution in such a way that you will become as fascinated as we were: don't expect exhaustive footnotes or highly academic language, and do expect the occasional anecdote about arson. We have narrated this story in a way that spoke to us, following the sources and characters that added to the narrative, but always trying to keep them framed within the broader context of their society and circumstances.

Our voices may emerge as you read. We sit towards different ends of our careers and bring two different, though complementary, perspectives to this story. Eleanor is female, in her thirties, and is an associate at Allies and Morrison. She is deeply fascinated by the history of the profession and has led on the writing of the chapters that follow the profession from its beginnings through to the turmoil of the 1980s.

Paul is male, in his sixties, and has been an architect for over 30 years. He has worked for some of the largest names in British architecture over a varied career, and is now Head of Professional Practice at the Architectural Association in London. He is passionate about the future of British architectural professionalism and has used his wealth of personal experience to cast an unflinching gaze over the evolution of the British profession since the 1980s.

The experience of researching and writing this book has caused us to reconsider some of our deeply held assumptions about the profession we both practise. As we have read and conversed our way through the writing process we have discovered divergences, where our experiences and education have caused us to think differently, but common ground has grown steadily between us as we found the historical roots of some of the more damaging aspects of contemporary British architectural education and practice.

We hope though that one voice, one story, will override us both: that of the essence of the architect charting millennia of history and human development. We hope this is a story you will follow, learn from, and maybe one day play a part in yourself.

Eleanor Jolliffe & Paul Crosby
London, 2022

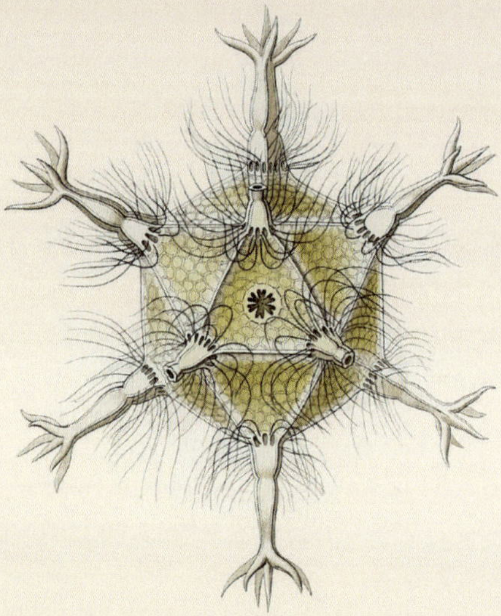

CHAPTER 1

The Ancients

Ancient Egypt: sacred design and significant influence

The ceremony of laying foundations for temples and monuments was considered so sacred in ancient Egypt that only the gods' direct representative on earth, the pharaoh, was able to perform it.[1] Architects were there to add, to embellish, to continue the work of building – but not to begin it, and never to take ownership of the design. A tomb inscription from the architect Menkheperreseneb suggests how this might have looked in practice, describing the laying of the foundation stone for a monument to Thutmose I in c.1455 BCE:

> 'This god [Thutmose III] assumed the station for the extension of the [measuring-line]. He set his majesty before him at this monument, which his majesty had exacted. The majesty of this god rejoiced in this monument [the majesty] of this god proceeded; the beautiful feast was celebrated for my lord. Then I went to do the extending of the measuring-line.'[2]

Figure 1.1 Reconstruction of a foundation deposit – part of the laying of the cord ceremony, c.1479–58 BCE, Metropolitan Museum of Art.

The design of buildings was considered to have been handed directly from the gods to the kings. These divinely inspired designs were then stored in secret books of sacred knowledge to which few people had access.[3] Egyptian society placed little value on architectural originality. However architects, among the few who had access to the sacred architectural plan books, had tremendous social influence and an entry into exalted social circles, moving easily alongside the king and the high echelons of the priesthood. In the theocratic government of ancient Egypt, great power lay in proximity to the priesthood. Architect and vizier Hapnseneb made use of this proximity, becoming the first 'Chief of the Prophets of North and South'. Clearly influential, he is considered the first person in Egyptian history to unite the disparate powers of the nation's priesthoods under a single authority, in c.1480 BCE.[4]

A close, almost intimate, relationship between king and architect can be seen in multiple tomb inscriptions describing architects. For example, Ahmenotep (c.1425–1356 BCE) was described as 'the hereditary prince, count, sole-companion, fan-bearer on the king's right hand, chief of the king's works even all the great monuments which are brought, of every excellent costly stone, steward of the King's daughter. Chief of the prophets of Horus'.[5]

Senmut, Queen Hatshepsut's chief architect in the Eighteenth Dynasty (1550–1292 BCE), was so close to his patron and queen that there are stone portraits of him behind every door in her funerary monument at Deir el-Bahari.[6] He was also known to have raised her daughter, and describes himself in his own tomb as:

> ... foreman of foremen, superior of the great, overseer of all the works of the house of silver, conductor of every handicraft, chief of all the prophets. I was the one whose steps were known in the palace; a real confidant of the [Queen]'.[7]

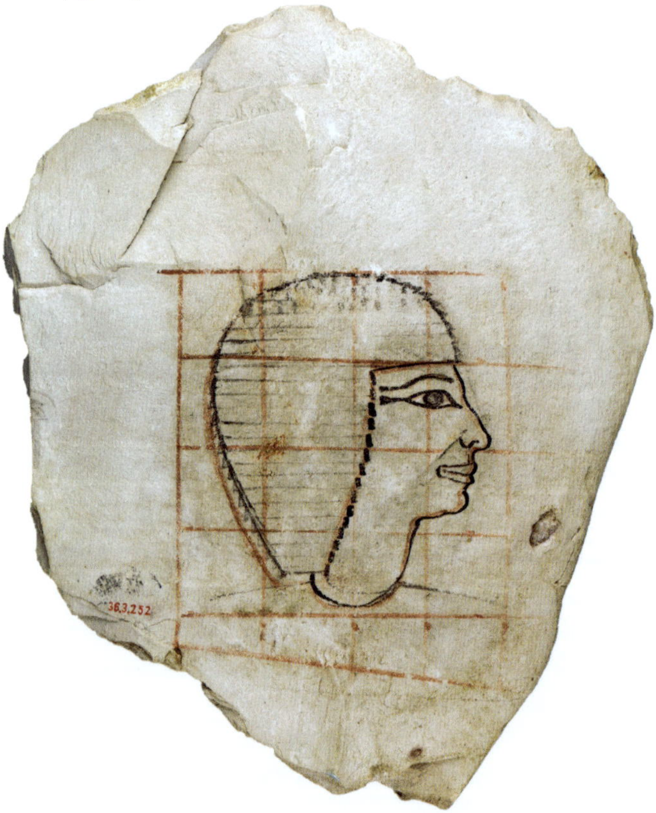

Figure 1.2 Portrait of the architect Senmut, c.1479–58 BCE, Metropolitan Museum of Art.

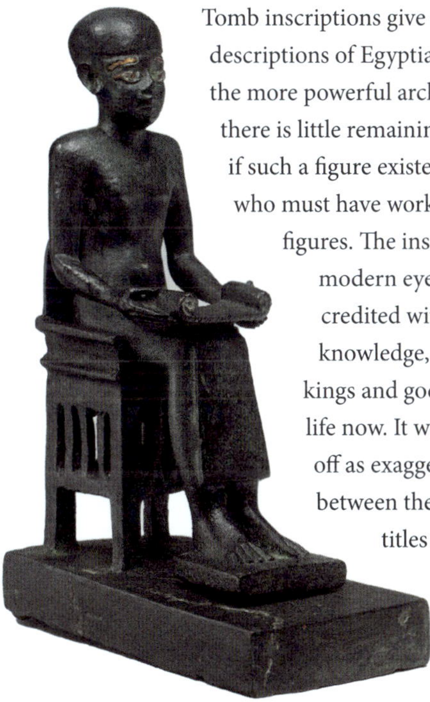

Tomb inscriptions give some of the best glimpses and descriptions of Egyptian life, and illuminate the roles of the more powerful architects of the period. However, there is little remaining record of the jobbing architect, if such a figure existed, or the assistant architects who must have worked alongside these more famous figures. The inscriptions seem grandiose to modern eyes. The men they describe are credited with almost superhuman levels of knowledge, and their intimate relations with kings and gods are unfamiliar to our way of life now. It would be all too easy to write these off as exaggerations or semi-fictional, but between the formal language and extended titles there are glimpses of real people of great learning and with polymath tendencies.

Figure 1.3 Tomb inscription of Intef, the overseer of the fortress of King Mentuhotep II, c.2000–1988 BCE, Metropolitan Museum of Art.

Figure 1.4 Statue of the architect Imhotep, Metropolitan Museum of Art.

The way knowledge was held – secret and sacred – encouraged a dynastic, precedent-driven approach to the practice of the architectural profession, though some have also speculated that Egypt's relative geographic isolation and lack of competition also did little to encourage innovations in construction.[8] Imhotep is one of the most significant figures of ancient Egyptian architectural life, and seemingly one of the few Egyptian architects to have innovated. The stepped pyramid he built for King Djoser in the 27th century BCE was the first masonry construction of the Old Kingdom.[9] Little is known about his motivations or inspirations, but this innovation catalysed the construction of the pyramids and temples that still astound us today. Imhotep was also High Priest of the sun god Ra, Chief Justice, Chief Treasurer and Chief Architect to King Djoser. He was deified after his death. So revered was he that, according to tradition, Egyptian scribes would honour him by sprinkling ink around themselves before beginning to write.[10]

While we know little about the motivations that catalysed the new technology in his stepped pyramid, one may have been the material it was built from. Stone was a symbol of power in Egypt, perhaps due to the wealth symbolised by the monumental amounts of work and craftsmanship associated with building with it, or perhaps its longevity. To work with it in a new way must have been a celebrated and exhilarating act.

The tomb inscriptions that introduce us to these famous architects also offer glimpses into their working lives. The foundation ceremony described at the beginning of the chapter shows the 'line' to be a cord knotted at 12 equal intervals, allowing accurate measurements to be taken and staked out – measurements likely to have been derived from the human body.[11]

Few drawings survive, but scraps of papyrus and flakes of limestone have been found apparently showing plans and working sketches.[12] A painting of an Amarna palace in the tomb of Mery-Re, high priest of Aten, suggests that presentation drawings were done. The painting shows a merging of both plan and section in its representation, depicting key rooms and ceremonies and functioning more as a drawing of the essence of the palace, rather than showing what it looked like or how it was built.[13] No working drawings have been found, suggesting that instructions were given verbally on site. However, this is an interpretation of what survives, and working drawings by their nature may have been discarded, destroyed, or even erased and the papyrus or equivalent reused.

While some elements of ancient Egypt are well preserved in funerary monuments, we must interpret what we find – and interpretation, being through the lens of the interpreter, is liable to misunderstanding. Possibly the closest we may come to understanding how ancient Egyptians understood architects is to take note of the gods they assigned to watch over them: for example, the goddess Seshat, lady of builders, of writing and of the house of books. She is sometimes replaced in representations by That, god of science, and Ptah, god of craft.[14] Whatever the realities of daily life for the architects of Egypt, it is clear that Egypt considered her architects polymath civil servants, practising a profession without a divide between arts and technical skills. They were expected to have a broad understanding of society, sciences, crafts and construction, underpinned by an understanding of the sacred texts and the knowledge of their forefathers.

Ancient Greece: legendary skill and burgeoning bureaucracy

Moving across the Mediterranean Sea to Greece, and the future conquerors of Egypt, we can see that this polymath expectation was not unique to Egyptian architects. Plato, who lived between c.424 and 347 BCE, correlates architects and kings as exemplifying executive, practical knowledge over purely critical or scientific knowledge in an allegory on leadership.[15]

Looking at the myths and legends the Greeks told to explain and communicate the world around them, we come across Daedalus, the first legendary architect of the Greek world. There are historical parallels with the Phoenician civilisation that spread across the Mediterranean between 1100 and 200 BCE. Daedalus is credited not only with designing the Minotaur's labyrinth at Crete (possibly the first palace of Knossos), but also with the creation of a machine in the shape of a wooden cow. Pasiphae hid in this cow to mate with the bull the sea god Poseidon had given to her husband Minos (King of Crete and son of Zeus). The issue of this union was the Minotaur;

Figure 1.5 Daedalus attaching wings to the shoulders of his son, Icarus. Stipple engraving by GS and JG Facius, 1779, The Wellcome Collection.

a bull-headed man-beast who lived at the centre of Daedalus' labyrinth. The plan of the labyrinth he is supposed to have purloined from the tomb of an Egyptian pharaoh. Daedalus, rather fittingly, means 'the cunning worker' or 'the skilful one'.[16]

Daedalus' story suggests that successful Greek architectural life was fraught with the dangers associated with being close to the powerful. Daedalus' most famous falling-out was with Minos, whose rage Daedalus fled by flying to Sicily on homemade wings. His son Icarus died in the escape when he flew too close to the sun (see Figure 1.5), but Daedalus survived to astound future patrons, becoming beloved of King Cocalus of Sicily for a reservoir and his underground steam bath.[17]

There is much that can be derived from this legend. Daedalus, a cunning and inventive polymath, is depicted as an architect. His wide knowledge encompassed hydraulics, the science of building, mechanics and aerodynamics. He was inventive and learned, as well as being charming enough to flatter and befriend kings, much as his Egyptian equivalents did. Architects thus could be seen to be considered by the Greeks as much more than overseers of building work. Socrates, in one of his dialogues, even writes 'in what employment do you need to excel, O Euthdemus that you collect so many books. Is it architecture? For this art you will find no little knowledge necessary.'[18]

From the writings of Socrates, Plato and other Greek writers quoted by Roman historians it is clear that Greeks took their architects seriously and expected great things of them. Architects were design specialists who not only made the plans and *syngraphai* (specifications), but advised on the selection of the building's location and measurements, oversaw and instructed the works and the payments to contractors, and collated as-built information.[19] Architects were sometimes master sculptors, sometimes something closer to an engineer, other times theoretical designers, marine architects or designers of public festivals.[20] It was not a closely defined role. Hippodamus, architect of the temple at Rhodes (5th to 3rd century BCE), was also credited with some of the earliest examples of urban thought and masterplanning, as well as being one of the first non-politicians to advance thoughts and theories on the role of government. He was also infamous for his flowing hair, expensive jewellery and a tendency to wear cheap winter clothing year-round.[21]

Perhaps surprising, given this breadth of expertise and practice, is how little we know of Greek architects, and how few of their names have survived to posterity. Painters and sculptors enjoyed much wider admiration in Greek society, perhaps due to the more certain authorship of their work. It is also plausible that, given the likely scale of an architectural team, later writers preferred to use only the more famous names. Another theory, described by Roman historian and geographer Pausanius, is the tendency of many Greek towns to ascribe their origins and authorship to mythical heroes or local worthies.[22] While this may sound superstitious, it is not dissimilar to how we credit buildings today. Though Norman Foster is a well-known name outside architectural circles, his Stirling Prize-winning office building will be described to posterity under the name of its patron, as the Bloomberg Building.

Given the breadth of the role of architects in Greek life, their education must have been considerable. Plato, in Book 1 of his *Laws*, suggests that a sort of apprenticeship route was favoured, advising that young aspiring architects should be furnished with miniature tools and employed in the erection of doll's houses,[23] and it is probable that the architectural arts were learned in the office or employ of a practising architect. Temple records in Delphi evidence this, recording payments from 343 to 340 BCE to a *hyperarchitekton* (architectural assistant).

Architecture was largely considered an upper-class occupation. However, some men seem to have risen to the role from the ranks of craftsmen. There are records at Delos of a man called Phaneas who was first paid as a workman, and later as an architect.[24] Some architects also seem to have monetised their knowledge of construction by contracting as both builder and architect. This is controversial in scholarship, however, as much has been interpreted from the records of a single architect called Callimachus being named as the contractor of the long wall at Athens.[25] Callimachus was credited too with the modelling of the capital of the Corinthian classical order from a basket of growing acanthus, and was also lauded for the invention of a lamp that burned for a year without needing to be refuelled.[26] Short of electricity having been invented significantly earlier than is currently known, this seems more likely to indicate his powers of persuasion and illusion than his powers of invention.

The architect's multifaceted education is supported by surviving writings. Until at least the 4th century BCE architectural books covered theory as well as the technical matters of construction.[27] Vitruvius, a Roman architect,

Figure 1.6 Cypriot limestone relief showing what is believed to be workers at a stone quarry, 3rd century BCE, Metropolitan Museum of Art.

quotes many Greek writers in ways that suggest that in the Greek mind, literature and art were fully conjoined arts.[28] Socrates also states that 'it is only by scientific as well as artistic knowledge that the architects of the Parthenon could have erected the most perfect building known to us'.[29]

While it is clear that architects were highly educated and multifaceted professionals, there is less evidence of exactly how they worked. It is widely speculated that working drawings and models (*paradeigmata*) were made,[30] however almost none survive. This, combined with the standardisation of form in Greek civic buildings, led one scholar, J Bundgaard, to suggest that Greek architects did not make plans but only issued verbal instructions on site.[31] This would seem to be unlikely, as it is based on the absence of drawings rather than proof of this methodology, and it would not seem reasonable to expect working drawings to survive a building site, and then further thousands of years. However, this theory cannot be entirely discredited; we do not have definite proof to advance either hypothesis. Drawings were certainly part of an architect's craft, though. The description of an architectural competition for the design of a *temenos*, or sacred enclosure, on the Acropolis in 448 BCE, invited drawings 'not less than one cubit large' (roughly equivalent to 1:10 scale).[32]

The process by which work was won and tendered is a little clearer. For civic and religious buildings, a commission made up of responsible citizens renowned for their financial and administrative competence was selected to oversee the commission and erection of the works. The commission was not the client. It functioned instead as a governing body, with the money and initial brief coming from the city or religious order. Architects worked as technical advisers to this commission on matters of aesthetic convention and design constructability, collaborating on designs suited to the architectural tastes of the day, and in line with the budget. Technical advice was not simply a matter of buildability; the ancient world also had building regulations. Records have been found at Pergamon outlining regulations for party walls, dangerous structures and the penetration of damp from one property to another.[33] All these factors, and likely more, would have been considered during the design process.

Once the design was agreed it was put out to tender. This seems to have been done piecemeal – much like modern management procurement routes. Similarities continue in the tendering of public works. Today, public works above a certain value must go to public tender through national and international journals. In ancient Greece tenders were invited by a public announcement by the herald in the marketplace. The architect and the commission would review the tenders and award the contract to the best bid. The architect then drew up a detailed specification for each piece of work, though the contractor was responsible for procuring materials and labour. Each contract was further backed by a guarantor, invited on the strength of his financial and social standing. The commission would then administer the contract and ensure proper accounting of the funds.[34]

There is a suggestion in Vitruvius' accounts that the more extravagant flourishes of architects were also legislated for, with a law at Ephesus stating that were the architect's 'extras' to exceed the contract sum by more than 25%, he would be held personally liable for them.[35] This would have been effective as, according to inscriptions at Pergamon, architects were not wealthy. In one case in 407–6 BCE an architect was paid the skilled workman's wage of one drachma per day – not as much as his responsibility might have suggested, but more than a clerk.[36]

One especially notable story of winning work is described during the premiership of Alexander the Great in c.330 BCE. The imperial ambitions of Alexander were creating significant demand for architects, and Dinocrates – finding his letters of introduction and recommendation to the court unsuccessful – took a somewhat theatrical approach to winning work (see Figure 1.7). As Vitruvius recounts:

> [Dinocrates] undressed himself in his inn, anointed his body with oil, set a chaplet of poplar leaves on his head, draped his left shoulder with a lion's skin, and holding a club in his right hand stalked forth to a place in front of the tribunal where the king was administering justice … In astonishment [Alexander] gave orders to make way for him to draw near, and asked who he was. "Dinocrates", quoth he, "a Macedonian architect, who brings thee ideas and designs worthy of thy renown. I have made a design for the shaping of Mount Athos into the statue of a man, in whose left hand I have represented a very spacious fortified city, and in his right a bowl to receive the water of all the streams which are in that mountain, so that it may pour from the bowl into the sea."'[37]

Alexander, delighted with the idea of his design, immediately enquired whether there were any fields in the neighbourhood that could keep the city in corn. On finding that this was impossible without transport from beyond the sea, '"Dinocrates," quoth he, "I appreciate your design as excellent in composition, and I am delighted with it, but I apprehend that anybody who should found a city in that spot would be censured for bad judgement ... Therefore, while thinking that your design is commendable, I consider the site as not commendable; but I would have you stay with me."'[38]

Unorthodox but effective, it seems.

Successful Greek architects, from the records available, seem to have been inventive, adaptable, highly educated leaders of thought and of people. As in ancient Egypt, no clear divide is drawn between the artistic and technical elements of the practice of architects; action cannot be divorced from theory, but equally cannot exist in isolation: architects are oriented towards external

Nomen idem, at maior uirtus, facit ausi bu artem

action. 'To architect', a term used by both Plato and Aristotle to describe civic and intellectual leadership, was to apply knowledge in practical ways for the common good,[39] and shows a civic regard for architectural skillsets beyond the purely built.

Figure 1.7 Cristobal Lozano presents to Pope Alexander VII an engraving of Dinocrates' proposal to Alexander. Engraving by F Spierre after Pietro da Cortona, The Wellcome Collection.

Ancient Rome: military organisation and managerial roles

Much of our understanding of Greek architectural thought comes from writing quoted by Vitruvius in *De Architectura*, but now lost (see Figures 1.8 and 1.9). Marcus Pollio Vitruvius was an early Roman architect, famous for his 10-volume *De Architectura*, most likely written between 30 and 15 BCE. These 10 books cover significant ground and demonstrate both Vitruvius' learning and his practical knowledge. It would be unfair to suggest that all Roman architects were like him, but it is probable that the fact his book survives suggests it was useful and its suggestions broadly agreed with.

One of Vitruvius' most famous opinions relates to the proper education for an architect:

> 'The architect should be equipped with knowledge of many branches of study and varied kinds of learning, for it is by his judgement that all work done by the other arts is put to test ... architects who have aimed at acquiring manual skill without scholarship have never been able to reach a position of authority to correspond to their pains, while those who relied only upon theories and scholarship were obviously hunting the shadow, not the substance … Let him be educated, skilful with the pencil, instructed in geometry, know much history, have followed the philosophers with attention, understand music, have some knowledge of medicine, know the opinions of the jurists, and be acquainted with astronomy and the theory of the heavens.'[40]

Like the Greeks and Egyptians before them, Romans valued polymath architects. Vitruvius writes not only of education, but principles of town planning, hydraulic engineering, surveying, design of buildings, landscape design, and the design of military siege engines. Roman law and order also make an appearance in the practice of architecture, with Roman architects stationed to supervise stone cutting at government quarries[41] and serving

Vitruvii de architectura

Incipit liber primus. prologus

Cum divina tua mens et numen imperator cesar imperio potiretur orbis terrarum invictaque virtute cunctis hostibus stratis triumpho victoriaque tua cives gloriarentur et gentes omnes subacte tuum spectarent nutum populusque romanus et senatus liberatus timore amplissimis tuis cogitationibus consiliisque gubernaretur non audebam tantis occupationibus de architectura scripta et magnis cogitationibus explicata edere metuens ne non apto tempore interpellans subirem tui animi offensionem. Cum vero attenderem te non solum de vita communi omnium curam publiceque rei constitutione habere sed etiam de opportunitate publicorum edificiorum ut civitas per te non solum provinciis esset aucta verum etiam maiestas imperii publicorum edificiorum egregias haberet auctoritates non putavi pretermittendum quin primo quoque tempore de hiis rebus ea tibi ederem. Ideo quod primum parenti tuo de eo fueram notus et eius virtutis studiosus. Cum autem consilium celestium in sedibus inmortalitatis eum dedicavisset et imperium parentis in tuam potestatem transtulisset idem studium meum in eius memoria permanens in te contulit favorem. Itaque cum M. aurelio et P. minidio et G. N. cornelio ad apparationem balistarum et scorpionum reliquorumque tormentorum refectionem fui presto et cum eis commoda accepi que cum primo mihi tribuisti recognitionem per sororis commendationem servasti. Cum ergo eo beneficio essem obligatus ut ad exitum vite non haberem inopie timorem hec tibi scribere cepi quod animadverti multa te edificavisse et nunc edificare reliquo quoque tempore et publicorum et privatorum edificiorum pro amplitudine rerum gestarum ut posteris memorie traderentur curam habiturum conscripsi prescriptiones terminatas ut eas attendens et antea facta et futura qualia sint opera per te posses nota habere. Namque hiis voluminibus aperui omnes discipline rationes. Incipiunt capitula primi libri on building inspection committees. These latter functioned like a building control department, and neither architects nor builders were held responsible for latent defects in buildings that had been approved by them.[42]

Figure 1.8 Page from a 1400s Latin copy of Vitruvius' *De Architectura*. The original was unillustrated, but images have been added in other, later, manuscripts, Metropolitan Museum of Art.

While the education Vitruvius endorses seems perhaps too broad compared to the more focused approach of modern architectural education, Vitruvius does not suggest these subjects idly. Architects, he says, should learn history to be able to explain the semantics of their designs; philosophy to render them courteous, just and honest; music to give knowledge of mathematical theory but also to tune *ballistae*, *catapultae* and *scorpiones* (all torsion-based artillery) to the proper key;[43] medicine to understand the effect on the human body of climate and microclimate; law to know the principles relating to party walls, drains, windows and water supply, but also to assist in drawing up contracts that safeguard both client and contractor; and astronomy so that solar geometry and the 'theory of sundials' can be understood. Vitruvius does

Figure 1.9 Portrait of Vitruvius, artist unknown.

not insist on superhuman levels of expertise or knowledge, but that architects should have an understanding of all these subjects so they do not design in ignorance of the wider impact of their work.

Not all architects would have had this broad education in the liberal arts as part of an expensive education, however. Unlike Egyptian and Greek architects, most architects in Rome seem to have come from the lower social strata; there are even accounts of freed slaves becoming architects.[44] There were three recognised routes to professional architect status: to train in the liberal arts with an established architect (which sits closest to what Vitruvius describes); to train in the army, starting as an engineer or builder and moving through the ranks to a senior engineer/architect post; or to ascend through the levels of the imperial civil service.[45]

Interestingly, both Vitruvius and Cicero agree that architecture is a learned profession and, despite the low origins of some of its practitioners, is a profession suited to men of good birth. At least one Roman architect is known to have become a senator, another a counsel,[46] and the increasingly elaborate funerary monuments in the later days of the Empire suggest that at least some architects had wealth and social position.[47] It seems to have been the case that, as in ancient Egypt and Greece, men used the knowledge, learning and social cachet of an architectural career to help them rise through the social ranks. The polymath knowledge of the architect seems to have been a quality that was valued universally across ancient Mediterranean and Near Eastern societies.

As in other areas of Roman society, military organisation and service made their mark on the architectural profession. Vitruvius' town planning principles seem to draw their genesis from the organisation of a military camp. The expertise in surveying and hydraulics expected of architects would suggest experience in military service, and the way professions organised themselves into groups by specialities was reminiscent of the organisation of a legion.[48]

While architects are mentioned by numerous Roman sources and many tomb inscriptions, there are not as many records of architectural practice as might be expected from the obvious scale of works, and the implied scale of the profession. What scant evidence there is includes a tomb mosaic in the Bardo

Museum in Tunisia depicting a Roman architect and his assistant holding a five-foot measuring stick with a square and plumb bob and line depicted nearby, considered marks of the profession, and a description of drawing techniques by Vitruvius:

> '... a ground plan is made by the proper successive use of compasses and rule, through which we get outlines for the plane surfaces of buildings. An elevation is a picture of the front of a building, set upright and properly drawn in the proportions of the contemplated work. Perspective is the method of sketching a front with the sides withdrawing into the background, the lines all meeting in the centre of a circle.'[49]

He goes on to describe the importance of economy in architectural services and design, declaring that it 'denotes the proper management of materials and of site, as well as a thrifty balancing of cost and common sense in the construction of works'.[50]

There is reasonable evidence to back up his writing of plans and model-making, but Vitruvius does not mention, and there is scant evidence for, detailed or working drawings.[51] It may have been common practice to create working drawings and they have simply not survived, but the lack of evidence adds weight to theories that Roman architects were moving the profession away from the business of construction and towards an increasingly managerial role, or even to theories that precision of execution was less important in Roman architecture than the logistical management of large, ambitious projects.

It would be easy to read the rules of Vitruvius and imagine a perfectly ordered, paramilitary profession. However, as in all old texts, humanity appears between the lines of formal writing. Vitruvius bemoans the lack of rules governing the practice of architecture: 'Would to God that [protection of function for architectural services] were also a law of the Roman people ... For the ignorant would no longer run riot with impunity.'[52] He also despairs at the decorative stonework fashions of the day, 'for how is it possible that a reed should really support a roof, or a candelabrum a pediment with its ornaments, or that such a slender, flexible thing as a stalk should support a figure perched upon it, or that roots and stalks should produce now flowers and now half-length figures? Yet when people see these frauds, they find no fault with them but on the contrary are delighted, and do not care whether any of them can exist or not.'[53]

Aulus Gellius, a Roman author who lived between approximately 125 and 180 CE, describes both a common process of architects winning work, and the tendency of all building projects to go over budget, in an evening at a friend's home:

> 'When we arrived and were admitted, we found him lying on a Greek couch ... By his side stood several builders, who had been summoned to construct some new baths and were exhibiting different plans for baths, drawn on little pieces of parchment. When he had selected one plan and specimen of their work, he enquired what the expense would be of completing that entire project. And when the architect had said that it would probably require about three hundred thousand sesterces, one of Fronto's friends said, "And another fifty thousand, more or less."'[54]

Close relationships between wealthy patrons and their architect have been, and likely always will be, essential to the architectural profession, but these relationships bring risk. Like the cautionary legends of Daedalus there are stories of clashes between patron and architect in ancient Rome. The architect Apollodorus is described by Roman historian Cassius Dio in one notable exchange with Emperor (and amateur architect) Hadrian:

> '[Hadrian] first banished and later put to death Apollodorus, the architect ... The reason assigned was that he had been guilty of some misdemeanour, but the true reason was that once when Trajan was consulting him on some point about the buildings he had said to Hadrian, who had interrupted with some remark: "Be off, and draw your pumpkins. You don't understand any of these matters." (It chanced that Hadrian at the time was pluming himself upon some such drawing.) Later, on Hadrian showing Apollodorus a temple he had designed, the architect commented that the temple "had been made too tall for the height of the cella". "For now," he said, "if the goddesses wish to get up and go out, they will be unable to do so." … The emperor was both vexed and exceedingly grieved because he had fallen into a mistake that could not be righted, and he restrained neither his anger nor his grief, but slew the man.'[55]

Figure 1.10 Portrait of Emperor Hadrian – amateur architect and alleged murderer of the architect Apollodorus, c.130–8, Art Institute of Chicago.

Dio was known to be biased against Hadrian, and there is no record of this execution being ordered, but other elements of this tale ring true – the details are too specific. If nothing else this notes the ease with which Apollodorus at least moved in powerful and exalted circles, and the high stakes associated with designing buildings that could come to represent the legacy and reputation of powerful patrons. These risks seem to have been worth taking, however, for the power and projects they could bring. A fire in Naples in 64 CE led to the creation of a new building code, whose authorship shows some of the hallmarks of the work of Emperor Nero's architects, Severus and Celer. If it was their work it suggests a high level of architectural influence and leadership in late Roman society, similar to the theories Plato and Aristotle put forward about the role of architectural thinking, or indeed to the political influence of Senmut, Imhotep or Hapnseneb.

Roman architects, no less than the Greeks before them, were skilled, highly educated and adaptable individuals. The details we can find of Roman architectural life suggest that a similar education and skillset to that in the Greek world was required in the Roman world, with a similar coexistence of artistic and technical skills. There is no indication that architects believed one of these elements could exist without the other. However, in Rome the skillset was applied with a more managerial emphasis; an adaptation of the profession to suit the society it existed in and for. The hold of Rome over much of Europe gave the Empire the wealth and power to commission large building projects. The ambition and scale of these projects led to advances in building technology, often linked to Rome's military ambitions, and the manpower, time and money the Empire funnelled into its infrastructure and civic buildings created fertile ground for architects to flourish and for the profession to develop and mature.

CHAPTER 2

From the medieval to the modern

The fall of Rome and the rise of the master mason

The fall of the Roman Empire in c.400 CE plunged Europe into what has previously been termed the 'Dark Ages', when the 'light' of the learning of the Roman Empire was supposedly lost and an era of cultural decline began. The term is now considered outmoded, as historians discover more about the era, but it could certainly be seen as a dark age for the architectural profession.

The Roman Empire had provided architects with significant commissions, both state-sponsored and private. With this workload the profession flourished, developed and grew in self-confidence into a role and educational style that, while undeniably different, is not unrecognisable from that of the modern profession. With the withdrawal of Roman influence, and in 476 CE the fall of the city of Rome itself, the fortunes of the architectural profession plummeted. Recessions caused cities to shrink as economies reeled from the impact of interlinked and adverse conditions. In this climate of economic crisis and urban decline architects were not in high demand, and the skills and knowledge base of the profession in Western Europe declined rapidly. As the paramilitarily organised Roman construction industry failed it was replaced by village economies governed by local demand, local craftsmanship and local supply of materials. Construction methods were simplified, scaled down to a smaller and less complex workforce, usually without architects.[1]

The profession to the east of the Empire – in what is known today as the Byzantine and Ottoman empires – did not suffer as much. While the sources are limited, it is clear from descriptions of architects for projects such as the Hagia Sophia that the Byzantine architect's role and education continued along the lines of his Roman forebears; training through an apprenticeship route and often rising through a craft such as cabinetmaking or metalwork.[2] Byzantine and Ottoman architects are mentioned only in passing here, but travel and trade across the Mediterranean meant that these professionals would continue to influence their Western counterparts, ensuring that Roman ideas and craftsmanship did not entirely disappear from the education and influences of Western architects when the profession re-emerged in later centuries.

The power vacuum created by the fall of Rome was eventually filled by the consolidation of the power of Charlemagne and the Roman Catholic Church around 800 CE, providing the economic stability to once again commission large-scale architectural projects.[3] While the Roman organisation and Vitruvian ideals of the architect were lost for now, the evolution of village craft economies saw the re-emergence of the architect in the form of the master mason.

There are various misapprehensions and legends about the medieval era and the building of the great cathedrals of Western Europe: that architects did not exist; that there was no hierarchy on medieval building sites; that masons and craftsmen were attached to a religious order; and the list goes on.[4] It is clear from even the scarcest glimpse at the buildings themselves that most of this cannot be true. What is undeniable, however, is that religious orders played a significant role in architectural patronage due to their political, financial and educational dominance. While some masons and construction overseers may have been educated within the monasteries, the majority of the master masons honed their skills through an apprenticeship, training with masters experienced in their craft.[5] Master builders tended to rise from the craft of stonemasonry, with stone being the most prestigious and pre-eminent building material of the time. The apprenticeship route was formalised in the Masons' Guild: a seven-year apprenticeship to become a journeyman, followed by a further three- or four-year stint and presentation of proper work samples (or a portfolio) to attain master status.[6]

Master status is the point at which the modern architect in his medieval form emerged. Master masons were rarely literate[7] but their technical grasp of their craft enabled them to design whole buildings, oversee the workforce and solve complex structural problems, often in decorative ways. With this technical

Figure 2.1 Italian illuminated manuscript from c.1250 showing a king instructing a mason within the 'A', J Paul Getty Museum.

knowledge and the closely guarded secrets of the masons' lodges (usually geometry and how to generate an elevation from a plan) passed down through families, the profession flourished through the 11th to 14th centuries.

The technically grounded education of the master masons can be seen in the architecture itself. The architectural progression is the slow and evolutionary progress of innovation in forms born of knowledge of the material, rather than the reactionary or radical reforms of a designer who does not know their material 'by hand'. Ever eager for new designs, patrons would send their masons to 'copy' details and features from celebrated churches for use in their own buildings. Records show Beaulieu Abbey asking for safe conduct in 1220 for a French mason to build their apse, perhaps due to a lack of suitable English knowledge of vaulting, and in 1414 cathedral authorities in Valencia paid the architect Pedro Balaguer 50 florins to fund a journey to Narbonne in France and other cities to examine their towers and campaniles so as to find the most elegant design for their cathedral.[8]

On the building sites themselves travelling bands of masons, stuccoists, mosaicists and so on would congregate at the site of a major project and set up camp, training local talent and in time exporting it to new sites. The projects were not all churches but also palaces, stately homes, castles, military installations and fortified cities.[9] Competitions were sometimes held for architectural commissions, and towns have been recorded as competing for celebrated masons in the manner that modern-day football clubs might compete for celebrated players.[10] Once a mason was chosen contracts were drawn up, often specifying that the mason devote himself to this one job wholeheartedly. This document also appears to have acted as a specification, though a lack of a universal language and low levels of literacy meant this would have likely acted more as a contract document than written instructions. Specifications usually included the scope of work, including dimensions, number of doors and windows, arrangements for payment, penalties for non-completion and so forth. Sometimes the building was described in detail – the wall thicknesses, timber sizes and examples of existing buildings from which features should be emulated, alongside logistical concerns such as who was responsible for the supply of materials, bonds and sureties, and the provision of the mason's lodging.[11]

Figure 2.2 A mason at work on a 16th-century building site in Germany, attributed to Hieronymus Rodler.

The master mason's technical knowledge meant he was then called on to design the building or building element. There is evidence from the 13th century onwards of both drawings and models being used to give the patron an impression of the design. Once a design was decided on, the first task was in the tracing house, where the master mason would trace the shape of stones onto wooden moulds for his carpenters to cut out as guides for the stonecutters.[12]

The mason was also responsible for creating the outline of the building with rods and cords, a methodology all but unchanged since ancient Egypt, at which point the workmen could dig the foundations and lay foundation stones. Again, as for the Egyptians, the setting of the first foundation stone often catalysed large civic and religious ceremonies, which usually served a dual function as fundraisers for these long-running and expensive projects. The extended nature of such projects meant that the mason's skills were especially commissioned to keep the floor unencumbered, and to design in such a way that the building could reopen in sections, allowing the church to function (and fundraise) again before the project was complete. His skills were also needed to economise on materials where possible, for example by reducing temporary timber scaffolding. It is for this reason that many Gothic cathedrals have a system of passages and stairs within the thickness of their walls – to serve as both a circulation network for the workers and substructure for high-level scaffolding.[13]

The master mason was sometimes called on to take up the chisel himself for a particularly tricky bit of tracery or statuary,[14] to oversee and solve the numerous technical problems that arose daily, to administer the contracts and to supervise construction – sometimes simultaneously across multiple projects.[15] It is hard not to be impressed.

The structural responsibilities of the medieval architect are well illustrated by a story of the architect of San Martin's Bridge at Toledo in about 1212. He became aware that when his wooden formwork was removed the arches of the bridge would likely fall, and confided his fears to his wife. She took it upon herself to secretly set fire to the formwork, whereby the entire arch fell, with the destruction entirely attributed to accidental fire. The bridge was rebuilt (soundly this time) and the architect admitted his wife's actions to the archbishop, who apparently did not make the architect pay for the faulty work or the arson, rather congratulating him on the wits of his wife![16]

Working drawings have been found – both sketches on scraps of paper and large-scale tracings on plaster slabs or wooden beams, as well as working models in wood or plaster. The lack of detail shown seems to indicate that these were visual aids to support verbal instructions given by the master mason,[17] rather than full working drawings. As such, the ultimate design of the building may only have been fully known in the mind of one person. Villard de Honnecourt is the only medieval master mason we have a good record of, but if his sketchbook is in any way typical, masons of the period were accomplished draughtsmen, travellers and competent masters of stonecraft.

Even a brief look at medieval construction makes clear that there were highly skilled architects then, albeit with a different name and a more practical skillset to those seen before or since. There are few records of the sort of liberal arts education we saw emerging in Roman or Greek culture, but it would be ignoring the available evidence to declare the master masons unskilled or merely craftsmen. Their knowledge, design and managerial skills led to the building of some of the greatest architecture the world has ever seen.

In an echo of Egyptian times construction knowledge was carefully hoarded by the masters and guilds, but the invention of the printing press in around 1440 catalysed a leap in literacy rates and information began to circulate much more quickly than before. The knowledge monopoly of the guilds was broken, and their carefully controlled apprenticeships were eroded by greater access to education across European societies. A renewed interest in academic learning began to shift the architectural profession from an empirical craft apprenticeship to a liberal arts education, making the architect something of a scholar again as he had been in Ancient Greece and Rome. The years that follow from the 14th to the latter half of the 18th centuries are when the modern architectural professional could be said to have been born.

Italy in the 15th century: the re-intellectualising of architecture

The Italian Renaissance marks the beginnings of modern professionalism and inspired new intellectual and artistic attitudes across Europe. First published in 1550, *The Lives of the Most Excellent Painters, Sculptors, and Architects*, written by Italian historian, painter and architect Giorgio Vasari, gives us much of the information we have about individuals in this period. Architectural education in the 14th to 16th centuries, however, was not standardised – and unlike almost all the other professions there was no guild representing architects, with architecture not yet a recognised profession.[18] The architects Vasari details usually did not train in architecture, instead approaching the profession from a building craft or from painting or sculpture. Those from wealthier backgrounds seem to have had some general education prior to their architectural apprenticeships, but those who entered architecture from the building crafts often had little to none. In a passage apparently greatly influenced by the writings of Vitruvius, Vasari states that architecture should be pursued only by men possessing excellent judgement, a good knowledge of design, or extensive practice in either painting, sculpture or woodwork.[19] It is here we begin to see the shift away from the medieval mason.

There are no mentions of architectural schools or ateliers, but the work of the architects of the Roman Empire re-emerged in 15th-century Italy, largely driven by the humanists, as a model and inspiration for the building arts. From Vasari's *Lives* it can be seen that almost every architect he writes about spent long periods of time, often many years, measuring and drawing the remains and ruins of the antiquities in Rome.[20] Roman texts such as Vitruvius' *Ten Books* became required reading, justifying architecture as a worthy art for scholars such as Leon Battista Alberti, and giving a basis to an intellectual snobbery beginning to fan out across Europe, that suggested the master mason was no longer sufficiently educated to adequately carry out building design.[21]

Figure 2.3 Self-portrait in bronze of Leon Battista Alberti, 1404–72, National Gallery of Art.

Architecture was becoming an art for the educated and the wealthy. Alberti states in the beginning of his book on architecture that 'an architect is not a carpenter or a joiner … the manual worker being no more than an instrument to the architect, who by sure and wonderful skill and method is able to complete his work.'[22] It should be noted however that Alberti, Brunelleschi and other noted Renaissance architects, responsible between them for many of Italy's most celebrated buildings, were not particularly technically minded. All of them required help from builders and joiners on the problems of actual construction: the structure, jointing and building methods. There are arguably parallels between these arrangements and pre-contract services agreements or certain interpretations of design and build procurement in modern practice.

It was also in the 16th century that a wealth of drawings and models began to appear. As the designers were no longer also the master builders, onsite drawings begin to approach something recognisable to a modern draughtsperson's eyes in their level of detail, specification and instruction.[23] They needed to be instructions in and of themselves rather than visual aids to support verbal instructions. Written descriptions dominated contracts, and the provision of drawing dimensions seemingly overwrote those found in models of the same building (for example in the case of the 1518 contract for Michelangelo's San Lorenzo in Florence).[24]

Perhaps as a result of this growing disconnect between design and construction, and the new role of the professional architect, it was in this era that attributable authorship became a more significant issue. In medieval times, while not uncommon to find masons' names carved into their cathedrals, authorship was more often ascribed to the patron. In the early Renaissance, however, there was a transition from the artisanal authorship of those such as Brunelleschi: *it is mine because I made it*; to the intellectual authorship of Alberti: *it is mine because I designed it.*[25]

Figure 2.4 1733 study of Brunelleschi's dome on Florence Cathedral, Bernado Agrilli.

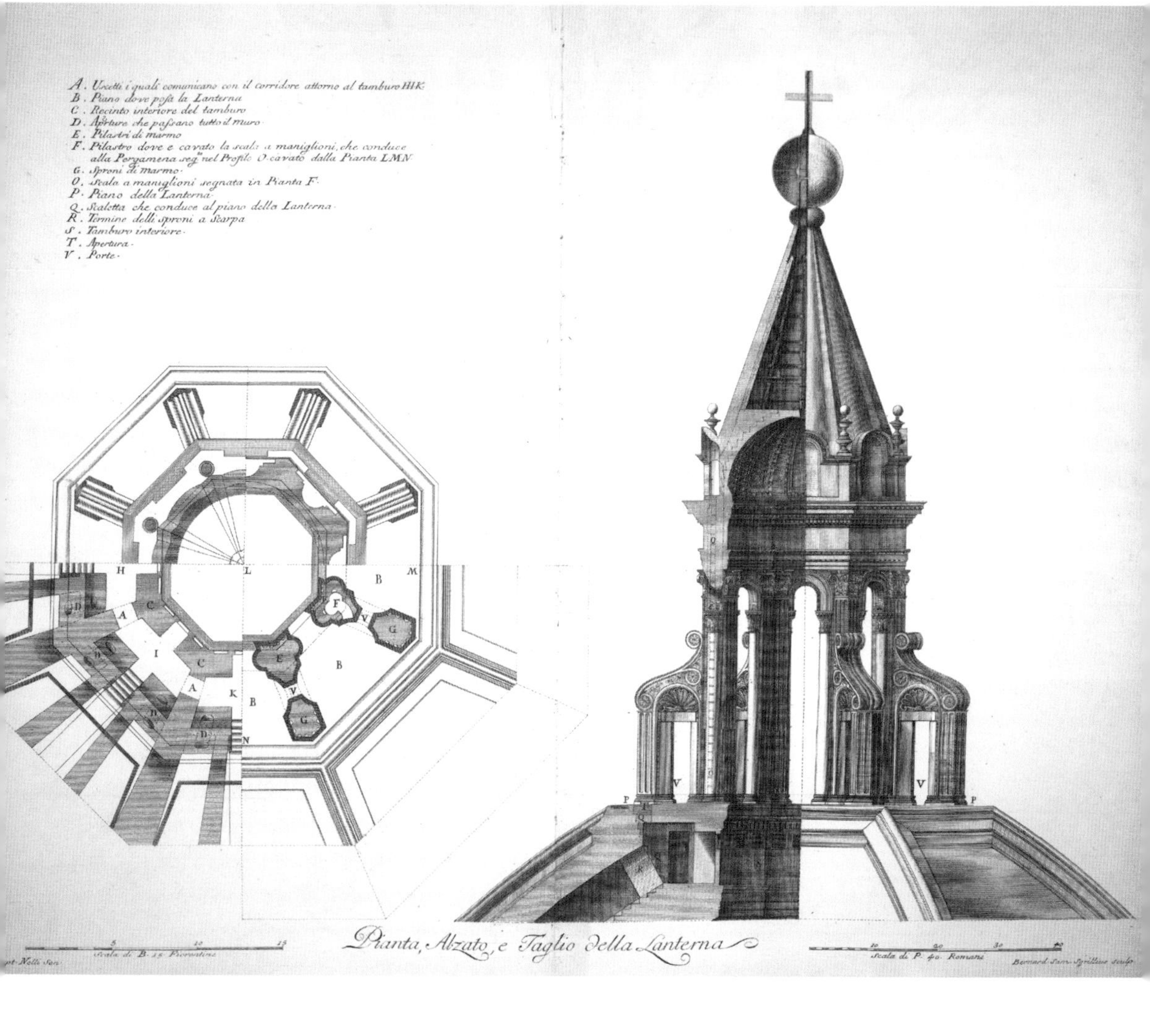

We can see the tensions and growing pains in this newly emerging 'profession' particularly clearly in stories of Brunelleschi and Alberti in 15th-century Italy. Brunelleschi favoured a more physically present approach to architectural practice, frequently leaving key gaps in his instructions to ensure that he would continue to maintain his commission. Indeed his building programme for Florence's cathedral in 1420 – after pages of detailed instructions – stops suddenly at the point at which instructions were needed for how to build the dome, ensuring his continued employment by preventing the builders proceeding without him.

Fearing that he might be replaced, in 1423 Brunelleschi stopped all construction work on the cathedral by feigning illness and remaining in bed. The master builders and the clerk of works came to him, unable to proceed and demonstrating – as Brunelleschi had intended – that he and he alone could lead the project. The tensions between Brunelleschi (of the new intellectual architectural profession) and craftsmen (of the old master mason tradition) continued to build, with the head of the stonemasons' guild imprisoning Brunelleschi in 1434, as the cupola of the cathedral was nearing completion, for non-payment of his membership fees to the guild, of which Brunelleschi was not a member.[26]

On the other hand, the more remote approach championed by Alberti was no less troublesome. Some of Alberti's letters to his site manager in Rimini survive. The tone and number of complaints suggest that although Alberti could send drawings and detailed instructions it did not then follow that these instructions would necessarily be understood or implemented on site.[27] It seems Brunelleschi's more theatrically present style, while also revolutionary, arguably better suited the transitional nature of the construction industry at the time.

Within this narrative we also come across the tantalising glimpse of an early female architect in the competition for the cupola design: '[Brunelleschi] could not prevent all the other Masters who were influenced from setting themselves, at the sight of this model to make others in various fashions, and finally a lady of the House of Gaddi had the courage to compete.'[28] Sadly, no other details of this courageous woman or her architectural pursuits are given.

Demonstrably it is in 15th-century Italy that we see the re-emergence of Roman and Greek ideas and of architects whose roles begin to more closely mirror modern practice. However, in this period we also see some of the turmoil caused by the imbalance of the artistic elements of architectural practice and technical knowledge. It was not until the amalgamation of these Renaissance ideas, and those of intellectual authorship divorced from first-hand craftsmanship, were combined with later developments in France that the birth of the modern profession was catalysed in Britain.

France in the 15th and 16th centuries: the birth of the architect's office

The Renaissance arrived later in France than in Italy. The Hundred Years' War with the English and political instability between the 1430s and 1550s meant that large-scale building activities largely ceased, and medieval masons were found there until c.1550.[29] However, with the French invasion of Italy in 1494 a constant influx of Italian artists arrived in France, introducing the court of Charles VIII to the new Italian ideas. By the middle of the 16th century we find both Italian and French architects in France, pattern books of the classical orders available across France, and students of the arts travelling to Rome to measure ruins.[30]

These new ideas, amalgamated with the position created by Charles VIII of France in the 1460s, Architectural Advisor to the King, led to the formation of the Bâtiments du Roi, or Royal Building Administration (RBA) under Francis I (1515–47).[31] The work and methodology of the RBA is the point at which we begin to see the genesis of the modern architectural office.

Inspired by the ideas emerging from Italy, Francis hired Sebastiano Serlio, an Italian architect. Records from 1541 show him being paid to visit building sites to oversee work, but also to travel to view and draw other castles. Francis' main motivation in hiring Serlio was to publish architectural treatises in France to improve the education of the masons of the RBA. Serlio's treatises became the first contemporary books on architecture printed in a modern language with illustrations, primarily created for the use of the architect, not the patron.[32]

Figure 2.5 Bartolomeo Passerotti, *Portrait of Sebastiano Serlio*, c.1570, Martin von Wagner Museum der Universität Würzburg.

While adult male literacy was still at around 5% in the 1500s it increased steadily with the first printing of the Bible in vernacular languages (c.1530s), rising to 75% by 1715. As a result of this growing literacy, by the 16th century specifications and written instructions were becoming increasingly detailed in France. The 1528 specification for the Royal Château of Fontainebleau's masonry and brickwork section extends to around 16,500 words, providing detailed descriptions of the building's dimensions, features, room sizes and chimneys.[33]

The intellectual status the Italian Renaissance lent to the study of architecture encouraged its uptake as a hobby of the aristocracy. This is aptly illustrated by stories such as that of Catherine de Medici (Queen of France, 1547–59) plaguing her architects with instructions, changes and interference at all stages of the process; commissioning among other things a Doric column in one of her homes with a newel staircase rising inside it, intended to form an astrological observatory.[34]

Women were not able to practise professions in this society, but architecture's acceptability as an aristocratic pastime meant that some wealthy women, such as the Marquise de Rambouillet, were able to practise by proxy. There are reports of her 'revolutionising' architectural plans in the 17th century by insisting on private and public circulation, service staircases, and bathroom and toilet spaces near bedrooms, and rejecting the cavernous chimney openings of the time, which sucked all the heat up the chimney in the building of her home.[35]

Figure 2.6 Adam-François van der Meulen's painting *The Building of Versailles*, 1680, Royal Collection. The royal party in the centre is demonstrating both aristocratic interest and patronage in architecture.

Figure 2.7 Sebastian de Clerc, *The Louvre under construction*, Paris, 1677.

During the political stability of the reign of Louis XIV (1643–1715) the RBA was enlarged and reorganised with greater specialisation of roles and a more hierarchical structure. During the building of the Louvre this further led to the establishment of the Royal Academy of Architecture (RAA) in 1671, to determine the training of architects and to centralise control of the French profession.[36] Its members met weekly to decide points of design or construction, and it became a sort of court of appeal for architectural queries. It created an orthodoxy of practice for French architects, and created a professional standing for its members above and beyond that of the master masons and amateurs practising at the time.[37]

The educational methods of the RAA – studying Roman classical orders, the works of famous architects past and present, and architectural treatises, and discussion of specific problems – influenced architectural education across Europe. It was an educational philosophy that held sway until the Bauhaus in Germany began to challenge it in the 20th century.[38]

Italy in the 16th to 18th centuries: reconciling craft and intellect

By the period of the 1550s to the 1750s we see the later and Baroque periods of the Renaissance in Italy. Architects were still entering the profession from the building crafts, but architecture was increasingly becoming a profession of the upper and professional classes. Training was more and more formalised, though still based on apprenticeships, but prestigious academies for additional study were being established in Rome, Bologna, Venice, Naples, Turin and Milan,[39] a formalisation and diversity of education that was not common in Britain until the later 19th century.

In later Renaissance and Baroque periods, the architect in Italy was better defined: a profession in itself, not an offshoot of painting or sculpture. Crucially, architects were no longer conflated with builders. The work also shifted: military engineering was mentioned less, though civil engineering remained an important part of architectural practice, and some architects also contributed to scenery and costumes for aristocratic and royal theatrical events and masques.[40]

Alberti's ideals of architecture practised almost as an intellectual discussion were being realised, aptly demonstrated by correspondence between Michelangelo and Pope Clement VII over the Laurentian Library. They discussed and exchanged drawings, studies, technical details and the finer points of design.[41] This also demonstrates the small but significant shift between early and late Renaissance practice in Italy. In early Renaissance architectural practice, the architect saw the materials and construction as an inconvenience to be overcome, but later Renaissance practitioners, such as Michelangelo and Philibert de L'Orme, treated technical problems as design problems, endorsing the view that the architect must concern himself with the materials and techniques as much as the ornament.[42]

The intellectualisation of the profession spurred by the Italian Renaissance increased the emphasis on completing design before construction was started and shifted the work of architecture further away from the building site; the balance of the profession's skillset was moving subtly away from technical experience. By the end of the 16th century we no longer see the architect perched on the scaffolding with chisel in hand; instead the profession is centred around the architectural office, with its leading characters, and the cast of assistants and draughtsmen that come with them.

Britain in the 16th to 18th centuries: the birth of the profession in Britain

The intellectual and artistic turbulence of the Italian Renaissance and its revolutionary impact on French architectural organisation did not go unnoticed in Britain. But it was not until the court of Henry VIII (1491–1547) and his break from the Roman Catholic Church in 1542 that change catalysed.

Henry's political and cultural rivalry with the kings of France prompted many of his great building projects, and his patronage of Italian architects and designers. The Italian influence on British design can be seen in the 1563 writings of John Shute,[43] but in reality much of the work of the Italian architects in 16th-century Britain seems to have been limited to the decorative details alone.[44] The English Reformation had caused a shift in political power, wealth and architectural patronage from the Church to the landed gentry, as well as a decreased supply of Italian talent to Britain. The new wealth generated from this Reformation produced an aristocratic society impressed by costly appearance and high fashion, and this may be why comparatively expensive Italian architects were generally employed only for the more immediately visible elements of design.

The Reformation theology of Martin Luther promoted work as a prime means of spiritual worth. The idea of a vocation for careers beyond the monastic or clerical was introduced, and elevated the acquisition of education and bettering oneself through work to an almost religious duty.[45] Coupled with the rise in aristocratic patronage and almost universal religious devotion it is unsurprising that a revolution in English architectural professionalism followed.

The plundering of the English Catholic Church during the Reformation created great wealth among the aristocracy and new patrons, but also ushered in new organisations of construction. Many churches and abbeys had previously employed a vast number of masons and other craftsmen on an almost permanent basis. With the dissolution of the monasteries and the seizure of Church property these men found themselves unemployed. Some were engaged by the Office of Royal Works, and others by the newly wealthy aristocracy, but it is plausible that a large number wandered the country looking for ad hoc work.[46] Large tracts of confiscated Church land were

➤
Figure 2.8 Design for a rose window drawn by Robert Smythson, 1500. The level of drawn technical detail demonstrates his competence as both designer and builder.

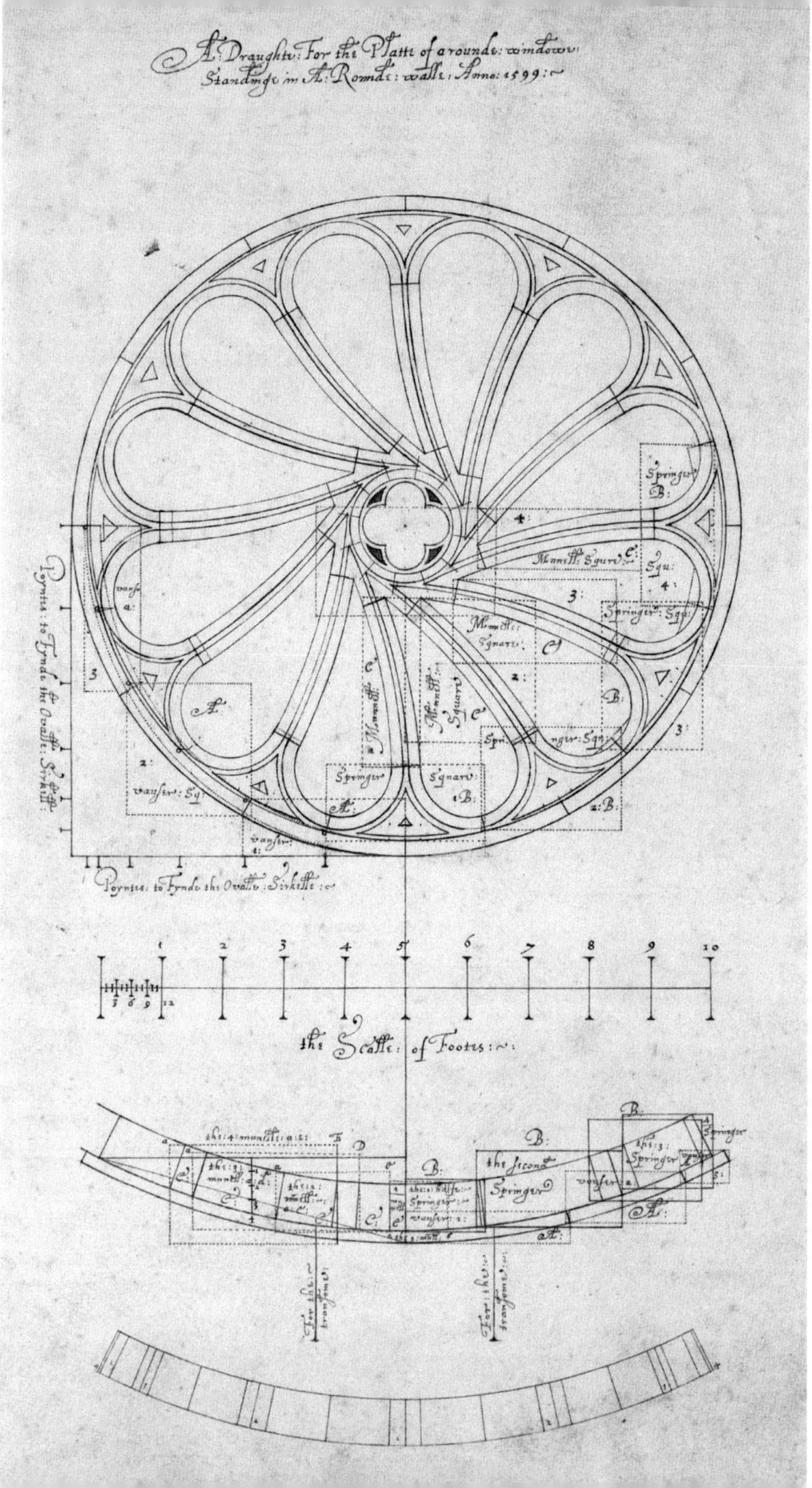
A: Draughte: For the Platte of arounde: windowe:
Standinge in A: Rounde: walle: Anno: 1599:
Springer
Squr
Poyntes: to Fynde the Ovalle: Sirkelle:
the Scalle: of Footes:
the: 4: munelle: a:
the: 3: munelle:
the second Springer
For the: transome:

sold at low prices to peers, public servants and so on, who resold them to speculators. The plots were further subdivided for sale to rising members of the yeoman class, leading to boom years for housebuilders that reached their climax in the reign of Elizabeth I (1533–1603).[47]

This boom in housebuilding saw the rise of the amateur architect – the patron acting as his own architect – advised by other specialist craftsmen and pattern books by Shute, but also by other less accurate transcribers of the classical orders, from French, Flemish and Dutch writers (the break with Rome having made it harder to source Italian architects).[48] The professional architect had yet to appear in England, though figures were beginning to emerge in the Royal Office of Works, and it is in the Elizabethan era that we see not only the beginning of the English architectural transition from medieval to modern, but also the establishment of the architectural amateur – a figure who plays an important role in the English profession until well into the 18th century. So widespread was this amateur methodology in the national consciousness that Shakespeare wrote it into a passage in the second part of *Henry IV* (in 1598). One particularly entertaining extract from a letter from Sarah, Duchess of Marlborough in 1732 typifies the attitude of the aristocratic amateur well:

> ‘I know of none that are not mad or ridiculous, and I really believe that anybody that has sent with the best workman of all sorts could make a better house without an architect, than any has been built these many years.’[49]

One architect who exemplified this movement from medieval to modern was Robert Smythson, who trained as a master mason. In this role he assisted patrons such as Sir John Thynne at Longleat and Sir Francis Willoughby at Wollaton. His drawing collection shows details drawn in ink, sheets with flaps to indicate different design options, and others showing dimensioned rooms.[50] While he was not an architect as we would recognise one today, he sits in the transitional role between the master mason and the professional architect.

Another interesting illustration of this transitional stage of English architecture is in contract documentation. The specification for the Fortune Theatre in London (1599) specifies the work in considerable detail, much as Alberti would have approved of, but the contract is fixed by reference to an existing building – the Globe Theatre – as had been common in the design and work of the medieval masons.[51]

Figure 2.9 Design for a two-storey bay window at Longleat House, Robert Smythson, c.1570.

CELEBERRIMVS VIR INIGO IONES PRÆFECTVS ARCHITECTVRÆ
MAGNÆ BRITTANIÆ REGIS ETC.
Ant. van Dÿck pinxit
R.V. Vorst sculp.
Cum priuilegio

By the early 17th century, the first British (for by now Scotland was united with England and Wales) 'architect' in the Renaissance sense had emerged – Inigo Jones. Jones visited Italy to study and collect books, and his work varied from theatrical set and costume design to garden design, to architectural work, all in his role as Surveyor of the King's Works. This included designs for Whitehall, the Queen's House at Greenwich and the Gothic chapel of Lincoln's Inn, besides a host more. Inigo Jones is particularly significant because, in the words of architectural historian Sir John Summerson:

> It is not simply the ability to draw which is significant, but the state of mind, the sense of control of which that ability is the outward sound. It represents, indeed, a revolution in architectural vision, and when we meet it with Inigo Jones' earliest surviving sketches in 1605 we know that we have finally crossed the threshold from the mediaeval to the modern.'[52]

Jones was by no means typical of 17th- and early 18th-century British architects, however. The craftsman-designer would exist alongside the amateur architect in Britain until the second half of the 18th century.[53] To make the transition from builder to architect, as Smythson had, meant making a social transition to an arguably more elevated but much riskier position in society.[54]

Jones's apprentice John Webb was the first person for whom we have a definite record of a British architectural education, the pattern of which was to persist well into the early 20th century. Webb spent three years in the Merchant Taylors' School, followed by his apprenticeship. Jones taught him mathematics as well as architecture, and though there are no records of Italian travels, collections of Webb's drawings show him to have been a keen student of Palladio. Webb's share in Jones's work is understood to have been considerable, and he continued in apparently successful independent practice after Jones's death in 1652, until his retirement.[55]

Webb's career overlapped with, and was overshadowed by, that of Sir Christopher Wren. Wren was appointed from a university-educated background in science to be promoted over Webb as Surveyor of the King's Works in 1661.[56] In 1666 the Great Fire of London catalysed significant

Figure 2.10 Anthony van Dyck's portrait of Inigo Jones (1573–1652), whose sketches brought English architectural practice 'from the medieval to the modern'.

From C to D is 45.0
Drawne by mr Webb

changes, setting British amateurs firmly on the path towards the professional. The scale of destruction was enormous, and the consequent rebuilding was far beyond the capacity of the masons and amateur architects present in London. Before 1666 only freemen of London could work as masons within the city limits, but after the fire Parliament relaxed the closed shop of the masons' company with an Act of Parliament declaring that from 1666 until the rebuilding was complete masons could come from outside. Despite the influx of masons this caused, there were still not enough to design and rebuild the city,[57] creating an opportunity for the fledgling architectural profession and for the King's Office of Works.

Figure 2.11 John Webb's elevational designs for Greenwich Palace, c.1660.

The huge rebuilding effort caused an expansion of both means and personnel in the King's Office of Works. This included greater specialisation of roles: surveyors to assess and confirm ownership of the ruins; architects for the thousands of designs;[58] and the emerging profession of the quantity surveyor to quantify materials and costs.[59] Wren was made responsible for the rebuilding of 56 churches, including St Paul's Cathedral, and though his masterplan for the city streets was never realised his office's work on the churches and cathedral bear testament to his skill, and to the breadth of his education.

The scale of rebuilding work after the fire crystallised the new professional role of architect – and the construction industry began to restructure. As the architect moved from occasional adviser to the client to overseer of the works, clients were compelled to find builders willing to work under the architect – thus forcing the construction industry's structure to change to something approaching the modern model. Clients began to enter into a contractual arrangement with the architect, who would then contract builders on their behalf to carry out the works, necessitating contractual forms to develop rapidly through the 17th century to suit these changes.[60]

By the end of the century professional architects were beginning to emerge from the cacophony of master masons, skilled craftspeople and amateurs. There was no recognised educational structure, but the genesis of the education we recognise today and of the modern architectural office can be clearly seen in the King's Office of Works. The influence of the French Royal

Building Administration was marked, but the King's Office of Works was a uniquely British interpretation and much less interested in the education of its architects. The technical experience of the master masons remained an important part of architectural practice, but the intellectual and artistic influences of the Italian Renaissance were beginning to make their mark on the balance of the British profession. As we reach the close of the 17th century in Britain we see none of the orthodoxy of architectural practice the French have by this point, and the ateliers of the Italians are nowhere to be found. It was the influence of the Industrial Revolution in Britain that would bring about the true formalisation of its architectural profession.

CHAPTER 3

Formalising the British profession

1815–1914, an age of Empire

One notable omission in the previous chapter is Britain's growing global power through the 17th and 18th centuries. The Industrial Revolution, which formed the catalyst for Britain's next leap in urban expansion and architectural evolution, was made possible through the wealth of trade goods and raw materials that flooded from all corners of the earth to this small island in the North Atlantic. It was not until the end of the Napoleonic Wars in 1815, however, when Britain was left without a serious international rival, that there was the money and manpower for the building boom that characterised the next few decades in Britain, and which saw the building of the National Gallery, the British Museum and University College London, among other institutions.

The years between 1815 and 1914 saw the formalisation of architectural education, the beginning of the closure of the architectural profession, the emergence of new construction professions and the expansion of the British Empire by roughly 10 million square miles and 400 million people. There is relatively little scholarship on the Empire and the architectural profession, though it seems to be a growing area of study; previous books on the development of the profession in Britain do not mention its influence. However, to discount the colossal impact of this power and wealth on developments in a profession that largely arose from those practising in the capital city of this Empire during this period would be to ignore the elephant in the room.

Architects and architect-engineers were often hired overseas by colonial entities, usually in their public works departments; there are RIBA records of men such as Francis Canning, whose address in 1886 is listed as

'Bloemfontein, Orange Free State, South Africa' and in 1887 as '13 Stratford Place, London'.[1] The interchange of ideas and influence on architectural design and practice that such transient professionals had both in Britain and its former colonies is physically apparent but little studied to date – especially with regard to architectural practice.

Figure 3.1 Group portrait in Bombay (now Mumbai), 1907, with architects John Begg and George Wittet at the front.

Figure 3.2 Construction of the ambulatory at Cathedral Church of All Saints, Khartoum, Sudan, 1900.

Britain in the 1800s – urbanisation and the problem of booming construction

Figure 3.3 Building under construction in Australia, 1880.

The money, technology and ideas that were flooding into Britain from its Empire began to change the type of buildings that were being commissioned in the early 19th century. No longer was the architect largely reliant on aristocratic patrons and the construction of their country homes. In the late 18th and early 19th centuries there was a rise in civic and public architecture; in clubs, museums, railways and housing for the millions of people who came from Britain's countryside to find work in its industrial cities, or to funnel goods and services to and from colonial outposts. London alone grew from one to two million people between 1800 and 1850.[2] The architect as aristocratic protégé all but disappeared, replaced by the professional man working from an office, fully staffed by junior architects and articled apprentices (students) competing with the myriad architect-surveyors, architect-contractors and builders, all seeking to capitalise on the capacious demand for construction in Britain's growing cities.

▲

Figure 3.4 Office of Ernest George and Peto, 18 Maddox Street, London, 1887.

➤

Figure 3.5 Junction at King's Cross of the Metropolitan and Great Northern Railways, London, 1861.

Capitalising on this demand, a new role began to appear by the early 1800s: men who often had no previous connection to architecture or construction, with a purely financial interest in the business. First they confined their activities directly to speculation, but after the stock market crash of 1825, many of these men began to undertake work for others. They subcontracted the actual construction work and so established the modern practice of general contracting.[3]

Figure 3.6 Early waves of the housing boom in the 1770s – a trend that would lead to the rise of general contracting.

The rise of the general contractor led to a decrease in articled apprenticeships in the building crafts, as these trades became less prestigious and more subservient to the general contracting role. This led to a decrease in build quality, and complaints of profiteering behaviour.[4] In the 16th and 17th centuries the master mason had combined the roles of architect and builder, meaning responsibility for the finished building lay with one person. However, as these roles began to diverge in the later 17th and 18th centuries this responsibility became divided between multiple parties – thereby offering more opportunities for defrauding the client.[5]

Figure 3.7 Cartoon of Seth Pecksniff from *Martin Chuzzlewit*, 1844.

The appearance and practice of fraud was not confined to builders, with one of the most frequent opportunities for fraud being centred around the practice of quantity surveying and measuring, in which bills of quantities were drawn up to allow for lump sum and competitive tendering. As architects' fees were usually defined as a percentage of the overall contract, quantity surveying came to be seen as particularly open to abuse.[6] So apparently ubiquitous was the poor behaviour of architects, especially with regard to fees and pupillage, that Charles Dickens satirised an architect as his villain, Seth Pecksniff, in his 1844 novel *Martin Chuzzlewit*.

Societies, dinner clubs and closing the profession

It was in this increasingly competitive and occasionally dishonest market that architects began to seek clearer public differentiation of their role. The first notable expression of this was a meeting on 20 October 1791 at the Thatched House Tavern of a group of Royal Academicians and architects, including James Wyatt, Henry Holland and Samuel Pepys Cockerell, to form the Architects Club.[7] This started as an academic and august monthly meeting, where topics such as professional qualifications, fireproof construction, the undertaking of another architect's unfinished work and professional fees were recorded as having been discussed.[8] However, despite it lasting 30 years, evidence of significant discussion of the profession dries up after the first few years, and what remained was apparently a convivial and exclusive, but perhaps not terribly significant, dining club.

Between 1806 and 1831 at least a further five architectural societies were founded – but aside from the odd volume of essays, little transpired from them beyond good intentions.[9] In 1834, a group of architects and surveyors met to create a Society for Architects and Surveyors: a group for 'such persons ... practising, *solely*, the profession of an Architect and Surveyor'.[10] However, given the public distrust of surveyors previously alluded to, some of the architects present at the founding meeting thought that such a society would not be able to achieve its aims of engendering greater public trust in architects. They drew up a rival manifesto for the Society of British Architects; open to those practising architecture, but closed specifically to those who did surveying work or had 'any interest or participation in any trade or contract connected with building'.[11]

This last point is particularly contentious. Not simply because of their desire to distance themselves from unprofessional conduct, but because throughout the 18th and 19th centuries many architects quietly practised surveying or had connections with building as a way to supplement and regulate their income.[12] Robert Adam, a leading and respected figure in the neoclassical movement, is a case in point, admitting late in his career to carrying out surveying work.[13] He and his brothers also purchased two patents for exterior stucco, as well as owning brickworks and pavement stone quarries in a series of complex business partnerships.[14]

The rival societies met, and negotiated, and argued; then the Society of British Architects brought about the ultimate defeat of its rival by remotely electing all the 'respectable' (non-surveyor) members to its own society and informing them after the fact. Little more was heard of the Society for Architects and Surveyors, but the founder members of the Society of British Architects, perhaps uneasy at their actions, decided to turn leadership of its society over to some senior members of the profession who had been interested bystanders until this point. Joseph Kay and Joseph Gwilt therefore chaired a meeting on 4 June 1834, in which the Institute of British Architects (IBA) was founded for 'facilitating the acquirement of architectural knowledge, for the promotion of the different branches of science connected therewith, and for establishing an uniformity and respectability of practice in the profession'.[15]

From here onwards we see a desire within the British architectural establishment to continue to control access to the practice of architecture. In order to do this, it defined practice more tightly than ever before in history, reducing the profession's ability to legitimately adapt to changing economic and social landscapes. In a rapidly globalising world this protectionist desire was understandable, but it is arguably this moment of definition and closure that began the decline of the fortunes of the profession in Britain – though it would take many decades to begin to see this play out.

The problem of pupillage

The history of the IBA, which on gaining the Royal Charter in 1837 became the Royal Institute of British Architects (RIBA), is by no means the exclusive history of the profession in the early 19th century, but the Institute's aims in establishing a uniformity of practice make it central to the profession's evolution during this time. Perhaps one of the most controversial matters was a prescribed and examined method of education.

Architectural education through the 17th and 18th centuries had largely grown out of the apprenticeship route laid down by the building crafts and master masons. It had evolved with the profession to the point that, by the late 18th and early 19th centuries, a form of articled pupillage was usual. A student would pay a practising architect a fee in return for four or five years' education in which the student would learn the art of architecture, often while living in the architect's home.[16]

Some architects took this educational aspect of their practice seriously, with architects such as John Soane being lauded for their diligence (see Figure 3.8). More usual perhaps were the experiences of George Gilbert Scott, who would go on to become one of the leading figures in the Gothic Revival. He found his education lacking and limited, and his romantic notions of the architectural arts channelled into the mundane building of 'second rate brick houses' in Hackney.[17]

Figure 3.8 John Wood's portrait of Sir John Soane (1753–1837).

It became usual for apprentices to augment their office studies by attending lectures in the evenings at the Royal Academy of Arts and to take sketching tours during their holidays. Travel still formed a significant part of education, but the grand, expensive and often dangerous European tours of earlier centuries dwindled, helped along by the canonisation of Gothic as the accepted architectural style of the 1830s and 1840s. Many easily studied English examples meant no Italian travel was needed to study them (see Figures 3.9 and 3.10).

Figure 3.9 A sketch executed in the early 1900s by Francis Cashmore when he was a student – probably on a sketching tour.

Figure 3.10 A sketch of a galleried hall from 1906 by Richard Creed as a student.

The students who became famous through their later success seem to have had a tremendous work ethic – devoting their working weeks to office training and evening lectures, and their weekends to sketching whatever architecture was within reach. GE Street (architect of the Royal Courts of Justice, and another leading Gothic Revivalist) and his brother spent their summer holidays walking around England, sometimes 30 miles in a day, sketching anything of interest that they saw. The younger Pugin, aged 15, made a full measured set of drawings of Rochester Castle before completing and publishing a monograph on military architecture.[18] In later life he would become best known for his design of the interiors of the Palace of Westminster.

Until the late 1820s neoclassical architecture, with its connotations of ancient Greek democracy and moral government, had been the favoured style of European powers and was imposed on their empires. In the 1830s, however, at the height of British Empire and self-confidence, the Gothic style began to be favoured in British public architecture. It was seen as a fundamentally British style, with roots in the history of the British Isles. This Gothic Revival further reinforced the idea of articled pupillage. Pupillage resonated with the image of the architect as medieval master artist surrounded by loyal followers, rather than a professional man or an elevated general contractor.[19] However, despite these lofty ideals, disquiet was growing among the students, compounded by the lack of educational facilities available to them. The Royal Academy offered just six lectures a year (which were not always given), and though Somerset House, King's College and University College London established part-time architecture courses between 1837 and 1841, the quality of these offerings appears to have been so poor that the students took matters into their own hands, founding the Architectural Association (AA) in 1847. It offered informal design classes of students critiquing each other's work alternately with lectures.[20]

In 1855 the RIBA began to take its first interest in education after a meeting at which architect William Tite described a gathering he had attended at the AA.[21] Two weeks later it was proposed that the RIBA should establish voluntary examinations, relating to technical competence rather than artistic taste, and grant diplomas, further suggesting that this should lead towards mandatory examinations supported by an Act of Parliament. With the support of the allied regional architectural institutes and the AA a board of examiners was eventually appointed in 1863.[22]

In 1887 the RIBA revised its membership charter to make Associateship dependent on the passing of the RIBA exam, and this had a considerable impact on training facilities. By 1891 both the AA and the Sheffield Architectural Society had begun to offer an evening course specifically to prepare students for the RIBA exams, followed by the establishment in 1892 of a three-year full-time course at King's College London. All of these served only to augment office training, rather than replace it, and it should be noted that the livelihoods of many of the RIBA members depended on pupillage fees.[23] The RIBA's interest in education created further opportunities for it to exercise influence over the direction of the British architectural profession. It aimed to standardise education and raise competence, but as the arbiter of the only professional exams it held the monopoly on the definition of the architectural profession, what activities were permitted of architects, and what balance of technical and arts knowledge was acceptable.

The mood in favour of compulsory examinations, however, was far from universal. There was considerable backlash not only from those Pecksniff types who made their living from pupils, but also from the artist-architects of the day who, worried by the growing power of the RIBA's specific definition of architecture, were so moved as to write a letter to *The Times*, followed by a volume of essays entitled *Architecture: A Profession or an Art*. The letter contains sentiments still heard in discussion surrounding architectural education today, suggesting that: 'while it is possible to examine students in construction and matters of sanitation, that artistic qualifications, which really make the architect, cannot be imported to the test examination and that a diploma of Architecture obtained by such means would be a fallacious distinction … We think that no legislation can protect the public against bad design; no good legislation help to prevent bad construction unless builders and all others who erect buildings were required to pass the test and examination as well as architects.'[24]

The formalisation of education met with its opponents, and the RIBA's closures caused a shift in the direction of the profession that is being felt to this day, but it was these formalised routes that allowed those who had been previously unable to access architectural education to slowly make their way into the RIBA's membership records. In 1889 Herbery Heelas Macaulay, a Nigerian-born indexer of the Crown Lands in Lagos, won a government scholarship to study surveying and engineering. He went on to study architecture through the RIBA exams, and on his return to Nigeria continued in public and private practice before founding the Nigerian National Democratic Party in 1922.[25] Whether a black immigrant would have been granted access to a less formally defined and examined profession in the 1890s is debatable, but the formal process Macaulay followed gave a clear path to those without connections or previous knowledge of the profession.

He was not the only non-white architect to appear in RIBA records in the late 1880s and early 1890s. It is not a long list, but in 1888, having studied at the Civil Engineering College at Poona (now Pune) in India, Muncherji Murzban was made a Fellow of the RIBA, and Ibrahim Akhmadi was made an RIBA

Figures 3.11 and 3.12 Ethel Charles' application form.

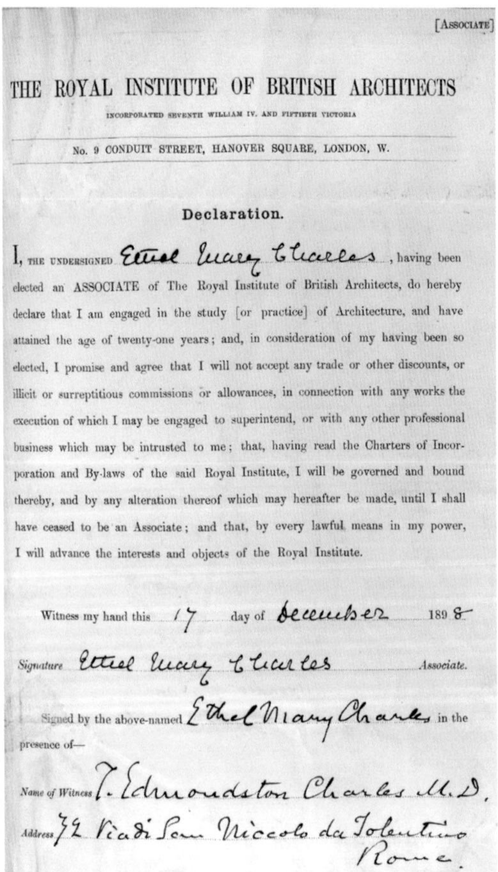

[Associate]

THE ROYAL INSTITUTE OF BRITISH ARCHITECTS

INCORPORATED SEVENTH WILLIAM IV. AND FIFTIETH VICTORIA

No. 9 CONDUIT STREET, HANOVER SQUARE, LONDON, W.

Declaration.

I, the undersigned Ethel Mary Charles, having been elected an ASSOCIATE of The Royal Institute of British Architects, do hereby declare that I am engaged in the study [or practice] of Architecture, and have attained the age of twenty-one years; and, in consideration of my having been so elected, I promise and agree that I will not accept any trade or other discounts, or illicit or surreptitious commissions or allowances, in connection with any works the execution of which I may be engaged to superintend, or with any other professional business which may be intrusted to me; that, having read the Charters of Incorporation and By-laws of the said Royal Institute, I will be governed and bound thereby, and by any alteration thereof which may hereafter be made, until I shall have ceased to be an Associate; and that, by every lawful means in my power, I will advance the interests and objects of the Royal Institute.

Witness my hand this 17 day of December 1898.

Signature Ethel Mary Charles Associate.

Signed by the above-named Ethel Mary Charles in the presence of—

Name of Witness T. Edmondston Charles M.D.

Address 72 Via di San Niccolo da Tolentino Rome.

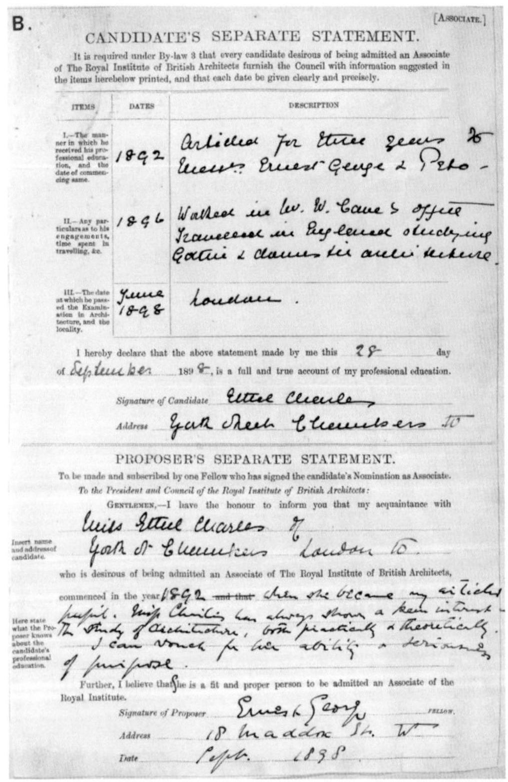

B. [Associate.]

CANDIDATE'S SEPARATE STATEMENT.

It is required under By-law 3 that every candidate desirous of being admitted an Associate of The Royal Institute of British Architects furnish the Council with information suggested in the items herebelow printed, and that each date be given clearly and precisely.

ITEMS	DATES	DESCRIPTION
I.—The manner in which he received his professional education, and the date of commencing same.	1892	Articled for three years to Messrs Ernest George & Peto –
II.—Any particulars as to his engagements, time spent in travelling, &c.	1896	Worked in W. W. Caves office. Travelled in England studying Gothic & domestic architecture.
III.—The date at which he passed the Examination in Architecture, and the locality.	June 1898	London.

I hereby declare that the above statement made by me this 28 day of September 1898, is a full and true account of my professional education.

Signature of Candidate Ethel Charles

Address York Street Chambers W

PROPOSER'S SEPARATE STATEMENT.

To be made and subscribed by one Fellow who has signed the candidate's Nomination as Associate.

To the President and Council of the Royal Institute of British Architects:

Gentlemen,—I have the honour to inform you that my acquaintance with

Insert name and address of candidate. Miss Ethel Charles of York St Chambers London W.

who is desirous of being admitted an Associate of The Royal Institute of British Architects, commenced in the year 1892 ~~and that~~ when she became my articled pupil. Miss Charles has always shown a keen interest in the study of architecture, both practically & theoretically. I can vouch for her ability & seriousness of purpose.

Here state what the Proposer knows about the candidate's professional education.

Further, I believe that she is a fit and proper person to be admitted an Associate of the Royal Institute.

Signature of Proposer Ernest George Fellow.

Address 18 Maddox St. W

Date Sept. 1898

Associate (both, however, apparently remaining in British-controlled India). In 1892 records indicate that Kotaro Sakuri was made an RIBA Associate while based in Tokyo, and in 1898 Ethel Charles enters the records as the first female Associate[26] (see Figures 3.11 and 3.12). It would not be until the years following the global upheaval of the First World War that this trickle of women and non-British men would increase, but it is doubtful whether an educational system that had remained purely on an articled pupillage basis would have admitted them at all.

Women, charity and the architectural arts

If women might not have been able to practise architecture professionally during the early 19th century, there are clear indications of their accessing the profession through other routes. The rapid growth of Britain's cities during the 19th century led to strikingly poor living conditions for the poor that flocked to them in search of work, and the philanthropic measures of the day often centred around housing and education for the working classes. In the mid-1860s Octavia Hill developed a method of housing reform largely based on the rehabilitation of existing slum properties and the provision of good-quality open and communal spaces. This pioneering approach inspired other charitable organisations such as the Edinburgh Social Union, under whose auspices women such as Jane Whyte and Lileen Hardy played pivotal roles in improving the built environment for Edinburgh's poor. These women were able to 'practise' the profession of architecture as charitable amateurs – without deviating from the domestic context that agreed with their socially accepted roles as wives and mothers.[27]

In 1834 the Poor Law Amendment Act sought to remedy the poverty, overcrowding and associated social problems that rapid urbanisation was causing in Britain, decreeing that no able-bodied person was to receive money or help from authorities outside of a workhouse. The building of these workhouses did not solve the problems of substandard housing for the working poor, however, and some wealthy industrialists sought to create better standards of living for their workers. Notable examples were further motivated by devout religious beliefs – such as the Quaker Cadbury's workers' housing at Bournville, or Edward Akroyd's villages at Copley and Akroydon (designed by George Gilbert Scott).

The Peabody Trust, established in 1862, was one of the first solely philanthropic associations that sought to alleviate the housing problems of the working poor, and also one of the first organisations in the UK to hire an 'in-house' architect. Between 1863 and 1885 Henry Astley Darbishire designed around 20 housing estates for the Trust.[28]

The growing gulf between drawing and construction detail, and the rise of the rendered perspective

The emergence of the general contractor had led to the general acceptance of lump sum tendering, and the relinquishing of the architect's construction management role to the general contractor. This is starkly shown by the accounts of the Bank of England during its construction between 1788 and 1833, which show no builder, and architect John Soane dealing directly with the various trades.[29] However, by the time the Royal Courts of Justice were built in 1874, contractor Bull of Southampton was working alongside architect George Edmund Street.[30]

As a consequence of their increasing remoteness from day-to-day management of the building site, architects' drawings and specifications necessarily became more detailed and prescriptive. This led further to a separation between the specification and the building contract, which until this point had usually been the same document. This separation allowed the general contractor to pass the specifications to his subcontracted labourers and craftspeople. The new contractual arrangement required more technical detail from the architect, and moved the responsibility for the detailed design from a collaborative process to a dictatorial one, where the architect was expected to fully design a building before handing over his designs to the labourers. Not only did this significantly increase the knowledge required for the architect's role, but it also contributed to the decline in prestige of the role of craftsmen, and their skill levels.[31] Further erosion of crafts skills was caused by the standardisation of details and building products brought about by the manufacturing prowess of the industrial factories, combined with increasing technical and legislative complexity, which forced a certain degree of specialisation on both designers and contractors.[32]

The growing level of detail now inherent in architectural drawings and specifications was used to great effect in the urbanism of Britain's growing Empire through this century. Pattern books published in London, still at this

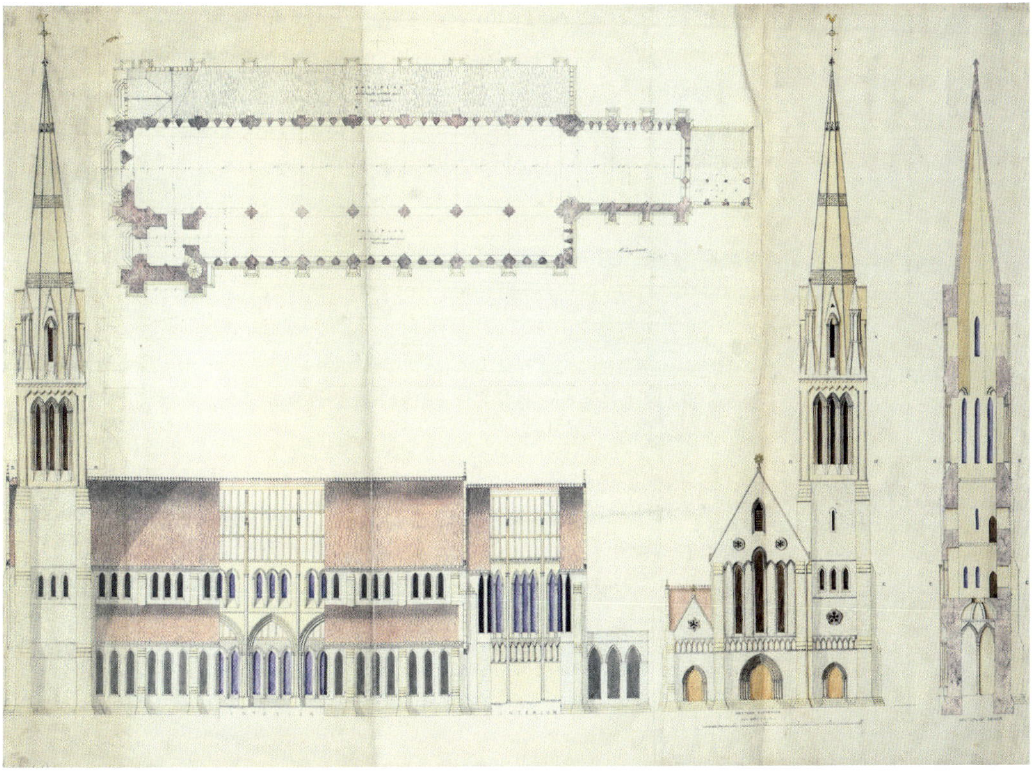

time a popular auxiliary income stream for British architects, were widely available in the British Atlantic world and known to be used by colonial craftsmen. Furthermore, organisations such as the East India Company, the British Army and the Church of England would commission detailed plans of forts, churches and entire settlements from architects in Britain, which were realised by local craftsmen and builders when those designs arrived overseas.[33]

Figure 3.13 An 1847 design by Henry Conybeare for the Church of Saint John in Colaba, Bombay (now Mumbai).

Another contribution to the increasing importance of architectural drawings and specifications was the declining architectural education of the architect's patrons. In earlier centuries architects more usually worked for aristocratic or noble families for whom architecture was an absorbing interest. These aristocratic patrons could usually read plans, elevations and sections. By the 19th century, however, the rapid increase in building typologies and types of client meant that committees of middle-class professionals or newly wealthy industrialists were a more usual client, and highly detailed and coloured,

Figure 3.14 Design for a church, 1850, possibly by Edward Lamb.

fully pictorial representations of buildings became the preferred way of communicating designs to this new class of patrons. The plan and elevation lost popularity to the coloured perspective. It is interesting to note that the growth of those listing themselves as 'architect' in provincial trade directories can be linked to the rise of the building committee, as lay-clients increasingly came to see an architect as essential to manage the project and its finances.[34]

This growing emphasis on the drawing as a product in itself caused problems. As today, a gifted artist does not necessarily make a good architect; drawing a building is not the same as constructing one. Until the 19th century drawings had been a means to an end, but the expectations raised by the beautifully hand-rendered drawings of the later 1800s too often led to disappointment when the building was finished and the client did not see the crisp shadows of the rendering but its more mundane realisation in brick and terracotta tile[35] (see Figures 3.14 and 3.15). The changing roles of architectural documentation reflect the driving ambition of the architectural establishment of the 1800s – to define it as a profession perceived as remote from the building trades and more closely associated with its wealthy and socially superior clients and patrons.

Figure 3.15 Fully coloured perspective drawing for Dixcot, Tooting Bec by Charles Voysey, 1892.

Style wars and questionable competition practices

The highly rendered drawing soon became a key component of the architect's arsenal, with the growth of architectural competitions as a means of commissioning architects and the rise of architectural journalism in the 19th century introducing an ever more literate public, and an expanding middle class, to an interest in architecture and design.[36]

In the early 19th century there had been a revival of Greek neoclassical design, breaking nearly 250 years of architectural continuity. This arguably stemmed from the publication of a book of measured surveys of Greek antiquities and ruins – *Antiquities of Athens* by James Stuart and Nicholas Revett in 1762.[37] It is perhaps no coincidence that this revival, inspired by the ruins of a 'new' classical civilisation, should have been catalysed during the decades in which Britain began to solidify its increasing influence and dominion overseas, seeking to define its rule as a 'new' democratic and civilising force. Perhaps also no coincidence was that the neoclassical style stemming from the Greek Revival, with its (British) associations of morality, godliness, education and good governance, was the architectural style Britain chose to export to its colonies. It became easily recognisable as the architecture of the British Empire, though to many of its subjects this architecture came to stand for something quite different, and more violent, than the lofty social values the colonialists apparently aspired to.[38]

By the 1830s the British middle classes were beginning to exercise their taste in another direction, tending towards the Gothic and its associations with homegrown British medieval craftsmanship and devout Christian faith. Starting with a school of architecture formed by Batty Langley for carpenters, and Horace Walpole's house at Strawberry Hill, it grew apace in the early 1800s with its eventual adoption by the Church of England and the work commissioned by the Act of 1818 to build churches for the growing British population.[39] This battle for stylistic dominance between the classical and Gothic revivals was a catalyst for one of the most contentious architectural competitions of the age, descending into infamy.

In 1834 the Palace of Westminster burned down, and in 1835 a competition was held for the design of the new palace. Competitions were increasingly popular with architects, as they gave them the opportunity to design without the interference of laypeople and clients (at least in the initial stages) – though the system was little regulated at this point. The Palace of Westminster competition was for a new building in the Gothic or Elizabethan style, and designs were invited, without an estimate of cost, to be submitted just five months after the competition was announced. Ninety-seven architects competed, and Charles Barry was announced as the winner in February 1836. However, cost had not been considered, and the inexperienced jury admitted to largely choosing on the basis of the elevation and the convenience of the floor plans. The designs were publicly exhibited and caused a furore in the press: firstly because the design was Gothic, not Greek; secondly because the jury were amateurs; and thirdly because they had favoured Barry because he was friendly with the head of the jury. The remaining 96 competitors held a protest meeting, but despite years of their petitioning Parliament the foundation stone for Barry's design was laid in 1840.[40]

Yet another fractious competition, this time for the Royal Courts of Justice, was held in 1866. Six architects were invited to compete, but later six more names were added. The jury of five laymen and six professional assessors announced that the winner was Edmund Barry's plan and George Street's elevation, which was manifestly absurd. It goes without saying that tension followed, but Street was eventually appointed without Barry in 1874.[41]

Figure 3.16 Charles Hussey and Thomas Rickman's competition design for the Houses of Parliament, 1835.

It was in matters of professional conduct such as these that the RIBA began to find its main role. It established the standard of architects' fees at around 5% of the contract cost, and set up a committee to oversee competitions to try to prevent disasters of the type detailed above. The RIBA insisted on a consistent set of drawings from all entrants, at the same scale and in India ink. Colours were only allowed in the differentiation of materials within sections, and models and perspectives were treated with suspicion. The RIBA then banned its members from entering competitions that it had not sanctioned.[42] This was, of course, controversial.

Inarguably, the RIBA and its members in the late 1800s were keen to forge a trusted and regulated profession aloof from the fractious and at times duplicitous construction industry it practised within. While this was a generally applauded aim, the implementation of the RIBA's policies caused many architects discomfort and disquiet. In accordance with its ambition to professionalise architecture, the RIBA sought the full closure of the profession and the protection of both the function and the title of 'architect'. Bills to this effect began to be introduced into Parliament, unsuccessfully, from 1884, but

Figure 3.17 Lewis Cottingham's competition design for the Houses of Parliament, 1835.

Figure 3.18 Charles Barry's revised design for the Houses of Parliament, 1836.

this campaign was interrupted by Britain's declaration of war on Germany on 4 August 1914. The devastating impact of war would bring seismic change to the global and social context in which architecture was practised.

The late 18th to the early 20th centuries in Britain were a time of great wealth and tremendous upheaval, where the structure of British society was reformed and the global power of the country rose to heights unseen through most of history. It was a time of great disparity of wealth but also of tremendous opportunity, which the architects of the time capitalised on. Architectural practice was marked by naked opportunism, professional rivalries and squabbles, and by the collegiate interchange of ideas and the beginnings of the regulated profession it has become. This all happened within a time period and moral context which are difficult to grapple with objectively. While the British government abolished slavery in 1833, it also took direct British rule of India from the East India Company in 1857. On the one hand the 19th century saw the implementation of Poor Laws and great technological progress, but on the other child labour was common, slums were ballooning in size, and only men of property could vote.

This environment of change brought new clients and styles, social and architectural influences from across the world, and the money that allowed such influences to be debated and built on. Architects came together and brought about a formalisation of the profession that sought to decrease fraudulent behaviour and hold them accountable to a recognised set of standards – tangentially beginning to allow access to the profession from those previously unable to practise it. It is a complex period complicated by egos, well-documented squabbles and architectural *coups d'etats*, but it is the point at which the fundamental cornerstones of modern British practice – prescribed qualifications, distinct professional standing and clear differentiation from the construction trades – were established. While the motivations of the profession seem clear, and perhaps noble, the profession's millennia-long negotiation of the balance between art and technical application was upset, and the narrowing of the definition of architectural practice contributed to a less agile, less polymath, less architectural profession.

CHAPTER 4

Democratisation and commodification

The First World War and its aftermath – devastation, and opportunities for women

Following the declaration of war between Germany and Great Britain in August 1914, the RIBA set up the Architects' War Committee (AWC) to oversee the profession's response. While the President of the RIBA did make a formal offer of help to the government, this met with no official reaction. Architecture was seen as a luxury, and there was little appetite for architects in a country at war, except for enlistment in the armed services.[1]

Throughout the years that followed the *RIBA Journal* printed a roll of honour, listing those members who had enlisted, been promoted and been killed. Membership fees were waived for all those who enlisted, and Belgian architects who had sought refuge in England were granted the privileges of the Institute during the war.[2] More than 1,300 of around 4,330 RIBA members served in the armed services in the First World War, and the 230 who died are memorialised on a wall at the RIBA's current headquarters in Great Portland Street in London.[3]

The Architects Benevolent Fund was especially active during the war, supporting architects in difficulty – a country at war led to low demand for architectural services and high unemployment. Loans were made and the Professional Employment Committee, a subcommittee of the AWC, organised the subsidisation of architectural work, also applying to the government Committee for the Prevention and Relief of Distress for funds to promote civic surveys in more densely populated areas of the country. The government responded favourably to this, and surveys were carried out in Greater London, South Lancashire, South Yorkshire, Exeter and Plymouth, largely by architects.[4]

Figure 4.1 Sir Aston Webb & Sons' design for a war memorial outside the Royal Exchange, London, 1920.

It was not only practitioners who were hit hard. With young men called to join the armed forces, educational institutions suffered a drop in applications, and fees. Though women had been allowed to register with the RIBA since 1898 it was not until 1915 that the architectural school at University College London, the Bartlett, allowed them access to its education, and not until 1917 that the Architectural Association (AA) did the same. It is arguable that the financial motive was a stronger factor in the decision to enrol female students at this point than ideologies around female suffrage.[5]

The first cohort of women enrolled onto the AA course worked hard and excelled in winning AA and RIBA prizes. Winifred Ryle, one of this founding cohort, published an article in the *AA Journal* titled 'Women as Architects', which stated that in the future 'the woman architect will be not only a vague possibility, but an absolute necessity'[6] – an assertion which, though true, stoked resistance at the time, with one student opposing that 'what has been so clearly set forth from time immemorial by Nature herself and is so indisputable that even the most moderate and up-to-date "unfortunates" [female architects] cannot go against it'.[7] Despite the success of its female students, or perhaps because of it, the AA had introduced quotas by 1930, limiting female admissions to the school. These remained in place until the loss of male students again brought about financial difficulty during the Second World War.[8]

Figure 4.2 Students at the AA welcoming the Prince of Wales, 1921, AA Archives.

With high unemployment, a loss of expertise, skills and future students (who were in the trenches), and a struggling economy the RIBA convened a series of conferences in the later years of the war to consider the challenges and opportunities the profession was facing. The tone was optimistic but continued the protectionist aims of previous decades, with FM Simpson, a London University professor, speaking of the need for professional unity and a register of qualified architects.[9] Indeed, the unsettling impact of the war had galvanised the appetite for professional registration and more formal public influence. Sidney Webb envisioned a professional architectural society whose role was to publicly critique governmental policy and draw attention to and agitate for sufficient services to the community as a whole. Meanwhile William Lethaby, the influential Arts and Crafts architect, concluded the conference with the remark that 'it is only by getting the public's consent and interest that we can exist'.[10]

This group of visionaries formalised themselves as the Future of Architecture Committee, chaired by RIBA President Henry Hare. During the summer of 1918 they discussed areas of architectural policy, including inter- and intraprofessional collaboration, architects' fees and marketing of architectural services. They formulated a questionnaire which was circulated among the profession and received replies from multiple eminent practitioners. That of John Murray, Crown Architect and Surveyor to the Commissioners of Crown Lands, survives. His response would not be entirely unfamiliar to architects today, indicating concern over failure to deliver fully integrated services throughout the design and construction process, the low level of architects' fees and salaries, the inability of professional associations to keep their members abreast of technological advancement, the disengagement of younger architects from the professional process, and the lack of influence architects had over government policy or political decisions. His proposal was a consolidation of professional power in one place: a reorganisation of the RIBA, an amalgamation with regional societies, and closer collaboration with societies in which architects were heavily involved, such as the London Society or the Town Planning Institute.[11] Like the RIBA's members since its inception Murray's answer to professional vulnerabilities was not adaptation, but consolidation of influence and enforcement of what was becoming an increasingly rigid definition of the British architect.

Statutory registration – the battle for a protected profession

The common theme of much immediate postwar architectural conversation trended towards unity, formalisation and safeguarding the future. Statutory registration of both title and function in architecture, overseen by the RIBA, was seen to be the solution to all of these issues. This aim was not universal: architects both within and outside the ranks of the RIBA opposed registration either on the lingering grounds of the artist/professional debate or because of vested financial interests in the current system.[12] Registration controlled by the RIBA was also seen as a threat to those architects, significantly those outside London, who still practised as 'architect and surveyor' – a subset of the profession the RIBA had been, and remained, keen to eliminate on reputational grounds.

Statutory registration of architects bills were introduced into Parliament in 1889, 1890, 1892, 1895, 1900 and 1903 to no effect, but the desire for registration was becoming more widespread, with the International Congress of Architects in 1900 (Paris), 1906 (London), 1908 (Vienna) and 1911 (Rome) all passing resolutions in support of statutory registration systems.[13] Registration was usually promoted in terms of its safeguarding of the public interest, but the commercial protection and status such legal protection would offer to architects was a strong inducement for support in the economically uncertain 1920s and 1930s.[14]

War had interrupted efforts to pass a registration bill but efforts to finally close the profession re-emerged afterwards, leading to the RIBA forming a Registration and Unification Committee in 1920. It included representatives of the RIBA, allied societies and all the significant architectural groups of the day.[15] A great deal of internal politics, discussion and voting followed, culminating in the consensus that many of these smaller societies should merge with the RIBA so that discussions with political and governmental policymakers could be more authoritatively representative of the profession. In 1911 RIBA members made up a quarter of the architectural profession, by 1921 nearly half, and with each new member its authority to speak and to advocate on behalf of the profession increased.[16]

While there was consensus on the amalgamation of societies, there was debate about whether amalgamation should follow statutory registration, or registration should follow amalgamation. Those in favour of amalgamation first felt greater numbers would give greater weight to their attempts to introduce a bill to Parliament. Those in favour of registration first felt that it would better protect the standards of the profession if RIBA was felt to have higher entry requirements.

The debate led to the latter group storming the RIBA council chambers in June 1922 after significantly vocal outbursts in the trade press and forcibly dissolving the Unification and Registration Committee, replacing it with a new Registration Committee in their image. They were thrown off the council in 1923, and withdrew their opposition to amalgamation first following a postcard referendum in 1924.[17]

By 1925 a RIBA enlarged by its amalgamation with other societies drafted a registration bill, which included provisions for the RIBA to be in complete control of the Register of Architects, and stated that only those on the register would be able to use the title 'architect' and that entry to the register would be contingent on satisfying the RIBA council of bona fide practice and of subsequently passing RIBA's approved examinations.[18] This draft caused grave disquiet to architects still practising surveying, and they split from the RIBA to form the Incorporated Association of Architects and Surveyors (IAAS) in 1925, with the stated ambition of preventing the RIBA from eliminating surveying from the architectural skillset or controlling any statutory architectural registers.[19]

The IAAS joined forces with other aggrieved architectural figures including Edwin Lutyens, who had resigned from the RIBA, and Robert Tasker MP – a long-serving member of the London County Council, who bore a grudge against the RIBA from when it had refused to support claims he had made against the council's official architects' department in 1910. The Faculty of Architects and Surveyors (FAS) set up in opposition to the monopolist ambitions of the RIBA, registering concern that it should be given control over the legislative definition of an important national activity. These combinations of forces opposed and lobbied against the RIBA, its bills and its right to control the register of architects.[20]

In all this it is easy to forget that there would be a global impact to these squabbles, albeit perhaps limited to questions on the practice and status of architecture. Despite its slow dissolution following the First World War, by

1934 the British Empire still consisted of 80 territories or countries including Australia, New Zealand, India and vast swathes of Africa. Harry Barnes, a Fellow of the RIBA, writing in 1934 on the topic of registration, notes the global influence of the RIBA, stating:

> 'Its position is imperial. Not only is the whole surface of these two islands covered with a network of architectural organisations allied to and federated with the Royal Institute of British Architects, but you cannot go into any part of the British Empire, into any Dominion or Crown Colony where you will not find either already in being or coming into being an organisation of architects who, while directing their own affairs in their own locality, are yet linked not only by sentiments of interest but by more formal ties to the Royal Institute of British Architects.'[21]

These same considerations are evident in the debates surrounding the bills with minutes noting that registration bills for architects were already in operation in New Zealand, Canada and South Africa and under consideration for India and Palestine.[22]

The bill was introduced into the House of Commons in February 1927 by Sir Clement Kinloch-Cooke MP, and given a second reading in April of the same year. It failed to pass. Other bills were introduced between 1927 and 1929, also failing to pass, with particular concern among MPs about the attempts of the RIBA to directly control the register, and the detrimental impact this might have on working-class children who wished to join the profession. Then, as now, there remained the issue that the acceptance of a qualified individual onto the register is not a guarantee of their quality or competence to practice. A bad architect is equally capable of entry as a good one, and the MPs expressed disquiet over the high pass rate of RIBA exams – were such qualifications worthy of official protection? In 1927 a select committee modified the bill to change the protection of title from 'architect' to 'registered architect', thus making the principle of compulsory registration voluntary. The bill was further amended to ensure that no single professional body should be in charge of the register, and that registration authorities should not be solely professional bodies. The Architects Act was passed by both Houses of Parliament, and royal assent was given on 31 July 1931.[23] The 1931 Act protected the title 'registered architect', and the register was to be held by a new, independent body – the Architects Registration Council of the United

Figure 4.3 A cartoon showing senior architects and RIBA figures in the 1930s, around the time of the Registration Act.

Kingdom (ARCUK). Representatives of all Britain's larger architectural societies and groups sat on ARCUK, with the number of representatives proportional to each group's number of members.[24]

The bill was seen as a significant blow to the RIBA. Voices at the time suggested that the bill was a failure, with the concessions of 'registered' architect and ARCUK too great. Senior RIBA figures were less deflated, however; they felt that any bill on the statute books would enable incremental lobbying and amendments to a point where their aims – full closure of the profession and control of the register by the RIBA – could eventually be achieved.[25]

The make-up of ARCUK allowed the RIBA, with its large membership, to quickly establish itself in control of the registration council and ARCUK's board of architectural education. In 1937 a new bill to amend the Architects Act was proposed, at which point pamphlets were circulated among MPs, alleging that the RIBA was seeking to force smaller societies to close. These allegations and the disquiet around the RIBA's control of ARCUK were raised in the parliamentary debates surrounding the Act. However, no modifications were made to ARCUK. The Architects (Registration) Act was passed in 1938, restricting the use of the title 'architect' to those on the register.[26] The practice of architecture itself remained unrestricted, and a contentious subject – as it does to this day. In the 2020s there are still those who believe that a monopoly position on the practice of architectural skills will safeguard the future of the profession. Arguments continue to be made in terms of public wellbeing and safety, but much like the initial arguments surrounding protection of title, the economic advantage such a monopoly would grant the profession is perhaps the more motivating factor. As in the 1930s there remains little to no political appetite to allow architects exclusive practice of their art.

RIBA exams, returning servicemen and the 'problem' of women students

The interwar years were not marked by leaps in architectural education – the profession at large seemed more interested in the fight for registration. Like most universities between 1914 and 1918, architectural schools were all but empty. Towards the end of the war they began to refill with demobbed soldiers eager to pick up their lives and careers. The RIBA recognised the difficulties of returning servicemen, granting them Associateship on easier-than-usual terms with a Special War Examination – which lasted with modifications until 1922.[27] Tensions around female students began to rise again with the perception, despite the remarkable success of some of the early female cohort, that they were 'hijacking' places that by rights belonged to the men.[28] Suggestions were even made at the AA of establishing an all-female architectural school to train women in interior design, freeing up these 'hijacked' places, with the additional advantage of reducing 'distraction' for male students. Nothing came of this, however; instead, the AA imposed a quota – no more than 12 women per year were to be admitted.[29] It was a step backwards, and one which did not favour the profession. The 'distracting' influence of these female architects would lead to professional and private partnerships that would spark some of the defining moments of British architectural practice in the decades that would follow.

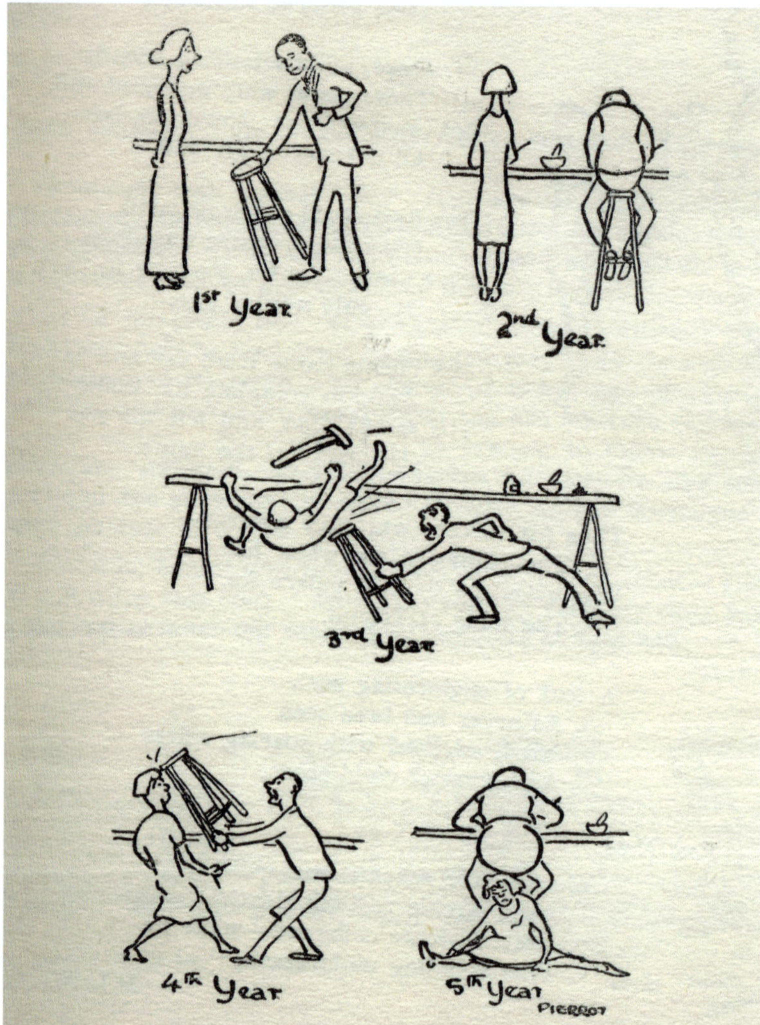

Figure 4.4 Battle of the sexes cartoon from the AA Archives, 1924.

Also appearing in tiny numbers in architectural schools are students from Britain's Empire, such as women from Australia and New Zealand, and sisters Angelique Yuen Mo-Ting and Esther Yuen Mo-Ting from the British Crown Colony of Malaya. Unfortunately, financial trouble interrupted their studies, but Esther returned to London in 1948 on a scholarship after a stint at the Kuala Lumpur Public Works Department. She returned to Kuala Lumpur in 1950, marrying a Scottish emigré architect, whereupon they set up in joint practice as Yuen and Todd.[30]

Despite a system designed to favour white British men, these women and international students made a small mark on British architectural history; arguably it might have been greater if their energies had not been partially consumed in navigating a profession that seems to have barely tolerated their presence. The impact on British architecture and practice had the schools not sought to artificially restrict their intake could have been monumental at a time when the world was rebuilding after devastating global upheaval. However, what that impact could have been will now never be known.

From 1919 onwards various architectural schools began to be recognised by the RIBA, such that a degree from them would exempt the student from the RIBA final examination for Associateship. These schools based their syllabuses on guidance from the RIBA Board of Education and were subject to RIBA inspections. Despite conferences in Paris and London in 1920 and 1924, it was not until 1939 that the RIBA Board of Education formed a committee which began to overhaul the mix of pupillage and university-based education that had characterised the interwar years, though by this point the RIBA had lost its fight to define the educational standards of the profession to the government's formation of ARCUK. In 1945 the committee reported that pupillage could not be considered to give a balanced and comprehensive education, suggesting instead a system of five years' full-time education, of which four and a half should be in schools, the rest in an office. While novel to British architecture, this system had been adopted by most other European countries before 1926.[31]

This is not to say that individual schools were not looking towards Europe for inspiration. Despite a lack of official policy from the central institutions of the profession, the AA, Glasgow School of Art and Liverpool University all altered their curriculums and ways of teaching in response to the exposure of some of their leading professors to the École de Beaux-Arts methods employed in France and America. The system was based on an education grounded in the classical civilisations of Greece and Rome, and was heavily academic.[32] The emphasis on an architectural education 'free from commercial pressures' began to increase the distance between the architect and knowledge of the materials from which buildings were constructed, distancing the modern Western architect ever further from the polymath profession that had weathered the millennia between ancient Egypt and the Industrial Revolution.

Between 1924 and 1926 an almost unprecedented number of books of architectural theory were published in England, suggesting an active search for a doctrine of architecture in the turbulent times of the mid-1920s.[33] Between 1932 and 1935, however, under the influence of Modernist thought, enthusiasm for total obedience to laws of aesthetics inherited from the principles of the Bauhaus movement in Germany began to emerge. Slowly a shift in formal education started, away from the individually competitive nature of the Beaux-Arts schools to collaborative 'units' of students working together in a more democratic fashion.

Legal and standards reform

Some of the most significant changes to architectural practice in the interwar years were in legislative reform. By 1917 the focus of the British state was turning away from war and towards reconstruction, and the RIBA was determined that architects should play a key role. A new Ministry of Reconstruction was formed by the David Lloyd George administration and, after a forceful deputation from the RIBA, architects were appointed to positions at the Local Government Board, the Ministry of Munitions and the Board of Trade.[34] In 1919 the Addison Act sought to respond specifically to the postwar housing crisis, promising government subsidies to finance the construction of 500,000 homes within three years. Though funding was cut and only 213,000 homes were completed, it was a significant step on from the Poor Laws of the 1800s, making housing a national government responsibility for the first time, with homes for working people to be developed by their local councils. Further Acts in 1924 and 1930 provided further subsidies, obliging councils to clear all remaining slum housing, and leading to the building of 700,000 homes. Interwar housing Acts overall were responsible for the building of 1.1 million homes in the UK, with space standards developed by the Acts eventually picked up by private sector builders.[35]

Figure 4.5 Housebuilding in 1932.

Figure 4.6 The Becontree Estate, London – interwar social housebuilding at its height.

These Acts gave opportunities to architects in practice but also to academia, with architectural and planning theory developing around the homes that were built. The mood of the country looked for housing 'fit for heroes', and as the country rebuilt after the war various regulatory changes began to be made to safeguard the quality of this rebuilding. The Public Health Act of 1875 had been a milestone in the development and consolidation of British public health legislation, with further Acts in 1890 and 1907 to encourage local authorities to adopt building by-laws.[36] These were not dissimilar to modern building regulations, and might include the minimum size of window or how drainage was to be designed. However, despite a public interest in higher-quality building after the war, there were no standardised national by-laws; rules varied from council to council. Indeed, by 1930 there were 660 local authorities which had still to enact a single by-law.[37]

The opportunity for local discrepancies, abuse of power and corruption in application of the local by-laws was satirised in HB Creswell's *The Honeywood File*, a fictional and satirical account of the letters surrounding a building project in the mid-1920s. Architect James Spinlove ARIBA is depicted constantly at war with a tricky district surveyor, Mr Potch, who also happens to practise as a local architect and is apparently determined to make life as hard as possible for the London-based Spinlove by less-than-fair application of his local by-laws.

It seems that Creswell was not the only person to whom the system seemed ridiculous. A governmental committee convened during the war allowed the building of homes under the Addison Act to be exempt from outdated by-laws. By 1936 the Public Health Act was passed, requiring all local authorities to adopt building by-laws based on a model set drafted by the government by 1939, in order to standardise building quality and reduce opportunities for abusing the system.[38]

As a result of the number of new houses being built progress was also made in the discipline of planning. Though the overlaps with architecture are irrefutable, a separate discipline of town planning was established around 1914. The RIBA and its members had been active in discussions on the Garden City movement and influential in lobbying for planning reform in the wake of the first Planning Bill in 1907. However, the RIBA formed a planning committee which tended to work independently of local governments. A Town Planning Institute separate from the RIBA and its committee was established in 1913 and, although the RIBA was influential in discussions around planning for several decades, and Raymond Unwin served as president of both the TPI and RIBA, the two disciplines drifted apart. The desire of the British architectural establishment to control and safeguard all functions of architectural practice had led to them being sidelined, and a new discipline forming. This was to be a common pattern as the process of construction grew more complex in the following decades.

It was not only in control of urban planning that architects sought to exercise their influence. The first standard form of building contract was issued 'in agreement with the RIBA' in 1903, giving pre-eminence and quasi-judicial power to the architect.[39] Consolidating their position the RIBA formed the Joint Contracts Tribunal (JCT) in 1931, – issuing, for the first time, a standard form of contract between the RIBA and the National Federation of

Building Trades Employers. This standard form was to prove popular, with a local authorities version published in 1937 and revisions discussed and published in 1939, 1963, 1980 and 1998.[40] JCT contracts remain popular to this day, with the suite of contracts now expanded to include different scales of work and procurement routes. These first contracts were all tailored to a 'traditional' procurement with a bill of quantities. The standard terms within them were seen to save much time as – until this point – it was most usual for a new contract and set of terms to be drawn up for each individual project.

Standardised forms became ever more popular following the First World War, as pressure increased on the architect to complete a full set of drawings and contract documents for each project. Architects were called on more and more for deep technical understanding, at a time when the profession's inherited knowledge of building skills had suffered a severe blow and the decline in building skills seen in earlier decades had been exacerbated by the loss of life in the war. The loss of these skills, alongside the increased demand

Figure 4.7 A lab at the Building Research Station.

for building occasioned by the war, increased pressure on the specificity of written and drawn descriptions of building projects, contributing to even greater specialisation of the building professions, industrialisation of the building industry and more formal quality standards to be associated with building products.[41]

The problems with shoddy construction work prior to the war had not gone away either, and in 1921 the UK government funded a research laboratory – the Building Research Station – which carried out research into emerging building products, including early research on reinforced concrete in floors, the development of British Standards for brick, and the first national standards for construction materials.[42] The context of declining technical knowledge, new building technologies, increased pressure on programmes and greater demands of building documentation created a new context for architects that required a level of polymath skill and adaptability that the UK profession had been moving away from for nearly a century.

Figure 4.8 The reading room at the Building Research Station.

Worldwide depression, unemployment and new avenues of architectural practice

In 1929 a worldwide depression, beginning in the United States of America, wiped 15% off worldwide GDP. Personal income, tax revenue, profits, prices and international trade all dropped. In 1931 it overwhelmed Britain with financial upheaval so significant it caused the minority Labour government to fall. A national government under Ramsay MacDonald followed, as did severe declines in heavy industry and unemployment as high as 20%. Work in architecture became ever scarcer, and an estimated £70–80 million of construction work was abandoned.[43]

In these days before the welfare state the RIBA, the Association of Architectural Surveyors and Technical Assistants (AASTA) and the Architects Benevolent Society set up an unemployment fund, working with the London Society to commission a survey of London to find opportunities for slum clearance and development in line with the Housing Act of 1930, and holding an exhibition of their findings in 1934.[44] Exhibitions and public displays of building problems and their solutions became popular throughout the decade, also providing opportunities for women to engage more publicly with architecture.

Judith Ledeboer for example was appointed organiser of the 1934 Building Trades Exhibition New Homes for Old exhibition, which visitors entered through a reconstructed slum sourced from salvaged parts of a recently demolished slum in London's East End. There was then a display of cutting-edge solutions to the problem. Ledeboer was also appointed to this role in 1936, when rural housing was the focus. To illustrate her point more forcefully she arranged for a condemned farmworker's cottage to be transported to the exhibition hall in Olympia – its smell causing much comment in the press. A new model cottage designed by Justin Blanco White (a fellow female AA graduate) formed the counterpoint to this smelly display.[45] This research and exhibition work provided female architects with opportunities at a time when the global depression had made jobs scarce and society increasingly called on working women to return to the home.

The challenges of the Great Depression also catalysed the formation of the Building Industries National Council (BINC) in 1933, from a series of conferences convened by the RIBA. The BINC sought to formalise

Figures 4.9 and 4.10 Trade stands at the 1938 Building Trades Exhibition.

collaboration between various sectors of the building trades and professions and to increase public interest in the building industry as a way of stimulating work. Initially the BINC sought to mitigate the impacts of government austerity policies in the first years of the Depression. Its work promoted industry rationalisation and economic stimulation, and lobbied for long-term policy with an evidence base formed from its research. Later it published a series of articles in *The Times* calling for a policy of public works. BINC was keen to emphasise the broader impact of construction work on local economies, claiming that not only did the building industry support the British industry of producing raw materials, but that the construction industry provided the largest national weekly circulation of money through weekly wages.[46] These arguments had a noticeable effect on local authorities, with Kingston-upon-Thames spending £150,000 on new offices, a town hall and police courts which opened in 1935, and a Somerset local authority reversing its decision to postpone the construction of its new offices in Taunton.[47]

While the exhibitions and research institutes had raised the profile of architectural services, the use of publicity and public relations as a means to alleviate the worst impacts of the economic depression was problematic. The RIBA Code of Professional Practice at the time stated that an architect 'must not advertise nor offer his service by means of circulars or otherwise, nor may he make paid announcements in the press'. This clause had arisen from the efforts of the RIBA to distance the profession from the less reputable elements of the construction industry in the 1800s and to maintain a professional persona. However, by the Depression era of the 1930s, this inability to market their services was a significant challenge to architects.

Particularly disadvantaged were architects in private practice, as they relied heavily on lobbying by the RIBA to raise the profile of architects and for the statutory protection of their services. Additionally, work arising from conservation campaigns was reliant on the awareness of such campaigns, and private practice was coming under increasing pressure from the growth of the 'salaried' architect within local authorities. It was felt that architectural skills and priorities were being suppressed by non-architect management.[48]

Reginald Rix, a provincial architect, argued forcefully in a report submitted to the RIBA Council in 1930 that the public was largely ignorant of the

functions of an architect and that well-directed publicity would not only promote the role of the architect but public appreciation of architecture and the reputation of the RIBA. He contextualised his report in the efforts at the time to get the Architects (Registration) Act passed, which it eventually was in 1938, arguing that professional advertising by a collective association was not overly commercial and might assist in the passing of the bill. His suggestions were dismissed as impractical, but they added to the shift in attitudes towards publicity surrounding professional services.[49]

Figure 4.11 Ideal Home Exhibition, 1936.

The RIBA's Public Relations Committee (later the Film, Broadcasting and Television Sub-Committee) lobbied (to no effect) to include a clause in the 1935 Housing Bill to require all large-scale public housing schemes to be supervised by a registered architect. The emergence of the documentary film movement in the 1930s gave an arguably better opportunity for the RIBA to engage the public in matters architectural, working with film company Gaumont-British to produce five films on architecture.[50] Subjects included 'the house through the ages'; 'airports and airways' and the RIBA building in Portland Place. The RIBA also offered access to its photographs to the BBC and provided advice and help to a 1937 BBC series of 'television talks on architecture'.[51] The embrace of television could have been a great opportunity to engage with the public but serious attempts seem to have fizzled out after this, and today the vast majority of popular architectural programming in the UK is fronted by non-architects.

The Building Centre – a department store for building products

There has been consensus since that Britain's recovery from the economic recession of the 1930s was largely based on the growth of the consumer goods and construction industries.[52] While there has been little discussion of the impact of the architectural profession, it is clear that architects played a role in this, and that one particular rising trend contributed both to this recovery, and to changing the way architects practise and specify buildings – the commodification of building products.

Until this point in time an architect might have specified – say – a tiled roof with a certain performance or colour, but it is likely that a tile laid on a roof in Northumberland would be different from a tile laid in Dorset, depending on locally available materials. With industrialisation and standardisation, as well as the rising interest in new construction technologies, this began to change. Perhaps the clearest example of this was the opening of the Building Centre (BC) on New Bond Street in London in September 1932.

Following the public success of the Building Trades Exhibition, the BC was founded by Frank Yerbury, the secretary of the AA, to stimulate public interest in building for the benefit of the architectural and construction industries. By placing the BC on a central shopping street, Yerbury intended not only architects but the general public to browse its displays, particularly hoping to appeal to women. It displayed not only guttering, paints and roofing products, but also curtains, washing machines and refrigerators – all displayed in attractive ways, rather like a department store. The window displays changed seasonally, just as in the neighbouring shops, and the products were usually placed in situ to make it easier for those browsing to imagine them in their own home. For example, panels of brick were hung on the walls and tiles were laid on small sections of roof. The BC even opened with a private view, much as a private gallery might open an exhibition.[53]

Nothing at the BC was for sale, though. Manufacturers applied for their products to be displayed and paid an exhibition fee. Architects and clients would then browse the products on display, noting the number of the items that interested them. At the desk information sheets could be picked up for each of the products so that a file could be assembled of all the products to be used on a particular job.[54] This role of 'architect as shopper' was new, and to name a particular branded product in building specifications was also new territory for the architect. It added a new dimension to relationships within the construction industry, as product manufacturers sought to persuade architects to specify their products.

Creswell satirises this beautifully in *The Honeywood File* as Spinlove's client Sir Lesley Brash becomes enamoured of Riddoppo super-paint, which is marketed as 'inflammable' and acid-proof, 'cannot be scratched' by fingernails and, to the delight of Lady Brash, free from 'odiferous effects'.[55] After some back and forth, during which Spinlove objects on the grounds that it is unknown to both him and the builder and (horror) is advertised in the Tube, the paint is bought and used. The builder notes to the architect that 'the paint is beginning to creep … that [finishing work] ought to be done soon before Riddoppo super crawls out of the front door and off home, which is about what it's aiming for'.[56] Riddoppo super-paint appears at multiple points in the sequel, *The Honeywood Settlement*, as it fails and all parties seek to prove they are not liable for the cost of rectifying the paintwork. It is a humorous example but makes a serious point about the unknown and untested nature of many of the new products coming to market, and the design liability attached to them.

Many products, however, were sound and had been engineered to make more efficient use of resources whose availability was limited after the war. The range of materials and products expanded as a result of finding peaceful applications for technologies developed during the war, giving clients a greater range of choices than before. New electrical appliances were also introduced and marketed aggressively to encourage use of electricity. There had been huge investment during the war to increase electrical capacity and increasing domestic electricity consumption was seen as vital to justify the ongoing existence of this infrastructure. There are also suggestions that the proliferation of products was a response to the UK's shift from heavy to light industrial production, and that the new range of choice was as much an opportunity for manufacturers to diversify as it was to respond to a genuine demand from the building industry.[57]

It should also be noted that here – again – arose the question of how commercialised the architectural profession should be. In the same way that individual marketing of services was forbidden, the RIBA from its founding had sought to distance its members from what was perceived as a corrupt building industry, decreeing that its members should not be visibly associated with contracting. In recommending particular products to clients there was a fine line to be trod between providing information and promoting forbidden commercial building activities.

The Building Centre was another arena in which female architects were able to find 'acceptable' employment and opportunities for promotion, with those such as Mary Crowley, Justin Blanco White and Rose Gascoigne employed to research the BC's publication *Housing: A European Survey* in 1936. Cycill Tormley curated the 1937 display 'Prosperous working man's home' and Alma Dickens curated the 1936 exhibition Work of Women Architects. All of this was seized on and reported by an almost incredulous press at the time.[58]

The rise of the salaried architect

In spite of the battles around registration, the questions about commercialisation, and the rising levels of regulation and legislative frameworks, perhaps the most significant shift after the First World War was the rise of the salaried architect in public practice. The architectural historian John Summerson summarised it neatly in his 1942 essay *Bread and Butter and Architecture*, comparing a student leaving architecture school in 1925 with one leaving in 1938. The former might enter the office of a FRIBA for a salary, which may lead in time to a partnership. Most likely though in the meantime a relation or acquaintance would step in with a commission – perhaps a house from which you could work up to your own practice. This was the 1925 model of architectural success.[59]

The 1938 graduate, though, had tougher prospects, with the Depression having taken the glamour and scope of possibility out of private practice. Summerson describes it as 'almost fanciful to pursue the brass plate ideal, though it may be precariously achieved by a group of friends tacking half a dozen modest plates under a single bell pull'.[60] However, there was now an alternative – permanent salaried employment.

These official architect roles comprised full-time employment by councils or government, and were not particularly popular in the early 1920s. It was commonly held that these architects had little in the way of artistic autonomy; most of their time was spent inspecting, surveying and checking buildings designed by others. In this environment the artistic/professional divide seen in earlier arguments around registration was arguably resumed, with the former opting for private practice and the latter official.[61] The serious shift towards salaried employment coincided with the Depression, the housing Acts and slum clearance drives of the mid-1930s, which compelled local authorities to act. Most of them were ill-equipped for this job and sought to recruit architects to fill their knowledge gap.[62] As the numbers of official architects grew, so did their design prestige as they began to become known for enterprising planning and creative work. It also became a sought-after role for the socially and politically conscious students of the 1930s.[63]

Meanwhile the established members of the profession tended to remain in private practice, and paid little attention to the plight of the salaried architect; indeed, those in private practice seemed almost to set themselves in opposition to their official colleagues. The AASTA claimed to speak for these salaried employees and had collaborated with the RIBA on and off since its foundation. In 1934 a series of AASTA proposals, including a salary scale for architectural assistants in private offices, were rejected by the RIBA, at which point AASTA cut ties with it.[64]

In response, in 1935 a special RIBA committee on official architecture with Sir Raymond Unwin (RIBA President 1931–3) as chairman was founded. It recommended that design of important municipal buildings should be given to a private practitioner over a salaried official architect, as the former was more likely to be able to offer fresh design perspectives and contribute to advancing architecture, rather than be encumbered by the bureaucracy of the role.[65] These rather inflammatory comments were exacerbated by HS Goodhart-Rendel, who used his presidential address to liken the design abilities of official architects to machine-dispensed chocolate: 'repetitive and slightly stale'.[66] This, obviously, caused a colossal row – not only for the insensitive and superior remarks of Goodhart-Rendel, but because the tide by this point had turned: young architects were flocking to salaried posts rather than trialling the uncertainties of private practice. In 1938, approximately 31% of the RIBA membership were employed in the public sector. The London Passenger Transport Board employed architects, as did government ministries, which employed them to design defence buildings, post offices and telephone exchanges. Major banks and branded stores hired in-house architects, as did the Girls' Day School Trust.[67] The scope of public practice work was often broader than that of the private practitioner, calling on expertise in engineering, planning and surveying as well as architecture.[68] It could be argued that the public sector architect in the 1930s was approaching something of the polymath professional of the amateur architects of the early 1800s. The era of the sole practitioner sat behind his brass plate waiting for patrons seemed all but over.

The near 100-year history of the RIBA at this point had built up an interlinked system of myriad small private businesses, increasing respect for the profession, lobbying for helpful legislation, and creating standards of educational achievement and rules against internal competition. Though arguably protectionist behaviour, this nevertheless gave a degree of collective strength to architectural practice and a level of protection to architects' fees and their role within the construction industry. Public sector architects had less immediate concerns in these areas; their need was not to secure projects on good terms but to maintain their professional autonomy in the face of pressures from their employers.[69] The division in the profession marked a new style of practice. However, unlike previous shifts in architectural practice this one could not afford to be an existential shift away from small private practice. Whatever the needs of large companies and the state, there would always be individual commissions to be had. The two styles of practice, generally having both a political and stylistic divide, were almost diametrically opposed. However public and private practice needed to find a way to coexist.

In 1930 the RIBA published its first scale of annual salaries, in an attempt to mirror the RIBA mandatory minimum fee scales – providing 'pay scales' for both public and private practitioners. However, the priorities of the RIBA committees more broadly did not align with organisations such as the AASTA, and by the late 1930s the growing rift between public and private architects was becoming a serious threat to the predominance of the RIBA.[70]

Interwar democratisation and commodification

As in the previous chapter, the London profession has occupied most of this narrative. This is not because there were not individuals in practice in provincial areas of the UK but simply that then, as now, it is often in the concentrated professional atmosphere of a capital city that change is catalysed and new directions of travel taken.

One of the main themes of the interwar years was the democratisation of design. The unimaginable horrors of the First World War are widely acknowledged to have broken down many of the barriers inherent in the British class system and its highly stratified society. In February 1918 all men over 21 and all women of property over 30 were given the right to vote (accounting for around two-thirds of all women in the UK). The end of the war saw a growth of public democracy and the recognition that traditionally accepted societal roles and positions were breaking down. It was in this climate of greater democratisation that the model of architect as employed by aristocratic patron became increasingly irrelevant: in decline in the decades leading up to the First World War, it all but vanished in the years following it.

The commodification of building products and the increasing need of the construction industry to engage the public led to a significant shift in the architect's position. In previous centuries the architect's role had been to reflect aristocratic taste. In this newly democratised environment, and with an interested but largely less architecturally literate clientele, the architect shifted towards the position of arbiter of taste. This led to tensions between architects and accusations of individuals becoming an 'architect's architect' or of 'selling out'. While the democratisation and diversity of the interwar years ushered in new levels of standards and building quality, they also characterised some of the more turbulent and fractious years in the profession's history – which were increasingly publicly played out. The hard-fought right to protection of title and to define educational standards did not see a corresponding rise in quality of the education available, and in the latter years of the 1930s the pitched battle between private and official architects divided two sides of a small and arguably precarious profession against each other. New architectural ideas were beginning to percolate from Europe, but in the aftermath of one world war and in the lead-up to another the great figures of the time do not emerge as visionary designers. Instead, they appear as visionary bureaucrats protectively staking out their territory in an increasingly crowded and competitive market for professional construction services.

The continual debate around art and technical skill saw friction emerge as the profession by necessity moved towards a more technical definition of architectural practice in light of new building technologies, but was constrained by official definitions of practice codified in a previous era. As in every decade previously, those architects with the greatest adaptability seemed to chart these choppy waters most easily – turning their hand to research, planning and work on typologies and scales they had not seen before. Women began to make serious inroads into the profession though they still faced opposition, most notably as society called on them to return home once the troops came back from war. These are the decades in which the course of recent architectural history was set – they are just not quite as glorious as one might hope.

CHAPTER 5

Flawed utopia

War and the welfare state

On 3 September 1939 Britain declared war on Germany. The country was again plunged into a long and global war with a devastating impact. As in the First World War, architects were called on to join the armed forces, and construction all but ground to a halt as the labour, materials and technology were all diverted to military uses. On 8 May 1945 the Allies (including Britain) accepted Germany's unconditional surrender, marking the end of the war in Europe, and on 15 August Japan surrendered, bringing a global end to the war.

By the end of the Second World War Britain had been stripped of virtually all its overseas financial resources, and was deeply in debt to the tune of several billion pounds. The economy had been skewed by years of war, with industries such as aircraft manufacture far too large and others, such as construction, desperately short of materials, labour and investment. According to the Simon Report of 1944, an estimated 230,000 construction industry operatives had died during the war.

In this febrile atmosphere the Labour Party swept to power in July 1945 on a manifesto of social reforms, which saw the nationalisation of certain industries and the creation of the welfare state, extending measures enacted by the wartime coalition government. The ambition of these welfare reforms was to care for British citizens from the cradle to the grave, and included the creation of the National Health Service (NHS). Postwar pressure on education and healthcare infrastructure grew quickly, especially as birth rates increased. In addition to these new pressures, the bombing raids of the war had left the country's cities and infrastructure badly damaged. Bombing raids had killed around 43,000 civilians and made one in six Londoners homeless.

Figure 5.1 View of the bomb damage around St Paul's Cathedral, 1940.

At least 1.1 million houses and flats were damaged or destroyed across Britain's towns and cities.[1] Adding to the economic turmoil, US President Harry S Truman ended a lend-lease system in September 1945 on which Britain had depended to purchase necessities during the war. Britain was left essentially bankrupt with no way to pay for imports of goods, materials or even food. It was on its knees socially and economically.

In response to the desperate shortage of housing, exacerbated by slum clearance programmes, the UK government passed the 1946 Housing Act, which allowed local authorities to borrow more from the Public Works Loan Board in order to provide housing. These powers were extended in 1949, enabling local authorities to build for the population generally, rather than only the needy.[2] Quantity and speed of construction were key in the

immediate postwar years, and there was a huge amount of prefabricated, often low-quality, housing built in response. However, postwar shortages kept rationing of food and goods, including building materials, in place until the early 1950s, and building licences were required for all construction until 1954,[3] limiting the scope of what might otherwise have been a postwar building boom with rampant profiteering.

Figure 5.2 The Golden Lane Estate in the background of a bomb-damaged building in the City of London, 1957.

With the inception of the Housing Act the building activity of local authorities increased, leading to what became a 'golden era' for the British public architectural practice. Never before or since has the power and influence of the architect on their local communities been so impactful. The newly introduced 1947 Town and Planning Act required towns and cities across the country to make plans for their future. Many of these utopian visions would not be realised for decades due to the material and labour shortages; nevertheless, the allure of the possibility to change the shape of Britain's urban future

Figure 5.3 Lancelot Keay, RIBA President 1946–8 – the first public architect to be RIBA President.

proved irresistible to young architects of the immediate postwar generation, disillusioned as they were by years of war, death and shortages. They sacrificed the potentially higher pay and social standing of private practice for opportunities to work on grand and visionary scales and shape the face of the new welfare state through its schools, hospitals and housing estates.[4]

The powers and opportunities of public practice bought about something of a shift in perception within the architectural profession. The RIBA had until this point tolerated rather than embraced the public architects within its ranks, but in 1946 it elected its first President in public practice, Lancelot Keay. In his inaugural address Keay acknowledged the challenges the profession was facing – the reduction of intake of younger men into the profession; the shortage of trained and experienced men; the unparalleled upheaval in the building industry, and the difficulties to be faced including materials shortages, rising construction costs and full employment. This last may seem counterintuitive but full employment leads to inflationary pressures as demand for goods and services rises with no spare capacity available to increase supply at the same rate.[5] He also departed from more traditional RIBA sensibilities in his rallying cry for standardisation and mass production, declaring that 'if [standardisation] can be followed by mass production of certain essential components of best design and giving of high efficiency it will be for the greater good, for it will bring within reach of all many of the essentials which would otherwise be available only to the few'.[6]

Female architects – two steps forwards and one step back

The new material technologies that would go on to be showcased in the Festival of Britain – reinforced concrete, prefabrication and standardisation – were being increasingly experimented with in the creation of the housing, hospitals and schools that formed so much of the construction in this era. Meanwhile, however, other leaps towards modernity were being quietly backtracked. During the war female architects had been vital – drafted into public service in government departments, local authorities and voluntary roles. Jessica Albery, for example, was appointed to the Directorate of Post War Building at the Ministry of Works, co-authoring *A Survey of Prefabrication*; a work still consulted today.[7] Gertrude Leverkus worked in multiple voluntary roles through the early war years and was appointed Housing Architect in the West Ham Borough Architecture and Town Planning office in 1943[8] – a key role, as West Ham had been particularly badly hit by the Blitz and was used as a test subject for the new Greater London Plan. Jocelyn Adburgham (née Abram) began her architectural career in private practice in the office of WR Davidge and Partners in 1926, playing a leading role in the foundation of the Housing Centre in the 1930s. This expertise saw her appointed by central government during the war to consider housing policy, and her reports formed the basis of the housing manuals that shaped state housing design after the war.

On the private practice side of the profession strides towards gender equality also seemed to be being made; AA graduate Doris Robertson (née Lewis) was on the verge of a successful career, but gave it up to support her husband's architectural career, working uncredited on several of his projects until the outbreak of the Second World War.[9] Betty Pierce (née Scott) had begun a successful and creative architectural practice (Aiton & Scott) with fellow AA graduate Norah Tollenaar (née Aiton), noted for their work on a now-listed office building in Jersey, multiple private homes, a zoo and a printing works. Women architects seemed finally to be making breakthroughs, forging careers and becoming more widely accepted.

However, following the end of the war, as after the First World War, women were pressured to relinquish these gains, especially prominent ones in public practice. Albery faced opposition to promotion on account of her gender in Kent County Council, though she later found work in Basildon.[10] Leverkus left West Ham, returning to a modestly successful private practice in 1948 at Norman and Dawbarn in London, but was not involved further in the visionary public architecture of London's postwar building boom.[11] Adburgham left her policy-driving role and returned to private practice in Davidge and Partners.

Doris Robertson became categorised as a wife rather than a colleague, and was lauded in the press as her husband's 'critic on the hearth' and a 'superb hostess'; Aiton & Scott was wound up after the war as the male-dominated industry reasserted itself, and they struggled to find commissions. Aiton didn't practice architecture after the war, instead travelling widely in her new role as the wife of an insurance company director, and Scott worked as a draughtsman in film

Figure 5.4 Doris Robertson at an AA dinner in 1973 – she left a promising early architectural career to support her husband's career.

design under her married name until her architect husband's death in 1966, when she designed herself a house in Holland Park.[12]

To 21st-century eyes it seems a dispiriting anticlimax to the early promise and enthusiasm of so many talented architects. It is clear that though women had more than proved themselves in architectural practice during the war, society wished to reassert its previous norms and the route outside of wife and mother would be a hard one to follow for decades to come. Architecture has been one of the slowest professions to embrace women, and despite some progress since the 1940s, in 2021 71% of registered architects in Britain were still male.[13]

Perhaps the most noted success story of postwar female architects is that of Dame Joyce (Jane) Drew, who had begun a women-only practice in London in 1939. During the war she played a key role in RIBA debates on planning policy, and organised an exhibition on rebuilding Britain. She lobbied government to engage young Modernist architects, a policy which was adopted and which saw her husband appointed to a post as town planning

Figure 5.5 Jane Drew with local architectural associates in Chandigarh, 1950.

adviser to the resident minister in West Africa. She travelled as his assistant to Accra, where they lived and worked for three years. They continued to work in partnership both in the UK and abroad, and built a thriving architectural practice. She would become the first woman to sit on the RIBA Council (in 1964) and the AA's first female president in 1969. She held a variety of visiting professorships to US universities in the 1960s and 1970s, and was appointed a Dame of the British Empire in 1996.[14] She and her husband were some of the early pioneers of that archetypal model of British architectural practice in the 20th century – the husband and wife team.

It is clear that the strength of her practice after the war was key to the later trajectory of Drew's career. Given the experience of other notable female architects at the time, it is worth questioning whether the British profession would have suffered the loss of her considerable talents had she not been so fortunate as to marry a man who was prepared to share his practice and his limelight with his wife.

The last gasps of Empire

Jane Drew and Maxwell Fry were not the only architects who left the challenges of life in the UK immediately after the war to find work in one of Britain's colonies. The extract quoted on page 110 comes from an editorial in the *RIBA Journal* of June 1945 calling for architects to take their place in colonial administrations, and laying out in some detail what might be expected of them when they reached their destination. It speaks of a world that does not exist anymore, and sensibilities and concepts that feel alien and uncomfortable in the 21st century. It is odd to realise that this quote is less than 80 years old.

Figure 5.6 Christmas card from Jane Drew and Maxwell Fry from Chandigarh, 1953.

'There is now a demand, which is increasing, for highly qualified technical officers and the Colonial Officer is eager that the opportunities of colonial service should be known to architects … Architects are an integral part of the government administrative machine ... The architect may be concerned with the planning of large major buildings such as law courts and civil hospitals … post offices, police stations and residential quarters which, though smaller in scale, may be repeated scores of times. But whether the architect is concerned with the major or minor project much original thinking will be entailed ... In some Colonies there is no traditional style and the architect has to evolve his own standards, and help to formulate a technique of design suited to local conditions. But in other Colonies where traditional styles exist, the architect will find it intensely interesting to study their social and structural history, to assimilate so far as practicable what is useful and significant, and to apply to contemporary problems the resources of modern building science, in an intelligent and sympathetic way – no matter whether the ultimate effect be one of harmony or contrast.'[15]

In July 1947, amid the chaos of India's partition and independence, the *RIBA Journal* printed a letter which adds to this story of international British practice in a changing world, describing the opportunities that existed in India on the eve of partition.

'Sir,

I was disappointed that "Overseas Appointments for Architects" contained no reference to India … The private practitioner is now coming into his own. India is behind hand in all technical education so there are not enough Indians to fill the higher posts ... The result is that the few British firms of architects have all the work they can cope with. The Indian makes a good client in my experience and relies on his architect to save him from the rapacity of the contractor … I am home on short leave hoping to recruit some more staff so you may think I'm prejudiced but I have twenty-nine years of private practice in India and I go back joyfully for a few more. It is a very good country to work in – jobs are big, though costs are low, and three or four months leave in "Blighty" every three or four years is very, very good. But if you are to be happy in India you must make a home there and make friends with Indians.

Yours faithfully,

CG Blomfield'[16]

These examples do not suggest an Empire in decline, but the reality is that the Second World War significantly changed Britain's role in global politics. It had left Britain all but bankrupt and with a changed ideology. After six years fighting countries that championed extreme nationalism and the associated racist ideologies, it became less believable to the British people that Europeans were superior to Africans or Asians. The ideological and economic challenges associated with the British Empire saw it gradually dismantled, with India granted independence in 1947, and Britain withdrawing from parts of the Middle East in 1948. During the 1950s and 1960s many of the remaining mainland African and Caribbean colonies also declared independence, with others in the Middle East and the Far East made independent during the 1970s. In 1997 Hong Kong was handed back to China, marking the end of the British Empire.

British architects continue to practise overseas today but it is here, in the immediate postwar years, that the shift from the British architect practising abroad as a colonial official enacting the orders of an imperial government to the British architect practising abroad as an invited and commissioned consultant begins. This part of the history of the profession is, to say the least, uncomfortable. Nevertheless, the richness and international success of British architectural practice could be said to owe much to the cross-fertilisation of ideas, design influences, challenges and personalities that came about due to the centuries of international exposure the Empire enforced.

Postwar practice – visions of utopia, material shortages and a lack of pensions

For those remaining in Britain the immediate postwar years, especially for those in private practice, were incredibly challenging. Before the war architects had been involved with around 5% of UK construction work. With the demands of reconstruction and the building of the welfare state this had ballooned to 15 or 20% by the early 1950s.[17] The vast majority of this growth sat within the public sector, as building licences were initially reserved for essential works, which tended to be those commissioned by public sector practices. This took a significant toll on small private practitioners – the lack of work was compounded by soaring overheads, as full employment and welfare reforms saw both wages and taxation rise: many private architects barely made enough to cover living costs, and multiple letters and articles in the *RIBA Journal* of the late 1940s and early 1950s speak of the difficulty of supporting a family, and the impossibility of saving for retirement.

The technological advances in construction also created challenges for private practitioners. As the scale of projects increased, so did their complexity. The knowledge of a small number of fairly traditional construction techniques that had allowed the architect to practise before the war was not sufficient in an age of larger projects that demanded new, material-saving, often prefabricated construction techniques. Small practices rarely had the skills or resources to sufficiently research or experiment, and though some architects sought to remedy this by setting up group practices, most opportunities at the forefront of architectural progress sat firmly within public practice.[18]

However, public practice was not without its challenges. The *Architects' Journal* highlighted a particular problem in a vocal campaign between 1949 and 1950 in which it singled out London County Council (LCC) for criticism for its quantity over quality philosophy, and the sidelining of architects in the management of the Housing and Valuation Department. After a year of almost weekly attacks in the form of editorials, comment pieces, photographs, letters and articles, the LCC was eventually forced into action, returning control of housing design to the LCC architects in 1949.[19] This power struggle – not unusual, as many local authority practices appointed architectural staff under the direction of surveyors or engineers – was symptomatic of a broader problem across the industry. As project complexity increased and new construction techniques were increasingly adopted, greater specialisation became essential to practise. It was no longer feasible for the architect to design the structure, drainage, lighting, construction build-ups and technical details alone.[20] Increasingly there was a need to call on the services of consulting engineers and surveyors, causing significant unease among architects that they were losing their role. The RIBA, perhaps comprehending the path the industry was taking, or perhaps just picking up prewar campaigns, reassured its members in 1948 that though the time was not yet right, 'The RIBA has reached the end of the first stage in its registration policy … the ultimate objective is naturally to prevent anyone performing the duties of an architect unless he is registered.'[21]

Another consequence of the rapidly increasing workload in public practice was the phenomenon of public sector architects subcontracting design work out to their underemployed counterparts in private practice.[22] There are calls as early as June 1945 in the *RIBA Journal* for professional solidarity, as 'it would appear that some architects have taken on far more work than they can reasonably hope to carry out in the immediate future and this at a time when another architect has very little to do'.[23] These appointments were successful in terms of their distribution of work at a time of significant economic challenges, but did not lead to the healing of ever-increasing rifts in the wider profession between public and private practice. There were significant administrative differences between them, and each camp still eyed the other with suspicion.

Given the economic instability, some private architects sought to augment their incomes by working in collaboration with a contractor or house agent. Though this was not specifically forbidden there are numerous reminders from the RIBA in the professional press that architects should separate these functions to avoid conflicts of interest, and not combine them on letterheads or office signage. Architects were forbidden from becoming directors of building companies, and there was significant debate about the use of trade names, with the RIBA strongly recommending that the standing of the profession would be significantly reduced were architects to operate under trade names rather than the names of the principals of the practice.[24] As it had throughout its history the RIBA constantly sought to protect and elevate the societal and economic standing of the profession. Such attention to letterheads and practice names can read as mildly absurd to contemporary eyes, but the RIBA saw this 'respectability' as essential to its goal of persuading Parliament to legally protect the functions of an architect.

CONCERT HALL
ROOF GIRDERS
BY
REDPATH BROWN

The Festival of Britain – a celebration of the modern

In the midst of the challenges and tensions of postwar Britain came an opportunity to celebrate the future. A Festival of Britain was announced to mark the centenary of the 1851 Great Exhibition, originally intended as a London-based exhibition sponsored by the Council of Industrial Design to showcase the best of British science, technology, arts and film. It grew, however, to a nationwide celebration with well over 2,000 cities, towns and villages participating – planting trees, building bus stops, enhancing village signs, laying out gardens on bomb sites, or reconstructing or restoring damaged historic buildings.[25]

In the spring of 1949 17 architects were invited to submit proposals for the festival site on the South Bank in London, utilising the new materials and methods of construction coming into use at the time – both to showcase British ingenuity and to spare scarce traditional materials that were needed for ordinary building work.[26]

Figure 5.7 Royal Festival Hall under construction, May 1950.

Figure 5.8 Members of the AA visiting the site of the Pavilion of Natural Resources, 1950.

Figure 5.9 Preparations for the Land Traveller Exhibition, Alexandra Palace, 1950.

Figure 5.10 The Royal Festival Hall during the Festival of Britain, 1951.

ROYAL FESTIVAL HALL

By July of 1949 the challenges associated with the ambitious proposal were beginning to be known, with consulting engineers declaring that it would be impossible to open the site on time, as the designs were too complex to be simultaneously constructed on the constrained site. The architectural proposals were reworked and work started, only for more challenges to arise in the highly complex postwar construction materials market. Material availability fluctuated from month to month, with steel going from scarce to no longer controlled, and softwood from readily available to so scarce that usage on the festival buildings had to be more than halved. Labour strikes and rapidly escalating material and labour costs, combined with a winter and spring among the wettest since records began, added to problems and pressures that culminated in the site controller reporting that the main electrical service cables had been bitten through by rats.[27]

However, the festival opened on time and proved immensely popular with the public, acting as an effective advertisement for the benefits of modern design and construction. The RIBA set up an information bureau at its 66 Portland Place headquarters for the duration of the festival to provide information on modern buildings and architects, which was warmly received by foreign and domestic visitors. The staff also handled more obscure queries: could they, for example, describe the development of fish warehouses and methods of fish distribution over the last century?[28]

The optimism of the Festival of Britain proved prophetic. The 1950s saw the abandoning of building licences, the end of rationing and a Labour government that overcame the challenges associated with the postwar shortages. Such was the success of the postwar housing bills that Britain was building 200,000 houses a year by 1951.[29] The economy was beginning to pick up, unemployment was at a record low and many families began to have disposable income. Car ownership, for instance, doubled between 1947 and 1957.[30]

In this economic climate a new kind of client began to appear – property developers on a scale never seen before. Enterprising individuals had bought land, often bomb sites, cheap in the latter years of the war, and the 1947 Town and Planning Act seemed designed to allow great opportunity with its granting of reconstruction to prewar levels with a 10% increase in quantum. The building licensing system led to delays in the private redevelopment of these sites, but in 1954 both the licensing system and taxes on land value

increases were repealed. This, combined with a favourable economic climate and increasingly sophisticated credit systems, caused land values to increase rapidly and private development to boom, creating significant opportunities for these developers – and the architects they would employ.[31]

Figure 5.11 Battersea Festival Pleasure Gardens, 1951.

Educating a new profession

In this rapidly modernising world, the architectural profession began to question its role. Increasing scale and complexity of both projects and construction technology was driving specialisation of building professions, and architects saw a future in which they may become sidelined, losing their place as head of the design and construction team. The tension this caused with other construction professions began to effect changes within architectural education.

The contemporary belief was that in order to remain abreast of the increasingly complex and increasingly regulated construction industry, architecture needed to attract 'the best' students and trainees. The education system in the late 1940s was a mix of recognised schools (usually within universities) and architectural apprenticeships in offices, leading to some concern about the varying standards and scopes of education available. In the immediate postwar years there had been a rush to fill the vacuum at the profession's entry levels, with special exams in prisoner-of-war camps and for ex-servicemen,[32] but by the early 1950s the system and the relaxation of rules was becoming a cause of debate within the profession, with multiple letters and articles in the pages of the architectural press querying educational standards. The Modern Architecture Research Group collaborated with the Architectural Students' Association to publish a report in 1948 critiquing the stance it perceived the RIBA to be taking – far more interested in students of its recognised schools than in those who qualified through external examinations, despite the fact that this latter group outnumbered the former. The RIBA disputed the statistics, but the debate had been taken up with such enthusiasm by the profession that it became increasingly clear the education system was not meeting the needs of the profession and that the balance between university and practical (office-based) education needed revising.[33]

There was additionally growing concern within the profession that the calibre of students being attracted to architecture was not high enough. Entry requirements were limited to five passes at O Level (the exams taken around the age of 16, now called GCSEs), a standard significantly below the other professions – doctors, dentists, veterinary surgeons, etc. – not to mention below the entry standards for university undergraduate courses, or even the Higher National Diploma in Building.[34] Throughout the 1950s there were calls for a conference on education, with public sector architects the most vocal group. They had largely embraced the technocratic nature of the age and wished to see architecture as the root of all the building professions. They called for a general architectural course followed by postgraduate qualifications for specialisation – to planner, acoustic consultant, engineer, etc. Perhaps in an echo of the arguments between the professionalists and the artists of the 1840s, this new technocratically minded sector of the profession believed the future of architecture was scientific and lay with them as an increasingly specialised and technologically driven public service, rather than a private artistic or traditionalist pursuit.[35]

The debates culminated in an education conference in Oxford in April 1958, at which 50 delegates charted the future of architectural education in the UK, with the overriding aim of increasing the competence of architects at all levels. There seem to be no surviving complete notes or minutes of this conference, although the invited delegates seem to have been largely drawn from those sympathetic to the technocratic approach of the public architects driving the change.[36] An account of the conference and its recommendations was published in the *RIBA Journal* of June 1958:

1. The conference unanimously agreed that the present minimum standard for entry into training five passes at O Level is far too low and this level should be raised with minimum of two passes at A Level.
2. The conference agreed courses based on testimonies of study and the RIBA external examinations are restricting to the development of a full training for the architect and that these courses should be progressively abolished.
3. Ultimately all schools capable of providing a high standard of training and visits for the architect should be 'recognised' and situated in the universities or institutions where courses of comparable standard can be conducted.
4. Courses followed by students intending to qualify as architects should be either full-time, or on an experimental basis, combined or sandwich courses in which periods of training in a school alternate with periods of training in an office.
5. It may be that these raised standards of education for the architect will make desirable other forms of training not leading to an architectural qualification but which will provide an opportunity for transfer if the necessary educational standard is obtained.
6. The conference regards postgraduate work as an essential part of architectural education. It endorses the policy of developing postgraduate courses which will enlarge the range of specialised knowledge and will advance the standards of teaching and practice.[37]

The recommendations shifted architectural education from a vocational training to an intellectual one – definitively removing the last vestiges of the journeyman apprentice learning from his master. From this point on architecture was primarily taught as an academic subject in a university; architecture as a profession was to draw solely upon those who were willing and able to undertake an academic university-based education, and its roots and connections to the building trade were downplayed.

Of course, the RIBA did not have the legislative powers to unilaterally overhaul prescribed architectural qualifications; those powers belonged to ARCUK. There are few official archives in existence from this period, as much was destroyed when ARCUK became the Architects Registration Board in 1997, so there is little evidence for what ARCUK felt about the RIBA's suggested reforms. There is some evidence from the Ernő Goldfinger archive though that ARCUK in the 1950s and 1960s was very little interested in education policy, and gave the RIBA free reign. What can be easily found is not conclusive, but the course of history shows that the reforms suggested in the 1958 Oxford Conference were implemented and created the skeleton of the UK architectural education system that exists to this day.

The new system attempted to chart a new technological, intellectual course for the profession – with less emphasis on the mundane construction details and the process of building. However, this was not because the delegates believed this was not part of an architect's role, but rather because they envisioned a two-stranded future to the profession comprised of architects and architectural technologists.

Architects were the intellectual and theoretical branch of the profession – the only ones to be fully qualified and to enter the register of architects. They would hold specialised knowledge, undertake postgraduate study, lead the design and construction teams and oversee the vision and direction of projects. Architectural technologists were to be the branch that provided the 'highly competent technical assistance' – those who may not have reached the newly raised standards of entry to architectural training but who could train, potentially from the age of 16, in the more mundane matters of technical detailing and building process that did not require the same level of academic rigour as the 'architect' role.[38]

The recommendations were enacted at such pace that within 10 years 90% of students studying architecture were enrolled on a university-based course that comprised five years of study and two of office experience.[39] In a bid to further draw 'better' students to architecture, the RIBA created a travelling exhibition that toured schools in the late 1950s entitled 'Architecture as a career'.[40] There were further calls to safeguard the quality of architectural education within schools by ensuring that all teachers of architecture had a minimum of three years' experience in practice before starting their educational careers.[41] It is arguable that instead of strengthening the architect's role as intended, this academicisation and division of architecture significantly weakened the profession – but this is explored further in Chapter 9.

'The architect and his office' – crisis point

By the 1960s the changes that educational, economic and societal reforms had wrought on the profession were so considerable that the RIBA commissioned its first ever survey and report into architectural practice, 'The architect and his office', published in 1962. Women had by this point been entitled to join the RIBA for 64 years, but the title perhaps suggests how difficult a career in architecture remained for women at that point.

The report reached the following conclusions:

- Architectural education should be diversified in order to bring technical design skills back into the profession.
- Technologists should not be barred from RIBA membership.
- Closer relationships should be made with engineers.
- Education should be formed of an integrated 7 year period of practical training coordinated with a registered school syllabus.
- Office training is essential but there should be close cooperation between practice and school to maintain the necessary standards.
- Technicians/technologists are needed in architectural offices to raise productivity and standards of service. However, their role should not be concerned with design and their training should exclude this.
- Technicians should become members of RIBA but RIBA should sponsor an institute of technologists.[42]

Figure 5.12 Office of Hugh Casson and Neville Condor, 1956.

Figure 5.13 Eric Lyon's studio, 1958.

Within the body of the report it is not only these, almost expected, conclusions which appear – but there is significant concern about the level of architectural services being provided – and the competence of those carrying out those services. The report identified that the growth in project scale and complexity had created market conditions in which the traditional route in private practice – to work on small to mid-size commissions and buy into the partnership or start your own office – was increasingly impractical in contemporary practice. It noted that most private practices had expanded rapidly between 1951 and 1960, and that the vast majority were struggling with this change of scale.[43] It is the opinion of the report that just 11% of visited offices achieved all-round excellence in performance of management, technical efficiency and quality of design, and only 16 to 25% achieved high gradings for technical efficiency and quality of design, even if their management performance were ignored.[44]

Figure 5.14 G-Partnership Architects, 1956.

Figure 5.15 Partners and senior assistants of Architects Co-Partnership, London, 1956.

It was not purely the changes in architectural typology, scale or materiality that were causing problems – it was the speed of work and the administration of the office. The report reminds architects to 'take advice from their accountants on matters of financial policy'[45] and that 'methods of costing, overheads analysis and budgetary control should be developed'.[46] It calls on the RIBA to establish a management advisory service and publish a management handbook 'as soon as possible'.[47] It suggests that studies of the purpose and use of drawings that were being done be carried out to clarify the design process and that the possible advantages of group practices should be explored to achieve a 'more rational distribution of workload'.[48] Architects were getting more work but were proving themselves increasingly incompetent at not only carrying out the work, but running their businesses.

Within this context of construction boom it seems that it was hard to find qualified staff, and the report complains of the widespread practice of offices 'recruiting juniors without the educational minimums required for RIBA probationers', recounting that '40% of architectural assistants in private practice and 34% in local authority offices' had little likelihood of becoming architects, further suggesting that so stretched were some practices that there was significant danger that decisions that should be left to qualified architects were being made by unqualified juniors.[49] It further goes on to suggest that the (fairly new) educational system was not serving students well. It was not preparing them for any of the management or administrative aspects of architectural practice, or for the fact that a senior architect's role included less and less time drawing and more in meetings and discussions.[50] The lack of general organisation seems to have impacted on the morale of the profession, with almost universally high staff turnover, poor support for students completing their year in practice (Part 3 equivalent) and suggestions that better use should be made of administrative staff to free up overstretched architectural staff.[51]

On financial matters the report outlines an environment where generally the RIBA fee scales suit their purpose, though suggests they should be reformed to take into account the economies of scale inherent in the design process of some larger schemes , for example by a 'per unit' rather than percentage fee basis. It suggests that although career prospects were lower in public practice on account of the relatively few senior roles, they remained popular; the salary may have been lower but all public jobs came with a pension, which the majority of private salaried roles did not.[52]

The tensions that had been felt in the preceding decade between architects and other construction professionals are also addressed. Commentary and letters in architectural periodicals at the time suggest a general, if limited, optimism that if architects embraced postgraduate courses and specialisation further, they could reclaim the parts of the architectural role that had been lost to the specialist consultant engineer. The authors of 'The architect and his office' complained that architects had contracted out 'virtually all' of the major technical design skills on medium to large projects, but were clear that the idea that consultant work could be brought back under the scope of the architect was not realistic, stating instead that a 'substantial proportion of the technical design skills should be brought back into the profession itself, through the diversification of architectural education … to effect a better integration between the architect's office and the consulting engineer than exists at present.'[53]

From the findings of 'The architect and his office' a startling picture of architectural practice in the early 1960s emerges, showing a profession that has grown too big too quickly and is in crisis. The simultaneous rush of work from the public and private sectors, combined with near full employment and new technologies, created both fantastic opportunities and significant challenges for UK architectural practice – in terms of organisation, ongoing training and education. The report also seems to mark the point at which the benchmark and pinnacle of UK practice, the man sitting behind his brass plate working on small commissions, was no longer tenable.

Perhaps as a partial response to the findings of the report, the RIBA published the Plan of Work in 1963 – laying out the design and construction process from beginning to end in a series of lettered stages with suggested milestones and deliverables at each stage. It was widely embraced by the industry as a clarifying and standardising document and, though revised multiple times since, is still in almost universal use today.[54]

The reality of utopia and the beginnings of the end for public practice

As can be seen from 'The architect and his office' there was little shortage of architectural work by the 1960s, and large private practices were forming an increasingly important expression of UK practice. From the mid-1950s, however, the swing away from public architects was already evident,[55] and it was not only architects who were beginning to move away from public practice – it was losing its public appeal, too.

Immediately after the war the rush of construction in response to dire need had been appreciated and embraced. Modernist styles – rational, bare-bones, sparing of scarce materials, modern and forward-thinking – had been embraced as the wonders of a new age. In the following decades, however, this style came to be associated with austerity and the need for 'making do',[56] and problems associated with high-speed construction, new materials and a deficit of skilled construction labour became evident in the buildings where window frames rotted, or wall/roof interfaces leaked. Shortages meant that many of the Modernist utopian visions of the postwar years were only being realised by the mid-1960s, by which point the backlash against the mass clearance of historic building fabric under the guise of slum clearance was beginning to be felt, and there were the beginnings of widespread distrust of landlords and property developers.[57] Robin Hood Gardens in Tower Hamlets, a housing development of impeccable Modernist credentials, was ransacked in 1970 by some of its first tenants, leading to widespread questioning of the suitability of high-rise living for all ages and life stages,[58] and suggestions that the middle-class values Modernist architectural styles responded to may not be a universal aspiration. Architectural sensibilities and taste still moved towards the Modernist and comprehensive redevelopment,[59] but fledgling conservation movements were beginning to protest, with the establishment of the Victorian Society in 1958 and the publication of treaties such as 'The Sack of Bath' in 1973, which garnered wide public approval. Architects may have seen utopia in postwar Modernism, but society disagreed with them.

This mistrust of architects' instincts saw architects beginning to be associated with anonymous government departments, corruption and cronyism. In 1968 Ronan Point, a 22-storey tower block in Canning Town, east London, partially collapsed just two months after it had opened due to a gas explosion; in 1974 the architectural designer John Poulson caused a major scandal when he was convicted of bribing public officials to win contracts; and in 1966 the Centrepoint office building was completed but stood empty until 1975 as its owner profited from rising land values and rents while waiting for the right tenant – at a time of growing homelessness. Few examples were entirely the fault of the architect, but the aloofness of the profession from the construction industry and the years of public architects remote from the end users of buildings had left them precariously placed and easily scapegoated. Within this atmosphere of suspicion and failing buildings, legislation was introduced to standardise building regulation and reduce the potential for localised corruption. The Public Health Act of 1961 and the Health and Safety etc. Act of 1974 introduced national building regulations that replaced the local building by-laws. They started the transition from by-laws that regulated the method of construction to standards that focused on its results.[60]

➤ **Figure 5.16** Locals watching the construction of Thamesmead in outer London, 1970.

Figure 5.17 Centrepoint office tower and its surroundings, 1967.

Figure 5.18 Ronan Point collapse, 1968.

Public attitude towards architects is well, if perhaps exaggeratedly, expressed by a Monty Python sketch from 1976 in which two architects present tower block residential schemes to two besuited developers. The first demonstrates his 'abattoir' concept, in which residents are slaughtered on entry, collapsing into rage when it is rejected and decrying the developer's lack of artistic sentiment. The second architect presents a model which partially collapses and then bursts into flames before exploding, but is awarded the contract after demonstrating a 'masonic' handshake and the cost-saving measures inherent in the faulty structure. The developers agree that only slim tenants who didn't jump around too much would be able to live there. It's ridiculous, but clearly demonstrates contemporary sympathy with a view that architects were part of faceless and anonymous commercial entities that controlled the lives of ordinary people from high-rise buildings, with little thought or sympathy for the lives they were impacting. It is so far from the vision those same architects must have had when taking pay cuts to join public practices in the 1950s to envision a new and better world as to be almost absurd.

The climate of perceived 'cosiness' within the professions in 1967 saw the Monopolies Commission begin to investigate potential monopoly behaviour with regard to professional fee scales. RIBA fee scales were mandatory in the 1960s, as in many other professions, though there was some public suspicion that architects working on percentage fees made their living by inflating the cost of a building contract – much as there had been in the 1800s when architects acted as surveyors. In 1956 the Restrictive Trade Practices Act had made collective restrictive practices in the supply of goods illegal, and in 1963 this principle was applied to the supply of services in the Monopolies and Mergers Act. The commission's report, published in 1970, suggested that mandatory fees do not favour the consumer, as there is no incentive for innovation or competition between practices, and no guarantee of quality or differentiation in price due to competency of service. It suggested that price competition in the supply of professional services would be the single most effective stimulant to greater efficiency and innovation.

The road towards design and build procurement

By the 1970s the economic boom of the early 1960s had entirely subsided, with global inflation catalysed by the USA's budget deficits and war with

Vietnam. An oil crisis saw the price of primary commodities skyrocket and assumptions about cheap energy begin to be questioned.[61] The depression caused by this global inflation catalysed not only fledgling environmental movements but also the first concrete steps towards tackling the inefficiencies embedded within the design and construction process. Computing was in its early days and still rarely used in architecture, but discussions around photocopiers and repeating typical or standardised details across projects were increasingly seen in the architectural periodicals.

Perhaps most significant, however, was the impact this drive for efficiency had on building procurement. As early as 1944 the Simon Report had been commissioned to investigate a construction procurement system that had barely changed in several hundred years. The most common procurement route until a good few decades after the Second World War was roughly what is termed 'traditional procurement' today. A building was conceived, designed and detailed in full, then costed and tendered, usually through an open tendering process where anyone could submit a bid. However, the increasing scale and complexity of construction following the wars began to call this process into question, as it entirely divorced the construction process from its design.

The Simon Report noted this, suggesting the need for greater collaboration between contractor and architect in the earlier stages, but noted particular concern about open tendering, suggesting that this led to clients simply accepting the lowest price, creating an environment in which contractors would lower their prices and then make up their income by reducing quality or making claims against the contract.[62]

The Simon Report had little impact and was followed in 1950 by the Phillips Report, published at the height of the optimistic postwar reconstruction schemes, in an environment of high wages and material costs, full employment and the consequent lower productivity. It also recommended greater collaboration and coordination between the design and build sides of the industry, and called for an end to the widespread use of nominated subcontractors and a standard contract for projects procured with public money.[63] There is some evidence that following these two reports small numbers of projects began to be innovative with their procurement.[64] Influences and ideas from the USA also began to have an impact, and a limited number of negotiated tenders, where contractors were approached on the basis of their previous experience, and early design and build, where a contractor became responsible for both the design and construction of a project, began to appear.[65]

In 1962 the Emmerson Report followed in the footsteps of the Simon and Phillip reports, pointing to the shortcomings and fragmentation of the construction industry and its professionals. It reiterated calls for common forms of contracts and subcontracts, but praised the industry for its recovery and flexibility following the upheaval and devastation of the war.[66] Following quickly in 1964 and 1967 the Banwell Report and its subsequent review were published, expressing similar concern at industry fragmentation and tendering practices, but suggesting anonymised publication of all submitted tenders to aid bid managers in keeping their prices competitive.[67] While many of its recommendations were adopted by local authorities it was not taken up by the Ministry of Works, and the 1967 review did not find significant improvement, noting that the multiple guides published to assist clients in organising and planning their construction projects were barely publicised or circulated.[68]

Through the booming construction context of the 1960s there was much discussion about involving contractors earlier in the design process, and some experimentation with more innovative forms of procurement, but little actual progress.[69] Further reviews and studies were published as the economy worsened – including the Wood Review in 1973 and the Slough Estates case studies in 1976 and 1979. One study published in 1976 demonstrated that the UK took considerably longer to design and build large construction projects than all of the other seven countries considered, and that the eventual cost, exacerbated by the high inflation and interest rates, was higher than all but one. The reasons for this poor performance were considered to be unnecessarily lengthy and complex design, pricing and statutory approvals processes.[70]

The economic challenges of the 1970s saw a fast-decreasing pool of clients prepared to commit themselves to traditional procurement processes in a climate of high inflation and therefore highly uncertain and rapidly fluctuating material and labour costs. In a challenging environment further exacerbated by falling demand for built projects, delays and overruns the industry looked towards procurement that reduced the time and complexity of the design process and involved the contractor earlier in the process.

By the end of the decade, management contracting and design and build procurements accounted for around half of building contracts,[71] simplifying the process but necessarily bringing the architect back towards the collaboration and interdependency with building trades that the profession had been striving to avoid since the 1830s.

Postwar architectural practice – a flawed utopia

The decades that followed the Second World War in the UK were decades of renewal, regrowth and reappraisal. The Empire that had entered the war gave way to a more inward-looking Northern European welfare state. The global influences and powers of all the Western European nations declined in the rise of America and Russia as the next global superpowers.

Economically depleted, all but bankrupt, the UK spent the decades following the war regrouping and focusing inward. The legacy of war meant a hugely enlarged government, and this played out in construction with the highest proportion of architects ever employed directly by the state. State-sponsored rebuilding, combined with improving and then booming economies, saw the scale and complexity of construction projects reach heights rarely seen in the history of British construction.

Frankly, the British profession struggled with the pace of this growth. The reports, letters and journals of the time speak of idealistic, utopian and sometimes unscrupulous individuals embracing new materials, rapidly changing economic conditions and methods of working with unease. Friction built between construction professions as architects outsourced skills and specialities while fighting to retain leadership and influence within the industry and, despite the important and lastingly lauded work they had done during the war, women were largely pushed back to the margins of the profession. Symptomatic, arguably even representative, of the attitudes of these decades is the debate over the role of technicians – the wish of architects to outsource the 'boring' technical aspects of architecture to a professional inferior while retaining the 'fun' bits and the power and prestige within the profession itself. It was a crystallisation of the artistic versus technical debate that saw the profession definitively and formally split along those lines for the first time in history.

Unseemly squabbles and fights for power of local authority development offices and proximity to some of the scandals of the 1970s saw architects grouped together with governmental or development bodies, considered uncaring and unscrupulous and undermining the altruistic visionaries of these decades. This left a public legacy not of a profession that overcame significant challenges to rebuild the country as a better place, but of a mildly chaotic and incompetent profession more interested in its own glory and imposing its own conceptual visions on a disempowered populace. British architectural practice reached heights of public influence unseen before or since, and plumbed depths of public regard from which the profession has not entirely recovered decades later.

It seems unjust that perceptions of cronyism and incompetence became so ubiquitous, as some of the individuals and movements of these turbulent years were responsible for positive and needed reforms. Early sustainability movements and new research saw leaps forward in building technology; planning reforms saw unprecedented provision of decent-quality housing for the nation's poor; innovative hospitals and schools helped to build the foundations of a welfare state that, despite its challenges, has led to some of the highest living conditions of any country in history; architectural education reforms increased the consistency of education, aiming to raise the standards both of the education and the profession's competence; and the numerous reports and studies of the decades indicate socially aware, conscious and thoughtful individuals who sought to chart the profession's course from an individual running a small office behind a brass plate to a collaborative and engaged leader in a large and highly specialised team of construction professionals.

Ultimately it seems to have been this transition with which the profession most struggled. Since the professionalisation and gating of the architectural profession in the 1800s it had stood aloof from the building trades, formally defining itself in a way that prevented the adaptation which had allowed it to succeed in the preceding centuries. The thinkers of these postwar decades may not have expressed their recommendations in these terms, but they were essentially calling for a re-embracing of the collaborative construction models of the medieval and early modern eras and a return to the fluid balance that previous, looser, definitions of 'architect' had allowed – a call that, sadly, seemed to fall largely on reluctant ears.

CHAPTER 6
Recessions, diversifications and gradual change

Recession and privatisation – catalysts for change

By the 1980s Britain was facing double-digit inflation, powerful unions and a manufacturing sector that was becoming increasingly globally uncompetitive. Government policies led by Margaret Thatcher sought to remedy this precarious economic position via a deeply rooted belief in the free market, reduced state intervention and the reduced power of trade unions. These principles broadly aligned with monetarism economics – seeking to prioritise controlling inflation over controlling unemployment – and were characterised in government action to privatise state-owned assets, deregulate industries and reduce income tax. Thatcher's policies successfully reduced inflation but led to a deep fall in output, and saw unemployment rise as high as three million, the highest it had been since the global recession of the 1930s.

These policies had a significant impact on architectural practice. New competitive guidelines allowed private firms to tender for public work, leading to the closure of governmental and local authority architects' offices, and the Monopolies and Mergers Commission (MMC) report into architects' fee scales began to erode the legality of RIBA's mandatory fee scales. The MMC and Thatcher's government believed that the fee scales were too cosy, and bordered on price fixing – a conclusion which necessitated the publication of the 1982 RIBA fee scales as 'recommended' rather than 'mandatory'. In the early 1990s the government built further on its monetarism principles, introducing compulsory competitive fee tendering for public sector projects. Large private sector clients followed suit, and consequently the 1992 RIBA fee scales were published as 'indicative'. In 2009 the RIBA abolished its fee scales entirely, publishing instead a pair of books to aid practices in fee calculation. RIBA stated at the time that 'the RIBA practice committee felt that the application of percentages based upon fee survey data was an increasingly outdated method of calculating fees, and potentially harmful in the current economic climate'.[1]

The economy of the late 1980s and early 1990s was not easy for the public sector architect. Britain was no longer rebuilding bombed cities or establishing a welfare state. The demand for publicly built housing, schools and hospitals fell, and the reputation, deserved or not, of public sector architects as inefficient and somewhat corrupt had stuck. This suited the government policies of the time, and objectives of deregulating and encouraging innovation by pushing professional services into a more commercially competitive environment. The Greater London Council was abolished in 1986; the last vestige of the Office of Works, the Property Services Agency, was sold to private sector contractor and building materials company Tarmac (later Carillion) in 1992; and the Building Research Establishment was privatised in 1997.[2] Other council architects' departments followed suit and by the mid-2010s just 420 architects were employed in local authority architects' departments nationwide,[3] compared with the 1,500 staff the London County Council alone had employed in 1953. The day of the public sector architect had passed.

A founding partner of a successful London practice noted that when he started practising architecture the fee scales allowed them to get straight to the architectural work. Since what he termed the 'inevitable' abolition of fee scales, there has been so much in the way of negotiations about fees and appointments that they now employ an in-house lawyer. Architects, he said almost regretfully, are now much better businesspeople than they ever were before. Arguably Thatcher's policies have achieved their aim.

Few would deny that the market for architectural services became more competitive from the late 1980s. Whether competition in this market has driven higher quality or innovation, however, is less certain. A competitive market for fees saw a 'race to the bottom' in terms of quality in order to win work in a recession-hit UK, leading to significantly reduced overall investment in design services. The recession of the early 1990s proved to be a difficult time for architects, with mass privatisation, high inflation and an increasingly competitive market for fees; the government-commissioned Latham Report recorded a 39% drop in construction between 1990 and

1993.[4] The same founding partner remembers what he described as the 'precipice of bankruptcy', being just three months from insolvency for the better part of a decade. He was not an outlier; in the early 1990s architects' unemployment and underemployment climbed steeply.

It was increasingly difficult to make a living in a smaller practice. The trend that John Summerson commented on in 1942 stuck; the ability to 'work up a practice' from the commission of a house, to 'make good' behind your own brass plate never got easier from the date of that essay. The recession of the early 1990s further contributed to this trend, with high interest rates and low disposable income reducing the pool of smaller private clients. This, when combined with Thatcherite 'right to buy' policies that depleted public housing stock and local authorities not rebuilding at the rate they sold, did not make for a fertile environment for new practices.

Following on from earlier decades, the size of architectural practices increased; larger practices with a broader client base were better able to weather economic uncertainty. A trend emerged for smaller and medium-sized construction services practices to merge, creating large multidisciplinary services firms that engineered their growth to protect their methods of securing work. This shift resulted in increasing levels of policy, training and knowledge held within these firms, further marginalising the role of professional institutions such as the RIBA.[5]

The trend towards larger practices also saw increasing numbers of collaborations between practices and broader applications of architectural services. The court pageants, fancy dress and military engineering of the Renaissance and Roman architects may be beyond their more contemporary cousins, but increasingly architects began to engage in design commissions outside of buildings, including furniture design, temporary pavilions, exhibition design and sculpture. Zaha Hadid, the first woman to win the RIBA Gold Medal in her own right in 2016, not only designed award-winning architecture in her practice but, among other things, designed the stage set for pop-synth duo Pet Shop Boys' world tour in 1999 and exhibited her drawings and paintings at London's Serpentine Gallery in 2016–17. Increasingly, British architects, especially large London-based practices, sought to further stabilise their income by seeking international work, which is discussed in more detail in Chapter 7.

The diversification of UK practice

The general public mistrust in professions that emerged and grew from the 1970s[6] led the traditional 'gentlemanly profession' model of unassuming and impartial professional partnerships to seem increasingly irrelevant to the economic and social climate in which British architects were practising. As the RIBA slowly dropped its opposition to more commercially competitive styles of practice, architects began to embrace some of the benefits of commercial company incorporation. In 1989 nearly 40% of architectural practices were partnerships: by 2009 this had fallen to 9%.[7] Limited liability companies (LLCs), limited liability partnerships (LLPs) and employee-owned (EO) models, as they became available, allowed architects to practise, grow and work at an increasing scale and complexity without risking their personal finances.

Bob Allies, co-founder of London-based architects Allies and Morrison, remembers starting his career at a partnership in which all the staff were self-employed, which he reflected may be discouraged now. Slowly the business of architecture has matured and formalised, with increasing employment law and the ever-evolving legal and financial structures that go with it.[8]

Denise Bennetts, of husband-and-wife-founded Bennetts Associates, notes that when their small practice hit recession in the late 1980s with few financial reserves they 'realised the hard way' what the financial risks of the partnership structure involved, and their vulnerability to 'other people's failure, not just our own'.[9] After surviving the recession they incorporated as an LLC in 1992 – limiting their personal financial exposure but also appreciating the accompanying legal and fiscal discipline that came with this style of practice structure. In 2016 Bennetts Associates became employee-owned through an employee ownership trust, both to ensure the succession of the practice after the Bennetts retire, and to allow ownership of the business by its staff without prohibitive buy-in costs, which would be in opposition to their practice's ethos.[10]

Since the 1990s architects have embraced further diversity in their styles of practice and education, now working in planning, as professional clients, as design managers for contracting firms and within multidisciplinary practices, as well as traditional architectural practice. Architectural education is also no longer solely a path that leads to architectural practice. In 2011 slightly over 3,700 students began undergraduate studies in architecture, their cohort falling by just over 45% to around 2,000 entrants to postgraduate (Part 2) courses in 2016.[11] The transferable skills of this demanding design degree have led people to careers in art, industrial and product design, modelmaking and photography, as well as entirely unrelated disciplines. Architectural thought and training has more diverse applications than the apprentices of the 1800s could ever have thought possible.

It is not just practice styles and educational application that have become more diverse since the early 1980s. The human diversity of the profession has increased considerably too. In 1975 the UK government passed the Sex Discrimination Act, protecting men and women from discrimination on the grounds of sex or marital status in multiple areas of life including employment, training and education.[12] However, it wasn't until the 1990s and 2000s that professional institutions such as the RICS and RIBA began to commission studies into the challenges women faced in the construction professions.[13] While there will have been myriad stories of misogyny through the decades, some stories are so starkly shocking as to almost have passed into legend. Sticking to British examples, there is the considerable work on the British Library by MJ Long, which is usually attributed to her husband Colin St John Wilson; on the Pompidou Centre by Su Rogers, which is entirely attributed to her husband Richard;[14] and the infamous publicity picture of Terry Farrell, Norman Foster, Nicholas Grimshaw, Michael Hopkins and Richard Rogers, which RIBA Gold Medal winner Patty Hopkins was edited out of for the 2014 BBC TV series *The Brits who Built the Modern World*.[15] This is without mentioning the countless more everyday indignities women faced – the social acceptance of philandering husbands, and the casual dismissal by clients and builders: the 'mine's two sugars, love' and the wolf whistles.

Figure 6.1 Michael and Patty Hopkins.

Graham Morrison, co-founder of Allies and Morrison, remembers that when he started his architecture degree at Cambridge in the early 1970s two women started in his class but neither finished. The second employee of the practice he started with Bob Allies in 1984 was Joanna Bacon, also a Cambridge alumnus. Graham remembers her as being 'almost unique' in simply being around, so few women were there.[16] Joanna is now Allies and Morrison's

Figure 6.2 Ruth Reed, the RIBA's first female President 2009–11.

Managing Partner, leading a successful practice of around 300 people,[17] but is still unusual; few of the UK's 100 largest architecture firms are led by women in the early 2020s. It would not be until its 175th anniversary in 2009 that RIBA would elect its first female President. Welsh architect Ruth Reed stated in her inauguration speech that:

> In becoming the first female president of the RIBA, I am proud to be part of a change within the profession to recognise and encourage the skills and careers of women in the sector; I hope that by example I will encourage more women to remain in architecture. The profession as a whole needs to widen its membership to include architects from all social, racial and economic backgrounds to represent the diverse nature of our society.'[18]

In 2013 the RIBA appointed future President Jane Duncan as its diversity champion, and in 2015 launched its 'role model' campaign. In 2016 just 26% of architects were women, barely rising to 29% by the end of 2019. It was not until 2019 that gender parity for any section of the architectural profession was realised- and that only for architects below the age of 30.[19] A report commissioned by the RIBA in 2003 entitled 'Why do women leave architecture?' found that poor employment practice, difficulties in maintaining skills and professional networks during career breaks (including for maternity leave and for caring responsibilities) and paternalistic attitudes were among the main reasons women chose to leave the profession.[20] A paper by the report's authors five years later noted that though women architects had reached 17% of the profession (from 13% in 2003) there 'is still much more work to do'.[21]

It is not only women who are under-represented in the British architectural profession. The Architects Registration Board (ARB) began collecting optional equality and diversity information in 2012, and of those who chose to provide this data in 2019 84% identified as White or White British. While this roughly aligned with UK overall population of 85% white in 2019,[22] both Black and Asian groups were under-represented statistically. In 2019 3% of the UK's population was black, but just 1% of British architects were. And 8% of the UK population was Asian, but just 6% of British architects.[23] Meanwhile 79% of architects identify as heterosexual (with 18% preferring not to disclose sexual orientation), and the 3% identifying as homosexual or bisexual compares with 2.3% of the British population overall. This is an incomplete data set, however, as not all architects chose to disclose their ethnic or sexual background. Nevertheless, even allowing for the possibility that those architects who do not provide this data align exactly with the statistics of those who do, it is clear that the British architectural population does not accurately reflect the society it exists within.

In 1998 the Construction Industry Training Board (CITB) commissioned research which reported that while black, Asian and minority ethnic (BAME) communities were reasonably well represented on construction-related training and degree programmes, they were significantly under-represented in the industry itself. The reasons that were cited included a lack of awareness among the BAME communities about the range of opportunities in construction; a fear of discrimination and racism; a perception that the industry was dominated by white men and a predominance of word-of-mouth recruitment.[24] In 1993 a young aspiring architect, Stephen Lawrence, was murdered in an unprovoked racist attack. In his memory his family set up the Stephen Lawrence Charitable Trust (later Blueprint for all) to provide inspiration, opportunities and support to children from under-represented backgrounds. By 2020 it had helped 145 young people to qualify as architects,[25] using direct intervention to overrule some of the opinions and situations that the CITB report had identified as so damaging to BAME prospects in the sector. In 2007 the RIBA elected its first President from a

Figure 6.3 Sunand Prasad, RIBA President 2007–9.

non-white background, Indian-born Sunand Prasad. He was voted one of the *Independent* newspaper's 'top 100 environmentalists' for his role in greening the RIBA during his tenure.[26] As this book goes to print, RIBA members have elected their first black President – 31-year-old Muyiwa Oki, who will serve between 2023 and 2025.

These reports and rather dry data sets give numbers and headlines to the experiences of ethnic minority and LGBTQ+ architects from the 1980s to the 2010s, but more individual stories are hard to find. Perhaps because their numbers were so few, perhaps because many of these stories were quiet ones, perhaps for more nuanced reasons linked to the social culture of the day. Architects have always sat alongside the powerful in society, and architecture has always been an interest of the social elite, but it was not until the 1800s that architecture became a more exclusive profession to practise in the UK. In ancient Rome slaves became architects; in Renaissance Italy architects emerged from the studios of artists; in medieval Europe master masons came from the skilled journeyman classes; and prior to the gating of the professions in the 1800s the British tradition of 'amateur architects' saw skilled builders or those with an interest in design coming from all sorts of unassuming backgrounds to work in architecture. It was only when architects attempted to divide themselves from the building trades, when they tried to intellectualise and close the profession, that increased exclusivity of entry to the profession began in earnest. Arguably the trends in practice and education since that point have exacerbated this problem; who knows what richness these decisions have cost British architecture?

Design and build – a response to calls for collaboration

As public sector opportunities decreased and professional expectations and guidelines shifted, architects in Britain increasingly began to realign themselves with the building trades. More architects now work as part of contractor or client-side professional teams than at almost any point since the days of the medieval masons. Indeed, the shifting dynamic between architect and builder in recent decades has seen perhaps the most dramatic adjustment of this relationship since the formation of the RIBA in the 1830s and the enforced divide between the two professions.

Design and build (D&B) procurement routes had been slowly growing in popularity since the 1960s and 1970s, but in 1983 and 1988 two government-sponsored reports called for procurement reform in earnest. They noted that the process of procuring new industrial and commercial buildings was unnecessarily long and difficult, suggesting that approximate bills of quantities and negotiated tendering could lead to faster project implementation. The reports were based on studies in which roughly half the projects used traditional procurement methods and the other half roughly divided between D&B and management procurement methods.[27] The 1988 report pointed to the good results large professional client bodies were having on mega-projects in London and the southeast of England using bespoke forms of procurement methods tailored to their own needs and priorities, though it should be noted that the 1980s was the first point in time at which large professional client bodies with the in-house expertise and resources to manage substantial construction projects had emerged in earnest.[28]

As noted earlier, the recession of the late 1980s/early 1990s and the collapse of the property market saw a huge decline in property development and construction. Around 500,000 construction-related jobs were lost, and in excess of 16,000 construction firms became insolvent.[29] It was in this background of industry collapse and uncertainly evolving procurement, an industry which the author Sir Michael Latham described as 'ineffective', 'adversarial' and 'fragmented',[30] that the Latham Report was commissioned by the government in an effort to reform the construction industry to provide greater efficiency and better value for its customers. The report was damning, and set out a number of detailed recommendations which centred around the reforming of procurement and construction team relationships. Among other things it recommended that government should lead the way as a best practice client; that new (NEC) contract forms should be widely adopted due to their less adversarial nature; public sector registers of approved contractors, professional indemnity insurance, codes of practice, guidance documents, and latent defects insurance should be standardised, formalised and compulsory; risk should be allocated to the party best able to manage and carry it; conflict should be avoided with speedy dispute resolution; and teamwork duties should be firmly established with financial motivation.[31] Essentially, there was a call to a modernised version of the industry that had existed before architects sought to formalise their profession in the 1830s.

The report led to the creation of the Construction Industry Board in 1995, along with a series of other organisations which all combined to form Constructing Excellence in 2003.[32] It also led to the foundation of the Considerate Constructors Scheme to help improve the image of the construction industry more broadly.[33] Though the Latham Report called for an increase in partnering alliances, these have not proved to be especially popular. It was in these calls for procurement reform and greater partnership that D&B began to gain traction, however, with its underlying principles of early contractor design involvement.[34] The increasing scale and complexity of projects in the mid to late 1990s also contributed to the popularity of D&B, with its single point of control, directly responsible to the client.[35] It simplified client/construction team relationships and risk profiles considerably.

The rise of D&B was resisted by architects who saw it as a direct threat to their role within the construction industry, handing design responsibilities to the contractor more or less for the first time since the late 1700s/early 1800s, and increasing the prominence of the quantity surveyor role as cost became a more primary design concern. They foresaw decline both in design and build quality, as cost and time are necessarily prioritised in D&B contract arrangements.[36] Former RIBA President Richard MacCormac stated at a debate in 1993 that design and build in particular was responsible for the demise of good design in the British construction industry.[37] However, latterly support has grown for well-managed D&B procurement. The technical guidance of specialist contractors can considerably aid architects during the design process, and properly defined employers' requirements can help to safeguard design quality.

Perhaps one of the most notorious examples of poor build quality under a novel procurement route was what became known as the 'Edinburgh Schools', referring to the closure of 17 Edinburgh schools on safety grounds after strong winds caused a large section of an external wall in one school to blow down in 2016 due to missing wall ties. Procured under a 1992 government-created private finance initiative (PFI), the projects were financed by private funders and the buildings leased to the government for an agreed period before reverting to government ownership. The subsequent report into the construction of the schools found the defects to be 'fundamentally the result of a combination of poor quality of workmanship, inadequate supervision and ineffective quality assurance within the construction industry'[38] and concluded that the financing of the school was not at fault, but the construction quality. It further commented that 'there is an increasing shortage of essential skills and/or deskilling in the construction industry which is impacting on its ability to deliver and ensure the required quality of construction'.[39]

One of the arguably unforeseen consequences of the rise of D&B-style procurement routes, as can be seen at its worst in the Edinburgh Schools case, has been the split created in the architectural profession between 'design' architects and 'delivery' architects. The former are largely engaged by the client prior to the contractor's involvement in a project; the latter are employed by the contractor after the building contract is signed to draw the technical details and oversee construction. Furthermore, though the architect may be more collaboratively partnered with the contractor than under a traditionally procured contract, under D&B the contractor has control over the building site – and who may access it. Combined, the increasingly common split between 'design' and 'delivery' architects, reduced access to, and experience of, construction sites, and increasingly diverse and complex building techniques has seen a technical deskilling of the architectural profession over recent years. Arguably this has contributed to a decline in design quality, as buildings and details are drawn and agreed without a clear understanding of how they will be implemented on site.

There is an argument that this has allowed for more visionary work as architects design 'unencumbered' by the practical constraints of buildability, challenging building technology to rise to heights only limited by the architect's imagination and drafting abilities. In some projects – expensive and bespoke – this can create work of stunning beauty and originality. In many cases, though, it creates the sort of loopholes in the process that open a vulnerable construction system to exploitation by the unscrupulous, resulting in poor outcomes for building owners and occupants. This seems almost an echo of the progression of architects through the Italian Renaissance in the 15th and 16th centuries, as intellectual snobbery caused architects to sit aloof from builders. By the 16th century, though theirs was still a profession distinct from building, architects had embraced the challenge and craft of detailing to an extent that resulted in such works as the Palazzo Farnese and St Peter's Basilica. The renaissance of our modern profession, however, will take considerable will to achieve – and a level of 'upskilling' which the contemporary profession may not be willing to undertake. If the profession is to thrive and continue to adapt for centuries to come it must re-embrace the polymath adaptability of its past – and embrace the understanding of the craft of building that that would entail.

From the pencil to the parametric – the rise of computing

One of the other most significant changes to the architect's daily practice has been the almost exponential growth of drawing technology. In the late 1970s and early 1980s architectural drawing technology was more or less as it had been for the preceding centuries, if not millennia. Bob Allies and Graham Morrison both remember offices full of drawing boards when they started practising, recounting how the practice's partners would go around after they had gone home, lifting dust sheets and leaving notes on their drawings and details.[40] Following this was the entire basement room that was given over to the first computer in YRM's offices in the late 1970s. YRM seems to have been at the forefront of this new technology, as it was not until the introduction of personal computers in the 1980s that computer-aided design (CAD) became affordable for architects more broadly.

Figure 6.4 Early computing at the John S Bonnington Partnership.

CAD facilitated duplication of details, the representation of very large buildings digitally at full scale, and easier modification of drawings and details, as well as allowing multiple people to work on the same project at once. By the 1990s it had all but replaced hand drawing in architectural offices.[41] In the late 1990s three-dimensional digital technology began to bring about another change in drawing methods, allowing new ways for architects to represent their design and to work more collaboratively with the design and construction teams with the introduction of building information modelling (BIM).[42] BIM allowed buildings to be 'built' digitally in three dimensions for the first time, changing the way architecture is conceived and designed.

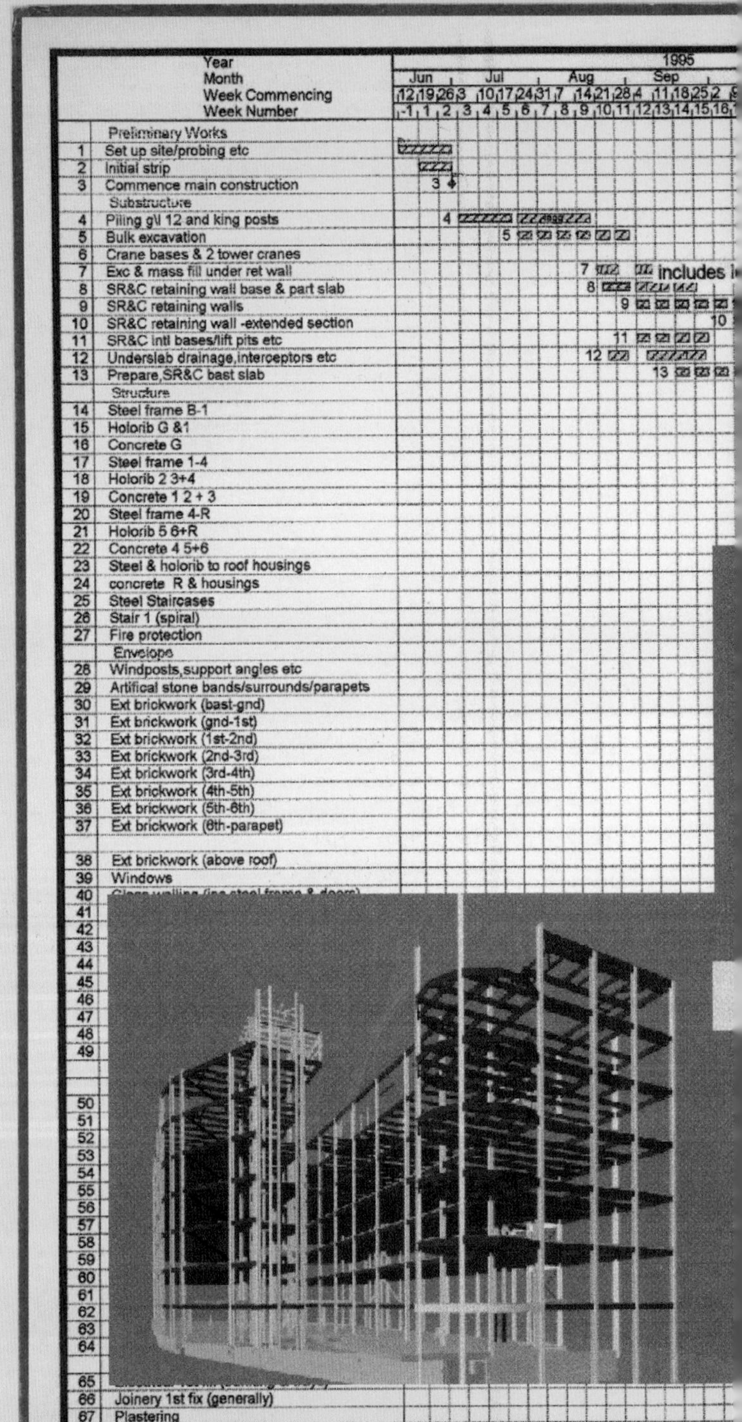

Figure 6.5 Early building information modelling (BIM), 1997.

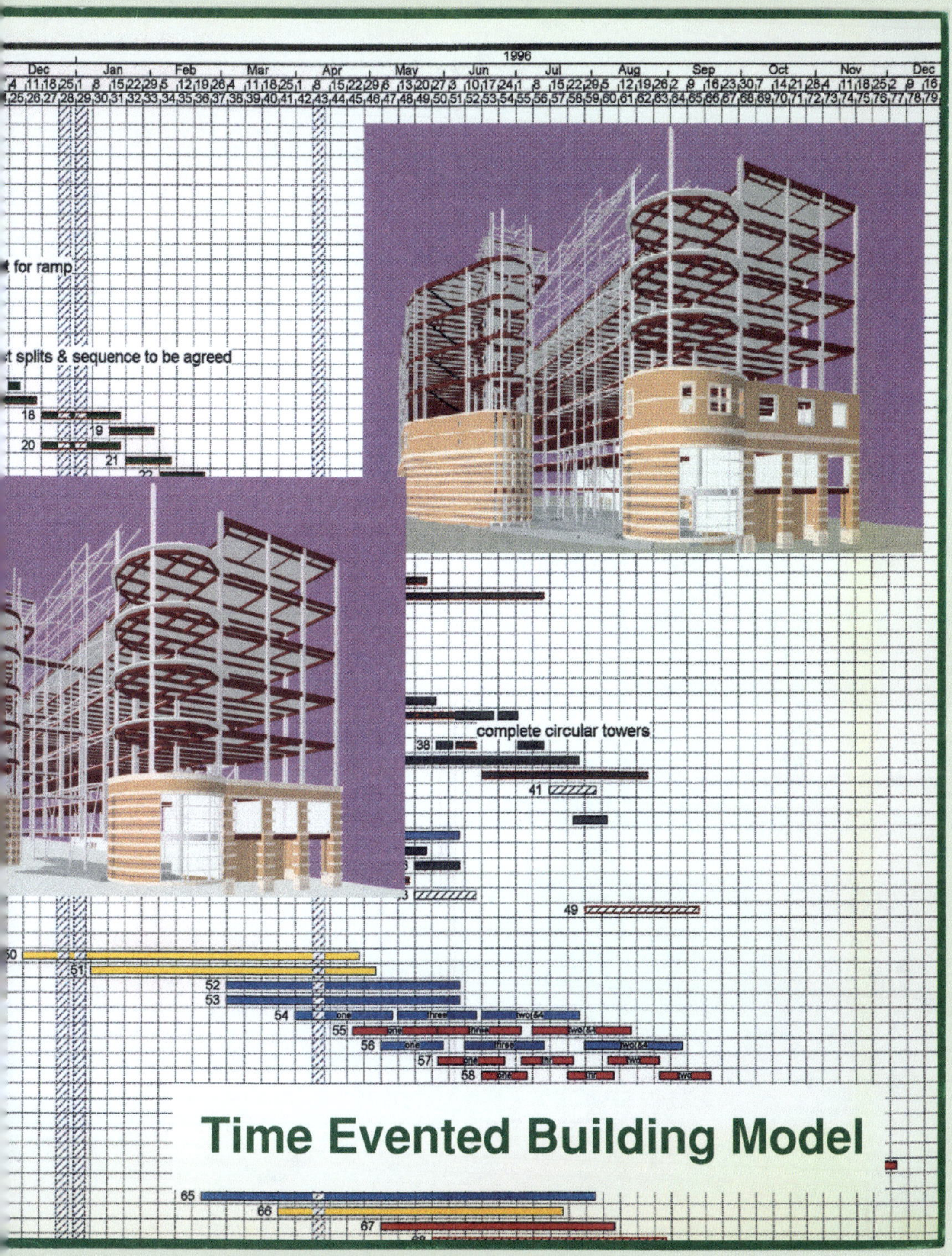
1996
splits & sequence to be agreed
complete circular towers
Time Evented Building Model

With each leap in technology architects' workflows changed – first to a faster, less tangible workflow and later to a three-dimensions-first approach. These changes in technology can be seen in some of the architecture of the period as architects come to terms with the opportunities and limitations of the software. On the one hand, the three-dimensional parametric curving forms so beloved of Zaha Hadid Architects, UN Studio and Frank Gehry, among others, were constructable and fully draw-able for the first time. On the other hand, most architects have an anecdotal story of a building – usually someone else's – that looks or is constructed a certain way 'because I couldn't work out how to do it the "normal" way in BIM'.

There are some who mourn the distance that increasingly digitised drawing puts between the architect and their drawings, and others who simply marvel at the ability of software to allow them to design, build and sequence construction without leaving their desk, while collaborating with people anywhere in the world. Software has also contributed to the increasing size of the average architectural practice. As running software has become essential to architectural practice, so has the entry cost of beginning a practice; software licences are considerably more expensive than paper and pens, and the creeping monopoly of the biggest software providers makes it difficult to seek alternative solutions. This monopoly has been aided by large clients – for example, Vectorworks became the most common CAD software in some of London's largest architectural firms due to it being the required drawing format for a station building programme by Transport for London,[43] and Autodesk's Revit is fast becoming the ubiquitous BIM software, with large clients requiring a 'model first' approach that necessitates all consultants and contractors working in the same software.

The increased speed with which drawings can be produced had initially been considered as a way to reduce office hours, but this has not necessarily been the outcome. The amount of legislative and statutory guidance and frameworks has increased almost exponentially since the 1970s, causing an increase in the quantity of documentation each project requires. Even planning permission has become considerably more protracted and complex to achieve, with Bob Allies referring to the 'novel like' design and access statements often produced by his own practice. Furthermore the introduction in 1974, and multiple amendments since, to nationwide building regulations; the 1984 Building Act; the 1997, 2007 and 2015 Construction Design and Management Acts; and the standards and procurement practices required through Britain's membership of and subsequent withdrawal from the European Union have all added to the complexity of practising architecture competently, and the difficulty of managing and maintaining this quantity of knowledge in a small practice.

The Architects Act 1997 – the end of ambitions for protection of function

Perhaps the most directly relevant Act to impact the practice of architecture was the 1997 Architects Act. Though the RIBA had stated in 1948 that 'the ultimate objective is naturally to prevent anyone performing the duties of an architect unless he is registered'[44] the following decades had shown this to be a political impossibility. The 1997 Architects Act consolidated the previous Acts and aligned Britain with the European Union's Mutual Recognition of Qualifications Directive – allowing registered architects elsewhere in the EU to join the British register without passing further examinations here. It also disbanded ARCUK and the Board of Architectural Education, establishing the ARB to regulate the architectural profession and keep the register of architects. Its work is overseen by a board of 11 people appointed by the Privy Council, of which only five may be architects.[45] This Act removed much of the residual power of the RIBA, which now functions closer to a professional members' organisation rather than having any power to regulate the profession or its education. The RIBA remarked in 2019: 'Our current policy is to support continued protection of title for architects as both an assurance to consumers and a benefit to the profession. We don't currently have a policy to actively campaign for protection of function for architects, something we believe any UK government would be highly unlikely to contemplate given UK competition policy.'[46]

The decades between the 1980s and the present day saw significant changes for architectural practice, with practice size, legislation and the impact of technology all rising with a backdrop of boom-and-bust recessions, privatisation of the professions and fast-changing attitudes towards the place of women and minority communities in society. For all the drama of the context, the change within the profession itself has been gradual and fairly undramatic, as architects have evolved to fit economic and social contexts. The last three decades have seen power in the design and construction team shift away from the architect and towards the project manager and quantity surveyor, as projects are increasingly governed by cost concerns and architects have lost influence on construction sites – they have increasingly relinquished design responsibility through new procurement forms and the impacts of reduced exposure to construction on site. The architect that has emerged into the 2020s works in increasingly large teams with increasingly large technical and legislative input, but with decreased influence and technical knowledge, dogged with worries about the profession's future.

CHAPTER 7

Global practice

Architects have always had wanderlust and a desire to travel abroad. From the 17th to the early 19th century, it was customary for architects and artists to embark on a 'grand tour', travelling around Europe to study neoclassical architecture with the aim of returning home to practise.

One of the earliest examples of royal patronage of an international architect was the design of the east wing of the Louvre in 1665. After inviting three Italian architects to bid for the project, Louis XIV commissioned Gian Lorenzo Bernini, who produced four designs, none of which were accepted. It is considered the 'greatest unfulfilled commission in the architectural history of France',[1] and has been characterised as a desire to appoint an architect based on reputation rather than locality, and to gain from the associated status of the Italian style.

Sir Edwin Lutyens, one of the UK's most revered architects, is among the earliest noted British architects to have worked globally, designing memorials, residences and public buildings in many countries including Ireland, America, Italy and South Africa. His largest commission was the design of the masterplan and associated government buildings in New Delhi in India. In 1911, while India was under the imperial rule of the British Raj, King George V announced the decision to move the capital of India from Calcutta to Delhi, intending it to be on the scale of Washington DC and Paris. For nearly 20 years, Lutyens led a team of British and Indian architects and engineers to design what is dubbed 'Lutyens' Delhi', its architecture representing a combination of the Western neoclassical and Indian Mughal tradition.

Lutyens, the RIBA Gold Medal winner in 1921, designed from his London studio, and despite his international works he is perhaps better known as an English architect and designer of country houses.

Figure 7.1 Viceroy's House, New Delhi: the main entrance.

As recently as 1994, Frank Duffy wrote that there is 'no such thing as a global practice'.[2] Although no architectural practice could truly claim to be global in the way of consumer goods such as food, cars or clothing brands, it can certainly be seen that the picture of international practice has changed from the early 1980s.

In 2022, US practices such as SOM (six US studios, five worldwide), HOK (16 in North America, six worldwide) and KPF (two in the US, seven worldwide) are truly considered international: the latter two have, in fact, more international offices than domestic.

1980s to early 2000s

In the period leading up to the early 1980s, UK practices were predominantly working locally, occasionally regionally and rarely internationally. Large, commercial practices were working mostly on office and retail developments and very few were working internationally, other than single projects such as banks and headquarters for large corporations. An example is the Bank

Figure 7.2 Bank of Commerce and Industry (BCI), Abu Dhabi.

of Commerce and Industry in Abu Dhabi (1978) by Fitzroy Robinson Partnership. With enough work to sustain a profitable business, there was little impetus or need for UK architects to cast the net wider.

Over the next 30 years, however, a number of factors – ranging from domestic politics to joining the EU, advances in technology and communication, and the reducing role of the architect – combined to fundamentally change the nature of practice.

In May 1979, Margaret Thatcher took office with inflation at 10% and the financial outlook bleak. Her government's policies directly affected the profession in terms of workload through the closing of many local authority architecture departments, and a consequent significant reduction in public sector projects[3] as well as the abolishment of the architects' fee scale.[4]

As well as being buffeted by the 1980s recession, architects faced a growing lack of trust from the public, who blamed them for the 'concrete jungles' of the 1960s and 1970s. When comparing the status of the UK profession with architects in Europe, America and elsewhere, it is little wonder that UK-based architects decided to search for projects abroad that were denied them at home. Potential work came from a number of sources, including the building programmes of European cities and the opening of new markets such as the EU and China, India and Africa with extensive urbanisation plans as a result of population expansion.

In 1973 the UK joined the European Economic Community,[5] which subsequently became the European Union. EU public procurement regulations determined that all publicly funded projects over a financial threshold should be open to all registered architects of member states via the Official Journal of the European Union (OJEU).[6]

On the other side of the world, in 1978, China reformed its economy and opened to international trade and investment.[7] The population expanded from 102 million at the end of the 1970s to 830 million in 2018.[8] Then, in the early part of the 21st century, China's government put in place policies to develop 20 new cities per annum until at least 2020.[9] The consequent exponential growth in construction realised many opportunities for architects and construction professionals on a scale previously unheard of.

Facilitating international practice

In the early 1980s the mode of drawing developed from the labour-intensive individual drawing to the beginnings of computer-aided drafting. This then developed into building information modelling[10] (BIM), which has become the standard means of designing and sharing information for architects working internationally.

Landline telephones and the fax machine, in common use in the late 1980s, started to become obsolete once the internet became available to the wider public in 1991. Its exponential growth within a few years meant that architectural practices could build their own websites, and therefore were able to market their practice to international clients without having to send hard-copy brochures in the post. From the early 2000s, the rise of video conferencing allowed architects the convenience of meeting online, thereby saving on cost and travel time to other countries, making international working possible for even very small practices. More recently, Covid-19 restrictions proved that architects could still function while working 'remotely'. The twin benefits of a reduction in carbon footprint and closer collaboration can only be positive.

International practice – the beginnings of new markets

In the UK, the deregulation of the financial markets in 1986, known colloquially as the 'Big Bang', ensured that London maintained its place as a centre of international financial trading. There was therefore an immediate need for up-to-date office space with large floor plates, and the need to accommodate the change from open outcry to screen-based trading. Various American finance houses set up their European bases in London, and commissioned their US-based architects such as Gensler, HOK, KPF, SOM and Swanke Hayden Connell to design headquarters in the City of London, Canary Wharf and Broadgate.

In Europe, cities such as Paris and Berlin began major state-funded urban regeneration projects such as Les Grand Projects (1981 to 1998) and the Internationale Bauausstellung Berlin (IBA),[11] completed in 1987. The IBA was conceived as a major urban and infrastructure renewal programme. Its director, Josef Paul Kleihues, commissioned over 20 of the world's leading architects to design buildings of many architectural styles, not dependent on an overall, singular vision.

Construction work in Berlin continued to benefit from the fall of the Berlin Wall in 1989, and the subsequent reunification of Germany, which gave additional opportunities for architects to participate in the renewal and repair of Berlin and other former East German cities such as Dresden and Leipzig. The subsequent moving of the seat of government from Bonn to Berlin ensured construction continued.

UK architects were particularly successful in winning important cultural and political commissions in Berlin, including the Börse Berlin AG (1998) by Grimshaw, the Reichstag (1999) by Foster + Partners and the Neues Museum (1997–2006) by David Chipperfield Architects. It is inconceivable – then and now – that the UK would appoint three architects from a single other country for equivalent projects of national importance.

Les Grands Projets, Paris

Paris has a long history of ambitious architecture and urban planning. Napoleon III commissioned Baron Haussmann in 1853 to bring light and air to the centre of the city and, although not fully implemented, work continued on this project until 1927. Though not comparable in scale, in 1982 President Mitterrand launched Les Grands Projets, a series of eight new buildings symbolising modern France moving with confidence into the 21st century. This was contemporary architecture on a scale and with ambition comparable to that of Louis XIV. Whereas the Palace of Versailles was for the privileged few (described by Voltaire as 'a masterpiece of bad taste and magnificence'), Les Grands Projets were public projects for everyone. The extravagance of the Baroque was replaced by the public language of minimalism. Mitterrand understood the cultural and social value of contemporary civic building, and power and knowledge is represented through simple monumental forms with a palette of contemporary materials such as glass and steel.

The final project, the Bibliothèque Nationale de France, was completed in 1995. There was an open, international competition attracting 244 entries, and the brief required the building to be the most modern library in the world, inclusive and accessible by the public. It emphasised an outward-looking desire to collaborate and share knowledge with international libraries as well as utilising modern technology. The winning entry contained an open public central square at the heart, connecting the four glass towers of the library with the city.

Whereas the Paris library projected confidence in the future, the British Library in London, designed by Colin St John Wilson and MJ Long, begun in 1962 and opened in 1997, was the culmination of indecision, delays and cutbacks, termed the '30-year war'.[12] The building was variously described as Modern, Postmodern and vernacular, and its brick cladding and pitched roofs referenced the past.

Bilbao – the beginning

Having witnessed Paris and Berlin's cultural profiles being raised by contemporary architecture, the mayor of Bilbao bid successfully to host a regional Guggenheim Museum. This is late 20th-century cultural imperialism; an alliance between the Guggenheim Foundation and Bilbao. The former, an internationally known and respected name, lends works from its collection as well as expertise in art and curating to the city, which in turn funds the building.

Figure 7.3 Guggenheim Museum, Bilbao.

In 1992, the Pritzker Prize-winning[13] American architect Frank Gehry won the invited competition. The shortlist was completed by Arata Isozaki Associates and Coop Himmelb(l)au, with all three known for creating unique, distinctive buildings. The competition required the building to have a strong visual image to attract funding, press and ultimately tourists. The formula for cultural and financial success was clear: organise a competition of international architects to generate publicity, then select a distinctive winning design. The architect has become a shape-maker; the more recognisable, the better.

The titanium-clad building, which opened in 1997, is purportedly redolent of the city's industrial past. It provoked international interest and positive reviews from architectural critics and the public alike. The city benefited from an immediate influx of tourists, with the associated financial benefits to the local economy.

Although just a single building, its effect was significant for the region as well as other cities worldwide seeking to emulate its success. The architecture profession benefited from positive public perception as well as future projects through what has become known as the 'Bilbao effect',[14] coined to identify new buildings, typically cultural, which have an immediate and positive impact on the local economy. Initially the building was received positively, but opinions on the Guggenheim Bilbao have become less favourable over time: in comparison to the ensemble of projects of Paris and Berlin, the Guggenheim Museum Bilbao is a single building in a regional city. Most tourists choose not to make repeat visits. Cities can never be sustained by one-off buildings, no matter how idiosyncratic the architecture. Nor can a city be sustained solely by seasonal tourists without wider investment in other, less-publicised projects. Davide Ponzini encapsulates this:

> 'There is no reason why we should believe the Bilbao effect works in terms of urban regeneration … These sorts of effects derive from more complex sets of investments and trends which cannot be done with one architectural project – no matter how beautiful or successful the building is.'[15]

Star architects

The enormous success of Guggenheim Bilbao elevated Frank Gehry to become, arguably, the first 'star architect' in the modern meaning of the word.

It is true that many of the mid-20th-century Modernists such as Alvar Aalto, Le Corbusier, Mies van der Rohe, Louis Kahn and Frank Lloyd Wright designed projects abroad. All were renowned and widely published, and had an identifiable, distinct style. However, Frank Lloyd Wright designed almost exclusively in the US with the exception of the Imperial Hotel in Japan, completed in 1923 and demolished in 1968. In 1937, Mies van der Rohe and his Bauhaus colleagues, Marcel Breuer and Walter Gropius, fled Nazi Germany and emigrated to the US. Mies built most of his work there before returning to design his final building, the Neue Nationalgalerie in Berlin, completed in 1968.

Only Le Corbusier built an extensive global portfolio of buildings in France, Russia, Japan, America and India until his death in 1965. He was the recognised leader of the International Style, identified by its universal architectural language unconnected to local context, and in this sense could be argued to be the real first 'star' architect.

It wasn't until the early part of the 21st century that 'starchitect' entered the lexicon, defining a small number of architects who travelled the world, feted by city mayors, cultural institutions and developers. More recently, starchitect has become a pejorative term levelled against those international architects living 'the life of the perpetually jetlagged',[16] flying in for the opening ceremony of their newest building, attending a press conference before having dinner and then flying out. Architecture, or, more particularly, the signature practice, has become a brand, selling a product more akin to luxury consumer goods such as handbags or cars, recognisable throughout the world.

Building as icon

The Sydney Opera House is one of the most distinctive and recognisable buildings in the world, emblematic of iconic architecture, having become a 'must visit' for tourists and a backdrop for fireworks and photographic shoots.

Designed by the Danish architect Jørn Utzon, it opened in 1973. Ove Arup,[17] the engineer, claimed Utzon was not a prima donna architect, more an architect-conductor. The former, he defined as an 'egocentric soloist throwing tantrums', the latter as one who is a visual artist requiring the technical support of others in order to realise the concept. Arup warned of the dangers of 'large technically sophisticated jobs' breaking down unless the 'architect-conductor has advisors and collaborators constantly at hand'.

The UK has been less consumed by the idea of the 'iconic' building and, aside from a few notorious exceptions, largely resistant to shape-making. The exceptions are projects such as The Public in West Bromwich (2008) designed by Alsop Architects, conceived in the 1990s and described as a monument to an ill-conceived ambition.[18] Originally an arts centre and now a sixth-form college, the government called it 'a gross waste of public money'.[19] Likewise, the National Pop Music Centre[20] (1999) in Sheffield, designed by Branson Coates Architecture, quickly became obsolete and eventually became a student union for Sheffield Hallam University.

Figure 7.4 Sydney Opera House, Bennelong Point, Sydney, seen from the harbour walk.

Turner Contemporary,[21] a contemporary art gallery in Margate, has been the result of two design competitions, with the first in the early 2000s ending in litigation that was settled out of court. The initial architect, Norway's Snøhetta, placed their design on the edge of the promontory overlooking the North Sea, meaning the steel required particular structural stability, leading to escalating costs. The client, Kent County Council (KCC), selected design and build as the preferred procurement method with the associated 'risk' priced by the tendering contractors, resulting in the budget overruns. KCC cancelled the project and sued the design team, who settled out of court.

Figure 7.5 Turner Contemporary, Margate

KCC launched a second competition, won by David Chipperfield Architects with a more straightforward design, which opened in 2011.[22] It sits on the quayside and is 'resolutely not an icon'.Chipperfield summed up Britain's attitude to architecture: 'There is a pressure on architecture to be interesting. The worst criticism you can throw at a building here is that it is boring.'[23]

All three projects, and others which have had similarly troubled stories, serve as reminders to think before you build. Architects are prepared to accept the accolades for successful designs, and so must also be answerable, at least in part, for those buildings deemed failures. But this raises the question: what is the professional's role and responsibility? Where does it begin and end? The architect is commissioned by and contracted to a client, but also has a duty and a responsibility to society. Architects are complicit – if only marginally – and this places an onus on the architect to ask direct questions at the commencement of a project. Put simply, if RIBA Plan of Work Stage 0[24] is 'strategic in nature', 'developing the business case' and 'whole life analysis', architects should be less passive and question the strategic aims of each project, and particularly if it is publicly funded.

The profession's public profile is represented through iconic, singular buildings by architects such as Norman Foster, Frank Gehry, Zaha Hadid, Herzog & de Meuron, Rem Koolhaas and Daniel Libeskind. The public image of the starchitect is supported by lectures, television appearances, books and exhibitions – all to maintain the profile and brand value. Donald McNeill notes that starchitects 'have a particular charisma that will draw a paying audience to a high-profile cultural institution to hear them explain their designs'.[25] Contemporary magazines and social media give credence to architecture as image, understating its importance to society. Academia is also responsible for maintaining the status of starchitects, encouraging students to visit their buildings and undertake precedent studies based only on image.

Buildings designed by starchitects are not wholly negative, for they generate publicity and provoke debate about the urban environment and, with it, raise the profile of a beleaguered profession. Theirs is an architecture of the one-off large museum with a generous budget and high-quality materials such as titanium cladding. However, the starchitect has a disproportionate influence and status: they are responsible for a very small amount of total design and construction output under the 'starchitect' model of practice. The architect is in danger of being reduced to being a form-giver and shape-maker, effectively giving buildings the status of an ornament, rather than addressing fundamental problems with the built environment. While serving an international audience with the grand, elaborate gesture, the profession is in danger of losing contact with the ordinary, unheralded and uncelebrated.

While much of the profession has been seduced by imagery and the latest iconic building, society is confronting issues of greater importance including the climate emergency, international conflicts and inequalities in many forms.

As the extravagant becomes the norm, the profession is conflicted. It raises the question of why starchitects aren't designing understated, low-budget projects such as social housing and celebrating those projects that form the mannered background and context to our urban fabric; the typical and the ordinary and the projects that are essential for a healthy society.

Kenneth Frampton, the Anglo-American architectural writer and critic, argued for critical regionalism[26] and for buildings to respond to local context and 'the idiosyncrasies of place'. He was opposed to universal, generic architecture and referenced the work of Alvar Aalto, Jørn Utzon and others on the fringes of the starchitect system, asking the question of how an international architect adapts to and respects regional culture and local practice.

In late 2014, President Xi Jinping announced that China would no longer accept 'weird architecture' and that art should 'serve the people'.[27] This comment followed the China construction boom that commenced after the economic reforms of 1997. China followed with policy, providing guidance on the design of major projects such as museums and stadia, with the aim that projects 'embody the spirit of the city, to show the style of the times, and to highlight Chinese characteristics'. As a consequence, replicas of well-known Western buildings were banned, and restrictions placed on tall buildings of over 500m.

Global practice – a changing picture

The UK has c.40,000[28] registered architects, whereas Italy has 150,000, Germany 118,000 and Spain 48,000. Despite the fact that the UK has the fourth highest number of architects in Europe, per 1000 population it has the lowest number at 0.6: Germany has 1.4 and Italy has 2.5. In many EU countries, 97% of architecture fee income is 'domestically focused'[29] whereas in the UK it is 95% with international work generating circa £500million in revenue.

The status of professional registration in the EU is wide-ranging. The UK has protection of the title 'architect', whereas Germany, France and Spain also have the protection of function, meaning that only an architect can submit drawings for regulatory approval. The title 'architect' is not recognised in Denmark,[30] where the standard of architecture and urban design is commonly recognised to be among the highest in Europe.

International work can also elevate young practices into the mainstream. The Centre Pompidou in Paris[31] (see fig. 7.6) was won by Richard Rogers, Su Rogers and Renzo Piano in 1971 in a competition that attracted 681 entries. Richard Rogers was 41 years old and had built very few projects, all of which were in the UK. Similarly, Norman Foster was 43 when HSBC commissioned Foster Associates for its new HQ in Hong Kong. At that time the practice, formed by Foster and his wife Wendy, was just 10 years old, had built very little and nothing over three storeys. The HSBC project was its first outside the UK.

Working on international projects brings a number of procedural and operational challenges, including managing the design process with a partner architect and ensuring a positive, collaborative environment.

Architecture, as a creative endeavour, is the only profession that celebrates a single figure leading the practice, whereas other professionals such as accountants and lawyers are defined by their practice. Much like fashion and film-making, architecture is the contribution of many talented people.

Figure 7.6 Pompidou Centre (Centre National d'Art et de Culture Georges-Pompidou), Paris.

Collaborating with international partners

Act global, think local is a cliché of international business, but the intention is well meant. Any successful project is the result of a number of factors. From the outset the international architect sets the tone as design team leader, engaging local consultants and showing leadership, fostering a collaborative design process while all the time respecting local cultures and methods.

It remains common for a practice working abroad to team up with a local architect variously described as executive, local, contact or partner. Nevertheless, the design architect receives the accolades, press coverage and awards, whereas the local architect is rarely given appropriate recognition for their contribution or credited with co-authorship. There needs to be more acknowledgement that often international buildings are the result of a collaborative effort.

In China, for example, all foreign practices are required to work with a registered local design institute (LDI). There are around 2,000 LDIs, and they must approve all new design and construction information. Most practices choose to team up with an LDI before design work has commenced so that they can work together, rather than the LDI being just a checking agency.

OMA teamed up with East China Architectural Design Institute (ECADI) to deliver the new HQ for Chinese Central Television (CCTV).[32] From the beginning of the design process, a team of architects and engineers from ECADI worked in OMA's Rotterdam office to embrace the working process and design philosophy as well as advise on legislative and technical matters. Likewise, OMA's architects worked in ECADI's Beijing office to help complete the design and conduct site visits in a true spirit of collaboration.

Communication

The partner architect supports the design process with their knowledge of local regulations and cultural interpretation as well as communication with clients and the planning authorities and engaging with contractors during construction. Of equal importance is the local partner being able to interpret the design intention for the client and regulatory authorities. This involves not just local language and dialect but understanding the nuances of communication.

All forms of procurement involve an element of design during construction, so for international projects it is important to work with a partner architect who understands and shares a common ethos and values.

Ideally, the local architect and design team members are appointed as early in the design process as possible, thereby becoming collaborating partners. The most challenging arrangement is a tag-team approach in which the concept architect completes the design to the equivalent of RIBA Stage 3, which is then handed over to a delivery team to produce construction information in preparation for tender and procurement. From the outset neither party is working together, and neither feels invested in the process. There will be an almost inevitable blame culture should the design not be carried out in accordance with the concept architect's intentions.

However, UK architects have found new ways of collaborating and integrating the skills and experience of others, allowing the concept design architect to focus on what they do best. This has led practices to reflect on their wider business plan and adopt international processes on their UK projects – namely, working on the early stages of a project developing the concept while preparing to hand over the technical and construction information to 'delivery' architects with more skills and greater technical expertise.

UK architects – international offices

In the late 1990s and the early part of the 21st century, UK architects were particularly successful in winning international projects. Rogers Stirk Harbour + Partners (now RSHP) followed up on its early successes in France, and by 2020 had four international offices, while Foster + Partners has 13 offices, four of which are in various regions in China. David Chipperfield Architects (DCA) and Zaha Hadid Architects (ZHA) among others won important commissions throughout Europe: both practices opened offices in Italy, Germany and China, initially as single-project offices which then developed into branch offices.

This, however, remains a low percentage of UK architects. In the period up to the early 1990s very few architects had offices abroad; even as recently as 2016 the RIBA reported that just 4% of UK architects have at least one international office.[33] Despite this, the influence and impact of international projects via the media is disproportionately high.

The business and management of architecture is not taught in schools, and most in practice learn on the job. Architects have used their experience and have become adept at working abroad and developing methods and processes to ensure that the balance of risk, design collaboration and the final building is as originally conceived.

Typically, there are two reasons for architects opening an international office, both of which are considered relatively low risk. Firstly, the practice has a new commission, having been approached by an existing client, or has won a competition and opens a project office for the duration of the design and construction, co-located with the local partner architect. Secondly, a senior architect in the practice decides to return 'home' and, keen not to lose an experienced team member, a branch office is opened around them. This has the benefits of the new regional office being led by a known member of staff and adopting the same management culture and ways of working.

Architect as design team leader – management, fee and risk

At home or abroad, it was previously unheard of for architects to directly engage consultants, thereby taking on additional design liability and commercial risk.

However, it has now become standard practice, internationally as well as within the UK, for the architect to directly engage all design consultants. ARB requires all UK-registered architects to hold professional indemnity insurance (PII) and 'ensure that any work undertaken overseas is adequately covered by your policy'.[34] Most UK policies do not cover working in the US and Canada due to the compensation-driven legal system and the damages paid out. If working there, a separate policy is arranged on an aggregate basis, limiting the size of any claim.

A solution to this may be single project insurance, which is more common internationally. Project insurance has the added benefit of encouraging collaboration, and is preferred by clients, designers and contractors alike as it is written specifically for the project and is retained by the owner of the building. A UK architect is still obliged to comply with ARB code and retain PII, but the project-based policy will cover claims of design fault and liability.

The FIDIC[35] range of contracts are internationally recognised by most regions and jurisdictions. Whichever form of contract is used, the management of risk and liability is to be negotiated between the parties. The UK legal basis of 'reasonable skill and care' is long established but unknown internationally, where it is more likely that 'fitness for purpose' will be required. The latter imposes a higher duty on the architect and an obligation to design to achieve specific results. This is problematic for UK architects and their professional indemnity insurance providers such that the local partner architect or another international consultant such as the engineer may be the lead contracting party.

How has working internationally affected UK practice?

If working solely in the UK, design management procedures are straightforward and follow quality management processes. Typically, this involves weekly design reviews of all projects which are based on familiar work stages such as the RIBA Plan of Work, a common regulatory framework and recognised procurement methods. However, management and design reviews in a practice with work in several international arenas demands contextual responses.

Architects working internationally face the challenge of adjusting established office structures and management processes to suit each project context, including the logistics of languages and time zones and respecting cultural, religious and seasonal holidays such as Ramadan and Chinese New Year. To facilitate efficient communication with the client and the local design team, language fluency is required ideally by those in leadership and project management positions.

As a result, and to utilise the knowledge gained and experience of a particular working culture, the practice might set up a team centred on language and culture that would be assigned all work in a particular region. This has the inherent danger that the team is defined by language and culture and as such becomes 'localised', acting independently and distinctly from the rest of the office.

International business culture – fees and cashflow

UK architects' fee levels are among the highest in the world, and broadly align with those in Germany and America. However, the commercial challenge of working internationally is not without financial risk, for in most other regions fees are lower and, in some cases, significantly so. This gives further justification for architects to partner with local practices, as they are then more able to work efficiently during the construction phases. Currency fluctuation is another business risk, addressed by fees being paid in the 'home' currency, thus negating potential losses.

Many regions first require a full set of information to be submitted at the end of each work stage and only on approval is the architect allowed to submit an invoice, which is then paid some months later. Some clients settle accounts only after the design team has submitted a contracted number of drawings. The professional is viewed as more akin to a supplier of goods rather than services, and the concept of design value is yet to be fully appreciated and understood.

The business culture in China and the Middle East determines that the architect and design team are paid in stages: typically on approval of completed work stages many months later. Consequently, the architect-led team must endure many months of financial risk. If the architect has engaged subconsultants the risk is even greater. Should the client delay or, worse still, renege on the payment of fees, under UK law the practice remains liable to pay the consultants. The risk can be absorbed by practices with significant cash reserves but even large practices may be unable to manage, as Austin-Smith:Lord (ASL)[36] found in 2011 when applying for a Company Voluntary Arrangement (CVA) in order to avoid going into administration, as a result of outstanding fees of £7 million on projects in the Middle East. The business lessons learned are to never become exposed to such large sums on one project.

To alleviate the risk to cashflow, UK practices have adopted the practice of issuing invoices for mobilisation payments before commencement of services. It is common practice for contractors to require mobilisation payments for the hire of plant, equipment and resources. Whereas lawyers and accountants issue such invoices as a matter of course, architects have been slow to adopt the practice, betraying a lack of business acumen, and only those confident in their own value will do so.

Authorship, copyright and brand value

Signature architects (what we would term 'starchitects') typically have separate contractual arrangements for which they charge a fee, over and above that charged by the practice for standard professional services. The additional contract confirms that the architect has had personal involvement in the project and has added their stamp of approval. Further, they agree to attend the opening of the building, much like actors attending the premiere of their latest film, thereby 'endorsing' the building as one of theirs. It is akin to a signature on a painting in that it authenticates the product and adds value.

A celebrity actor and a film are inextricably linked which – to a degree – guarantees box-office success. A film studio will know the style and idiosyncrasies of a particular star over another. Architects, similarly, are known for their design language or 'style', which defines their brand.

Herein lies the difference between the star actor and the star architect: the general public will know a building by its shape and nickname, such as The Shard or The Gherkin, but may not be able to identify the architect. Only two architects could potentially claim true star status: Zaha Hadid and Frank Gehry, both flamboyant and recognisable figures. Hadid was known for berating staff in public forums and ignoring interviewers' questions if she deemed them stupid or, as in the case of Radio 4, ending the interview if asked inappropriate questions. Gehry starred as himself in an episode of *The Simpsons* in which he was commissioned to design a concert hall. His design style was mocked when he was asked to crumple some paper.

And perhaps for the first time in history, practices are continuing to trade after the passing of their named architect.

A signature architect – like a famous chef, or fashion designer – cannot be everywhere, so the brand is based on the architect's endorsement and control of the output. They cannot work more than so many hours in a day, restricting the number of projects they are personally able to work on. This practice enables the practice to continue after the architect's death.

As the brand becomes recognised, there will be those wishing to copy and benefit from an imitation without having to pay the fees. Zaha Hadid Architects (ZHA) has been involved in a number of intellectual property (IP) and copyright disputes, for example in the case of a building in Chongqing bearing a close resemblance to one designed by ZHA for Wangjing SOHO in Beijing. ZHA believed that the copy was made possible by the illegal accessing of 3D computer files.[37] The Chongqing copy was quickly constructed and opened before the legitimate building in Beijing. Legal action was deemed pointless: even if the SOHO won, the judge would not instruct the copy to be demolished.

Zaha Hadid was regularly forceful in seeking compensation against those who copied products, and often registered international trademarks. However, in the case of a building, Hadid was phlegmatic, seeing it more as a reputation enhancer.

Zaha Hadid died in 2016 and despite initial concerns that the practice would see a reduction in new work, it has remained resilient and turnover has increased from £45 million in 2016 to £60 million[38] in 2021. The accounts show that 64% of turnover was from Asia, 23% from Europe and less than 1% from the UK. The transition from a single person to an international brand is complete.

Likewise, Richard Rogers Partnership has successfully managed the staged transition from a single-figure name to Rogers Stirk Harbour + Partners to RSHP, respecting the founder but acknowledging that the practice ownership and leadership have changed.

US practices such as SOM and others have followed a similar path, where the founders are no longer named and the practice title has become an acronym. SOM, formerly Skidmore, Owings & Merrill, is one of the world's largest global architects.

An oddity to note is that, with a handful of exceptions, few international practices have opened a permanent office in the UK. Those that have are almost exclusively from the US. European-based architects tend to team up with a UK architect, rather than open an office themselves.

Ethical practice

All practices have a dilemma when approached by a client whose funding and reputation are questionable. Working internationally heightens the potential risk of reputational damage that architects face when taking on a commission. Social media by its very nature facilitates immediate global protest: no architect wishes to be guilty by association.

Figure 7.7 National Stadium, Olympic Green, Beijing.

An architect may claim that the nature of the project justifies and warrants their involvement, no matter the regime or source of funding, and that they do not work for one person but for the betterment of society. In response to a number of migrant-worker deaths on a construction site for the Al-Wakrah Stadium in Doha, Qatar, Zaha Hadid stated that it was 'not her duty as an architect to look at it'.[39]

In February 2008, Steven Spielberg[40] withdrew from his role as an adviser on the Beijing 2008 Summer Olympics in protest against China's links to human rights issues in Darfur, Sudan. Herzog & de Meuron, the co-designer of the stadium, adopted a different position: 'It's very cheap and easy for architects and artists and film-makers to pull out or to make this kind of criticism.'

Jacques Herzog further stated:

> ‘All work conditions in China are not what you'd desire … It's easy to criticise, being far away. I'm tempted almost to say the opposite … How great it was to work in China and how much I believe that doing the stadium [and] the process of opening will change radically, transform, the society. Engagement is the best way of moving in the right direction.’[41]

It is impossible to define an international, homogenised code of ethics and professional behaviour. When practising locally or globally, architects are faced with ethical decisions, from whether to take on a client and a project to specifying materials and products. All have a professional duty to justify their decisions based on wider criteria than simply the commercial.

This argument that UK architects can help promote and indeed change a society for the better has also been used by the RIBA itself. In 2017, Jane Duncan, RIBA President, lauded the UK's ‘design culture that produces architecture of the highest quality. There are new challenges that the UK architecture profession is applying itself to on a global scale: dealing with the ethical and humanitarian issues prevalent in our globalised world, the digital industrial revolution and its impact on design and construction processes, and the need to create sustainable and healthy environments in an age of rapid urbanisation. The RIBA (as a signatory to the United Nations Global Compact) is supporting and promoting ten principles in British architecture, covering human rights, labour standards, the environment and anti-corruption.’[42]

Meanwhile, the Architects Code 2017 states: ‘You are expected to observe this Code wherever in the world you work. In a country where there are accepted standards of professional conduct for architects, you are expected to (and, if registered there, you should) also conduct yourself according to that country's codes and ethical standards.’[43]

The RIBA Code of Professional Conduct barely addresses ‘ethics’, stating that ‘Members shall treat people with respect and shall strive to be inclusive, ethical, and collaborative in all they do’.

The RIBA Ethics and Sustainable Development Commission recognises that practice is international, placing the RIBA's commitment to ‘public interest, social purpose, ethical behaviour and sustainable development at the heart of the institute's activities’.

The International Union of Architects defines an architect as 'professionally and academically qualified and generally registered/licensed/certified to practise architecture in the jurisdiction in which he or she practises and is responsible for advocating the fair and sustainable development, welfare, and the cultural expression of society's habitat in terms of space, forms, and historical content'.[44]

> 'A code of ethics and conduct establishes a professional standard of behavior that guides architects in the conduct of their practices. Architects should observe and follow the code of ethics and conduct for each jurisdiction in which they practice.'[45]

Given their status, prominent architects and practices in particular have a duty to lead by having a clear ethical position. This is more than protecting their brand for commercial reasons: every decision involves global issues such as the climate emergency. Architects also have an ethical responsibility across the whole life of a project. Projects funded by the oil and pharmaceutical industries are increasingly under the ethical microscope. At a smaller scale, but no less influentially, UK architects specifying global products should ensure that they meet transparent policies on anti-slavery and the environment.

Barometers of global architecture

The Pritzker Architecture Prize and the Venice Biennale are the two most important, respected barometers of international architecture.

Inaugurated in 1979, the Pritzker is awarded annually to a living architect who has produced a consistently high-quality body of work and has made 'significant contributions to humanity and the built environment'. Its jury is composed of past winners, internationally known architects, academics and lay members. In its first 10 years, US architects won five awards, three winners were European, and two winners each came from Japan and South America.

By contrast, since 2000 just one winner has been from the US and recipients have come from a wide geographical spread including India, China, Scandinavia and West Africa. This recognises that the best architecture is produced by many and is not the preserve of the established few.

In 2004, the prize's 26th year, Zaha Hadid was the first female architect recipient. Since then, a woman has won just four times and notoriously, in 1991, the prize was awarded to Robert Venturi while his partner, Denise Scott Brown, was ignored. In the citation, Scott Brown was patronisingly referred to as 'his talented partner ... with whom he has collaborated on both more writings and built works'.[46] In 2013, Harvard students, supported by architects and others worldwide, petitioned the Pritzker to retrospectively amend the award to 'joint', thereby acknowledging Scott Brown's equal contribution. In response, Lord Palumbo, Chair of the Prize and on behalf of the jury, rejected the request, writing, 'A later jury cannot re-open, or second guess the work of an earlier jury ...'[47] The letter continues: 'We should like to thank you for calling directly to our attention a more general problem, namely that of assuring women a fair and equal place within the profession.'

It took a further 13 years for another woman to win, when Carme Pigem was awarded the prize in 2017, albeit as one in partnership with two men. In the subsequent five years three female architects have won, notably in 2020 when Yvonne Farrell and Shelley McNamara of Grafton Architects won in recognition of the 'way they conduct their practice, their belief in collaboration, their generosity towards their colleagues, especially as evidenced in such events as the 2018 Venice Biennale'.[48]

The Chinese architect Wang Shu was awarded the prize in 2012, and the concluding words of his citation mention 'uncompromising, responsible architecture arising from a sense of specific culture and place'[49], acknowledging that China had developed its own contemporary creative excellence.

In 2016, the award marked a further change in emphasis, recognising architects whose work is not so much about the building as object but is more centred on process. The work of Alejandro Aravena with his practice Elemental is firmly rooted in social responsibility and engaging local communities.

In 2022 the prize was awarded to Diébédo Francis Kéré in recognition of his community engagement projects; his citation stated that his work 'is not about the object but the objective; not the product, but the process'.[50]

The Venice Biennale of Architecture, inaugurated in 1980, a year after the Pritzker, is an international exhibition held every two years and over a three-month period. Although curated by a single architect, it includes the work of many around a central theme.

Figure 7.8 Diébédo Francis Kéré next to his installation at the Sensing Spaces: Architecture Re-imagined exhibition at the Royal Academy, London, January 2014.

Similarly, the change of emphasis from the iconic to social is reflected in the themes of the Biennale. In 2012, 'Common Ground',[51] curated by David Chipperfield, aimed to demystify the role of the architect and explain the design process. It conveyed that architects are not the solitary geniuses as portrayed by the media, but professionals and members of society with shared goals and focused on looking at public architecture.

In 2016 Aravena, in parallel with the Pritzker, continued the theme of social and community engagement by curating 'Reporting from the Front':

> … to widen the range of issues to which architecture is expected to respond, adding explicitly to the cultural and artistic dimensions that already belong to our scope, those that are on the social, political, economical and environmental end of the spectrum …'[52]

Subsequent Biennale exhibitions have continued the theme of social engagement: Yvonne Farrell and Shelley McNamara curated 'Freespace' and, in 2021, Hashim Sarkis curated 'How Will We Live Together?' – titles which are self-explanatory.

In their early years, the Pritzker Prize and the Venice Biennale exclusively endorsed the iconic and the didactic, conveying the impression that buildings are produced by solitary (male) architects from a mostly Western tradition. Architects working in local and regional contexts were the exception.

However, over the past 20 years, the Pritzker and the Biennale have shifted emphasis away from portraying the building as object and have become concerned with communicating a wider role of the architect as the leader and coordinator of a process. Cynics may argue that this is in reaction to the now-pejorative term 'starchitect' and, ironically, they support an altruistic and public-spirited variant; after all, the award-winners and curators work globally and self-promote, giving lectures and publishing books in order to maintain a reputation and media presence.

International architects will continue to serve the insatiable desire of clients for global recognition. However, the positive message is that practice of architecture matters: although the profession is accused of encouraging the iconic and the theatrical, a balance is being readdressed. Architecture is not just for architects. It is a social and collaborative act, embracing the community, be it global or local.

Global practice – what's next?

UK architects have made a significant contribution to international design and architecture, but the relationship is not one-way. Working globally has also positively influenced practice in the UK through collaboration and change in methodology towards technical architects leading on the latter design stages and construction, while the 'design' architects concentrate on the earlier stages of a project.

The RIBA Plan of Work is sequential, and its eight stages too limiting for some cultures that want to commence construction in parallel with the early design stages. UK practices working in China are typically placed under pressure to deliver quickly and efficiently, and this has facilitated a design process of overlap rather than sequence. In order to keep up with demand and the need to build quickly China has developed construction methodologies such as pods and prefabricated building elements. Design and construction have much to learn and benefit from working in places such as China. UK construction has an over-reliance on wet trades, old technologies and carbon-heavy materials. Combined with the effects of Brexit, early signs suggest that with fewer certified materials and a smaller labour force,[53] construction is being forced to adopt prefabrication. Thirty years after the Egan Report,[54] one of its main recommendations may finally be realised: albeit not because of the construction industry changing voluntarily.

The Brexit[55] transition period ended on 31 January 2020, and the UK formally left the EU. The implications for architects range from being unable to compete for OJEU competitions to the loss of mutual recognition of professional status and qualification. While negotiations continue to finalise the terms of future trade, architects are trying to mitigate the risk of loss of income by seeking other international markets.

Architects such as DCA, FaP and ZHA are feted in Europe, the Middle East and the US but, proportionately, have built very little in the UK. They have built their best work abroad as a result of supportive and engaged clients who value their design skills, giving them creative freedom. The RIBA reports that 'one in five architects plans to respond to Brexit by exporting more overseas'.[56] The world is confronting issues of global importance, including the climate emergency, social inequality and political instability. The Covid-19 pandemic of 2020 taught us that we can work remotely in a functional way. However, it also reinforced the values of presence and togetherness. Global practice at its best is about collaborating with clients and consultants, enjoying open cultural exchange, while being critically regional and respectful of the local context and environment.

CHAPTER 8

The contemporary architect – the struggle to convey value

Defining the role of architect

As a profession, architects often struggle to define their role and their value and are increasingly unable to identify how they can make a positive contribution to improving the built environment. The reasons for this are varied and complex but, at its simplest, architects have been too absorbed by the building as an object. Image has taken precedence over process.

Even today, architects' websites are replete with project images and lists of awards won, yet an explanation of the design process is absent. It is as though architects are selling a product and not a service. By being unable to explain what they do, architects cannot articulate their value.

The public have strong views on a wide range of architectural matters: the built environment; tower blocks; the lack of investment in schools and hospitals. Although architects have a modest role and reduced influence in design and construction, still they are often blamed for its failure. The public mistakenly believe that architects are responsible for most UK housing, including the banal, standardised products of the private, volume housebuilders.

There is a lack of healthy dialogue about architecture and the amount there is is so polemicised that architects become over-defensive and unable to articulate their role and value. The profession was memorably satirised by *Monty Python's Flying Circus*[1] in 'The Architects Sketch': as one architect explains that he has avoided the use of flammable materials his model catches fire. 'Satire' appears on screen. This reflected the public view that architects were out of touch with society, lacked knowledge of construction and were profligate with the client's budget. But any irony or comedy value is cast aside when this is viewed after the Grenfell Tower tragedy of June 2017, in which 72 people lost their lives.[2]

Figure 8.1 Ove Arup.

Around the same time as the Python sketch, Ove Arup gave his 'Key Speech',[3] in which he discussed the values that underpin the work of practice and articulated his vision for the future. He made points that are as relevant today as they were when originally delivered, identifying the failings of the architect and proposing a number of solutions. He defined the term 'total architecture', setting it as an aim for all future projects.

It was usual at the time for the design team to consist of core consultants, which included the architect, structural engineer and mechanical and electrical (M&E) engineer, all directly appointed by the client. Also appointed, although not always fully integrated into the design process, was the quantity surveyor (QS), who advised the client on the estimated construction cost at the end of each design stage. Although common on most projects in the UK, in Europe and North America the QS role is typically carried out by the architect or project manager and costs are only verified once the contractor has submitted a tender. In Germany, on small- to medium-sized projects, the architect prepares a cost plan using industry-standard software.

The reputation of architects was further damaged in 1974, when John Poulson[4] was convicted of corruption related to building contracts. The case was widely reported in the press, and although he never formally registered as an architect the reputational damage to the profession stuck. Judge Waller said, in his summing up: 'To offer corrupt gifts strikes at the very foundation of our system. To accept them is a betrayal of trust.'[5]

On 4 May 1979 Margaret Thatcher became prime minister of the UK, and the actions and attitude of her government were to prove significant for the profession and construction industry for the next 30 years.[6] The lack of trust fostered during the 1970s and 1980s continued into the post-Thatcher era, when in 2011 Michael Gove, newly appointed Secretary of State for Education, told Parliament during a discussion on the design of new schools that 'it's a scandal … millions of pounds were spent on consultants'. He claimed, mistakenly, that 'One individual, in one year, made more than £1m as a result of his endeavours.'[7]

Gove's disdain for the profession continued when he announced the scrapping of the £55 billion Building Schools for the Future (BSF) programme. Although subsequently found by a High Court ruling to have been 'an abuse of power',[8] this had severe implications for practices and their employees.

Gove continued his attack on the profession, saying: 'We won't be getting Richard Rogers to design your school, we won't be getting any "award winning architects" to design it, because no-one in this room is here to make architects richer.' The RIBA issued a robust response from then President, Ruth Reed, but the damage was done.

Outside the political arena, the interventions of the then Prince Charles, beginning in the mid-1980s, also influenced public perception of architects. On 30 May 1984 he gave a speech at Hampton Court Palace, a Royal Gala evening in celebration of the 150th anniversary of the RIBA, in which he called on architects to build in a traditional way and to abandon Modernist principles.[9] His widely referenced quote about the winning competition proposal for the extension to the National Gallery called it 'a monstrous carbuncle on the face of a much-loved friend'. (Many believe he was, in fact, referring to Richard Rogers' hi-tech proposal and not the winning one: 'I would understand better this type of high-tech approach if you demolished the whole of Trafalgar Square and started again with a single architect responsible for the entire layout, but what is proposed is like a monstrous carbuncle on the face of a much-loved and elegant friend.')

The irony is that the words preceding the famous quote actually reveal that he had a valid and appropriate understanding of the idea of context. In 1989, energised by public and political support for his ideas, Prince Charles published his book, *A Vision of Britain: A Personal View*[10] as a reaction to the Modernist architecture of the preceding years. He proposed a number of solutions for the built environment, ultimately put into action by the commissioning of a new town called Poundbury, situated just outside Dorchester. Poundbury is an example of socially responsible patronage and follows a line of historical towns and villages designed with social purpose. Since the 19th century, Britain has built urban model villages such as Bournville and Port Sunlight, enabled by the benevolence of their patrons, entrepreneurs such as Cadbury and the Lever Brothers, respectively, with an explicit ethos of social responsibility.

The prince appointed Leon Krier, a neoclassical traditionalist, as lead architect. Construction commenced in 1993. The new town was well received by the public but less so by architectural critics. Stephen Bayley, writing in the *Guardian*, considered it 'fake, heartless, authoritarian and grimly cute'.[11]

Figure 8.2 Phase 2 housing, Beechwood Lane, Poundbury, Dorset.

Figure 8.3 Gardens precinct of low-rise housing, Hinksey Path, Lesnes, Thamesmead, London.

This debate raised the question of the future of architecture and social purpose, polarising and oversimplifying the debate between the traditional and the modern: Poundbury versus Thamesmead. Architects would have done well to listen to Prince Charles's words rather than being distracted by the supporting imagery of neoclassical architecture. A quarter of a century after his book's publication, no one can argue with the sentiment that a 'really good architect' should be concerned about how people live, and the environment they inhabit.

Prince Charles recognised the importance of engaging with people to help determine their own environment, and cited the increasing influence of housing cooperatives in the inner-city areas of the Northwest. He referenced Rod Hackney and Ted Cullinan as architects who, rather than imposing their singular visions, embraced the value of listening to residents and community engagement.

Prince Charles concluded the Hampton Court speech by lamenting that Mansion House Square – subject to a public inquiry into whether a Mies van der Rohe tower block and public square should finally be built – would have been better served if the community had been involved. The project was originally conceived in 1969 in a spirit of postwar enthusiasm for the 'modern'.

Ultimately it was rejected. The atmosphere of conservatism propagated by Thatcher and Prince Charles resulted in an ever-growing animosity towards architects, who were portrayed as lacking understanding of and empathy towards society. With irony, Jack Self in a 2017 article in the *Guardian* points out that the Gherkin is twice the height of the unbuilt Mies tower and, if built a decade later, would 'probably have appeared banal in the context of so many other corporate towers'.[12]

Shaping construction policy

Introduced in 1994, the National Lottery was conceived as 'the most significant change in the funding of Britain's arts and cultural sector since … the Arts Council'.[13] The Heritage Lottery Fund, a form of public patronage via the government, has been responsible for distributing over £8.3 billion on more than 49,000 heritage projects across the UK.[14] It has provided architects with many commissions of varying scales: the most well-known

Figure 8.4 Millennium Dome (now the O2 Arena), Greenwich, London, seen from the north bank.

include Tate Modern (2000) and the Eden Project (2001). Heritage Lottery Fund projects also include a few notorious examples, such as the National Centre for Popular Music in Sheffield, now a university student union, and The Public in West Bromwich (originally a multipurpose venue and now a school). The Dome and Millennium Experience, opened on 1 January 2000, is to date the largest project part-funded by the Lottery and cost c.£750 million. The project, 'a byword for New Labour hubris, squandered resources and hideously bungled planning',[15] was mired in political prevarication until Tony Blair gave the go-ahead just three years before the start of the millennium.

The UK government has sought to shape policy and attitudes in construction via many reports, 12 of which are covered in depth in *Construction Reports 1944–98*.[16] All identified common themes such as inefficiency of process and a lack of integration between design and construction. All made recommendations for change, which were mostly ignored by industry. The reports highlighted by omission the reduction of the architect's role.

The Banwell Report, published in 1964, criticised the separation of design and construction and what was perceived as inefficiencies. Thirty years later, in July 1994, after a period of severe economic recession, Sir Michael Latham was commissioned to review procurement and contractual arrangements, with a particular focus on clients as the 'driving force'.

Constructing the Team, more commonly known as the Latham Report, reaffirmed what everyone involved in UK construction already knew: that construction needed to 'set about Constructing the Team'. The report recommended several actions, including collaborative working, more particular forms of procurement, and contracts with an emphasis on partnering. The executive summary contained over 50 recommendations with common themes of quality, teamwork and improving efficiency. Latham reported that construction practices needed updating and that adversarial relationships on construction projects should be replaced with cooperation, trust and mutual understanding by all involved.

> 'Partnering includes the concepts of teamwork between supplier and client, and of total continuous improvement. It requires openness between the parties, ready acceptance of new ideas, trust and perceived mutual benefit … We are confident that partnering can bring significant benefits by improving quality and timeliness of completion whilst reducing costs.'[17]

The most radical recommendation was that government should lead by example and become a best practice client, and should be dissuaded from using bespoke forms of contract and instead adopt partnering-type contracts. Latham exampled New Engineering Contracts (NECs), which were launched in 1993, and are designed following three key unique characteristics:

- They stimulate good management of the relationship between the two parties.
- They can be used in a wide variety of commercial situations for a variety of types of work and in any location.
- They are clear, simple and written in plain English.

Although Latham had provoked industry initiatives such as CIC[18] and NECs, it was deemed necessary for government to force the construction industry to make changes. In 1997 John Prescott, then deputy prime minister, commissioned another report to review procedures from a client's perspective in response to continued concerns that construction processes were inefficient and not offering value for money. The task force was chaired by Sir John Egan, and included experts from industries other than construction, such as car manufacturing, hospitality and steel, and an investment manager. Given the members of the task force it is unsurprising that other industries were exampled as improving efficiency and transforming with new methods of production. These included car manufacturing, steel, retail and offshore engineering.

The executive summary opened by stating that 'The UK construction industry at its best is excellent'. That was the positive message. The next paragraphs paint a different picture, however:

> '... there is deep concern that the industry as a whole is under-achieving. It has low profitability and invests too little in capital, research and development and training. Too many of the industry's clients are dissatisfied ...'[19]

The report makes no reference to architecture, and the word 'architect' is used just once.

The architecture profession should not be under the impression that so few references in the report to architecture or the architect mean that it was considered that all problems lay solely with the contractor. Egan identified five drivers for change, all of which had a familiar ring from previous reports:

- committed leadership
- focus on the customer
- integration of the process and the team around the product
- quality-driven agenda
- commitment to people.

Egan and Latham called for sustained reductions in cost and time in the name of 'efficiency': all of these points are of relevance to architects.

Egan asked for reductions in capital cost and construction time, citing 'design and build firms in the USA currently achieving reductions in construction time for offices ... of 10–15% per year'. Although 'value' is mentioned more often than cost, there are no prescriptive solutions nor recognition of the contributions of the design team. Construction materials are easily measured and costed by the QS. However, an architect produces something else, generally called 'delight', and without mention in Egan or Latham.

The final report, *Rethinking Construction*,[20] was influential in effecting positive change in UK construction, bringing about a number of groups that merged in 2003 to become Constructing Excellence, whose members include clients, contractors, manufacturers and architects.[21]

Scope of services and procurement forms

We can see that the scope of services of contemporary architects has significantly reduced from that in the 1970s. The role and influence of the profession has diminished for justifiable and understandable reasons.

Architects gained an unenviable reputation of allowing projects to overrun, both in terms of cost and time. In tandem, cost consultants (QSs) and engineers expanded their scope of service to encompass other design and management services. The architect is no longer prominent in giving advice on securing planning permission, nor in leading negotiations with local authorities. And although considered a 'designer' under CDM legislation,[22] architects remain reluctant to take on the principal designer role, despite the RIBA encouraging all to do so.

Contrast this with the entrepreneurial spirit of the early 1960s and practices such as Building Design Partnership (BDP), one of the first to integrate engineers.[23] Its founder, George Grenville Baines, held a 'long cherished ambition of establishing the world's first interdisciplinary practice'. Grenville Baines did not have a conventional training, initially working for a QS from the age of 14, and did not start university until he was 25.[24]

BDP's practice ethos 'was always thinking with a socialist and progressive hat on … designing a lot of housing … and Pilgrim Hospital in 1961 … with a doctor or nurse on the design team to steer architects in the right direction'. BDP also pioneered the Design Teaching Practice in Sheffield to integrate teaching and practice.

Figure 8.5 Building Design Partnership offices, Sunlight House, Manchester, 1986.

In 1995, Yorke Rosenberg Mardell (YRM) 'set up its own engineering division to handle the design of mechanical and electrical services … out of frustration at not being able to find consultants with the same standards'. They believed that with a multidisciplinary practice, 'the client can be sure that the whole team is working to a common end'.[25]

The idea that architects might regain the role of QS has long since sailed. However, it is incumbent on the profession to become more knowledgeable about the cost of materials and construction methods and to be present at the table, engaging more fully in design. Without a good knowledge of building, economics is impossible, and other than touching briefly on this in Part 3 seminars, students are not taught about the cost of building types, materials and the different emphases in various forms of procurement.

As the architect gained the unenviable reputation for being profligate with the client's budget, the QS became a distinct role. Always directly appointed by the client to 'control cost', the QS is all too often not fully integrated into the design team. For all clients, keeping to budget is paramount and the QS role has developed from measuring quantities and surveying into one central to the project as 'cost consultant'. This is more than semantic, for in the early 1990s the 'consultancy' expanded into time management and the QS transmogrified into the project manager.

And if not a single service, it is not unheard of for the project manager and the QS to be appointed from the same company. Arup identified the QS as 'making a pitch to be all things – busy acquiring a new look', and further expressed his concern, suggesting that they are 'imposed on it [the project], preventing us from doing the job our way'.[26]

On large projects the architect is rarely asked their opinion on the form of procurement and, worse still, begins designing without knowing how the building will be procured. Leading into the turn of the century the prevalent form of procurement was design–bid–build, more commonly known as traditional procurement: a linear and sequential process in which the architect and design team prepared construction information before undertaking a tender process and then appointing a contractor. The contractor offering the lowest price was selected, inevitably leading to a confrontational attitude with the architect as contract administrator, as the former sought to mitigate losses (as identified by Latham). This placed architects in the invidious position of being contracted to a client for design services from commencement through to construction, as well as being contract administrator and obliged to exercise independent and fair judgement in determining onsite issues.

Prior to the 1990s, contractors were regularly (patronisingly) termed 'dinosaurs' by architects and others in design: this lack of respect only served to exacerbate a 'them and us' relationship. In response to the commercial need to build quicker, design–bid–build developed into a two-stage form whereby the design was complete to 60–70% – including foundations and structural main frame, enabling the contractor to commence construction earlier. The architect and design team prepared the balance of design information, which was priced by the contractor in the second stage. As a result, the contractor was 'on board' before the design was fully complete and able to advise on the construction method and materials, making a positive contribution to the design process.

This was then formalised with the idea that a contractor could be engaged to offer pre-construction advice to the design team, with the introduction of pre-contract services agreements (PCSAs). The contractor was engaged under a separate appointment and with no obligation from the employer to engage them for the build.

Taken a stage further: why have tendering at all? A fixation with cost being the sole determinant when selecting the contractor is the root of discord, and if collaboration is truly to be embraced why waste resources engaging in a process to achieve a price that is anticipated by the cost plan as prepared by the QS?

Egan and Latham identified fragmentation between all parties in construction and called for fundamental changes, encouraging forms of partnering or framework agreements:

> Public and private sector clients should begin to use the NEC, and phase out "bespoke' documents (Chapter 5, paragraph 5.30). A target should be set of ⅓ of Government funded projects started over the next 4 years to use the NEC.'[27]

A fundamental characteristic of collaboration is mutual trust born out of common, shared aims. Partnering in any form would help obviate conflicts from the outset by providing a defined, common purpose. The architect and design team want a beautiful building, and the contractor is focused on profit.

The client wants both: a quality building for a low price – but is this achievable or a naive dream? Tony Bingham is unconvinced that partnering is the answer, and to avoid disputes proposes to 'put the builder back in his [sic] place: A building contractor is very, very good at building buildings'.[28] And 'put the architect, the engineer in his [sic] place: An architect is very, very good at designing buildings'. Bingham continues by saying that D&B procurement is not the solution, and calls for an end to it, as it 'is a barrier to common purpose'.

Clients were receptive to D&B, as it transfers risk from the client to the contractor. Appointed by the client, the architect prepares design information, which is then completed by the contractor during construction. Typically the architect is novated to the contractor to finalise the design, although the contractor may select another architect. The relationship becomes murkier if the architect is engaged by both client and contractor and at risk of breaching the ethical wall. The client wants to 'protect design quality' and so engages the original architect in a 'design champion' or 'artistic supervisor' role.

A 2015 survey carried out by NBS[29] found that D&B contracts are increasingly favoured by contractors. Despite some architects preferring the domain of design only and having no role on site, many countered that it meant a dumbing-down of design quality. Prominent architects resigned from projects, not wishing to claim authorship of projects on which key design ideas were simplified by contractors.[30]

Latham states that 'the client whose commercial requirements demand an early start on site … should choose a procurement route which will accommodate those wishes in a flexible manner which avoids adversarial attitudes. A lump sum … or a design and build route would be a recipe for disaster, if the work on site is intended to progress while design is still proceeding.'[31]

To ensure that a truly collaborative design and construction process is successful, all involved need to have mutual respect for each other's skills and experience. It is lamentable that dialogue between clients, architects and contractors so quickly becomes confrontational.

By the beginning of the 20th century, practices such as Richard Rogers Partnership, Foster + Partners, Grimshaw Architects and Michael Hopkins and Partners had an international reputation for hi-tech architecture and were being appointed for major projects in the UK. Hi-tech used prefabrication, offsite construction and lightweight materials, necessitating

Figure 8.6 Lloyd's, City of London, seen from the south.

a fully integrated and collaborative environment with engineers and contractors. More an attitude than a style, hi-tech projects include Lloyd's of London and the Lord's Cricket Ground Media Centre.

In the determination to deliver buildings more quickly and efficiently, the developer of Broadgate, a large commercial development in the City of London, introduced the project manager, to lead the design and construction process. A role introduced from America to manage ever more complicated construction processes, the project manager is appointed prior to any design activity and acts as the client's adviser on all design and construction matters.

Latham identified that the role and duties of project managers required clearer definition, as previously these had been ambiguous: 'Government project sponsors should have sufficient expertise to fulfil their roles effectively.'[32]

Another consequence of the architect being largely unable to manage and deliver buildings 'on time and to budget' was the necessity for commercial clients to appoint a project manager. Architect Norman Foster acknowledges that the project manager role is pivotal:

> 'The role of a good professional project manager is to anticipate problems – to bring people together.
>
> - to get the best from everyone
> - to help resolve conflicts
>
> to create a team spirit
> To SOLVE PROBLEMS
> NOT TO CREATE PROBLEMS
> To have one face to everyone – not two faces.'[33]

However, he concludes his views in a sketchbook, with the commonly expressed view that project managers are prone to being remote from the design team and not engaged in collaborative problem solving.

The architect's role has diminished even further to the point where some medium to large practices appoint a design manager to assist with resources, fee proposals, design team programme, and the management and issue of design information.

All designers have a regulatory duty to comply with the Construction (Design and Management) Regulations 2015.[34] Alan Jones, then RIBA President, encouraged architects to take on the role of principal designer (PD), coordinating health and safety in the pre-construction phase. In support of its view that the architect is best placed to take on the PD role, the RIBA has published its own services contract separate from that for the architect. The architect, as design team lead and coordinator of design information, is best placed to coordinate the risk assessment of the project, from project initiation and throughout the design stages.

Architects have also become detached from the planning process, and have little or no influence in matters of policy and a diminished role in negotiating and preparing planning applications, to the point where the role of planning consultant was invented in the late 1990s. The reasons for architects relinquishing services such as cost advice to the QS, and management to the project manager are good, but it is mystifying how the profession lost knowledge of the planning process such that a specialist consultant was required to step in. Even on straightforward projects, not in a conservation area and uncontentious in terms of planning law – requiring neither Section 106[35] nor CIL negotiations – clients still appoint a planning consultant.

In addition, the National Planning Policy Framework (NPPF) makes no reference to the 'architect'. 'Architecture' is mentioned twice, as is 'architectural'. All of this undermines the knowledge and experience of the architect when it comes to planning.

UK planning is called 'development control', as if the architect and building should be tamed or restrained. In the UK anyone can submit a planning application, whereas in many EU countries planning is considered a strategic, positive process in which a registered architect is required to validate planning and building permit applications.

Some EU cities such as Rotterdam have a city architect leading large teams, influencing policy and developing urban strategy. Richard Rogers fulfilled a similar role in London between 2001 and 2008 as Chief Advisor on Architecture and Urbanism to the Mayor, though his appointment was not permanent and he was not replaced. Rogers contributed to the wellbeing of the city, and ideas on restricting cars, developing transport hubs and public green spaces were carried into The London Plan.[36] There are no similar positions anywhere else within the UK.

Living with Beauty,[37] the report of the Building Better, Building Beautiful Commission chaired by Roger Scruton, was launched on 30 January 2020 by the then secretary of state Robert Jenrick MP. Though no architect was involved in the report, it was generally well received by the profession. The executive summary proposes 'a new development and planning framework which will: "Ask for Beauty"; "Refuse Ugliness" and "Promote Stewardship"'.

There is nothing wrong with this, you might contend, nor anything amiss with the aim to 'work with our neighbours, not to impose our views on them'. It states that the planning process should be sped up but misses the point by suggesting that this will come about via digitisation and not by greater involvement of architects. It also highlights that quality is reduced post planning permission and calls on planners to insist on Section 106 agreements, requiring developers to pay a 'design monitoring contribution' as a fee for assessment and inspection to ensure that the finished building is as originally permitted.

The RIBA reinforces this point in its report *Design Matters*,[38] stating that the value of planning and the environment is such that the architect must retain status throughout.

> 'The … NPPF … recognises the problem of development quality deteriorating between permission and completion, which is often a result of the original architect not being retained after a development receives planning permission. Local authorities should consider conditioning planning permissions … to ensure that architects are retained until the completion of development.'[39]

However, local authority planning departments are powerless to insist that the design architect is retained, as has been evidenced by a number of projects built without the original architects. David Chipperfield Architects achieved planning permission on a sensitive site in Hampstead, and despite the inclusion of a planning condition[40] requiring that the practice be retained during construction the developer replaced it with another.

In 2020, a White Paper was published titled 'Planning for the future',[41] which states that planning 'has lost public trust', evidenced by a poll finding that 'only seven per cent trusted their local council to make decisions about large scale development'. Meanwhile, 49% and 36% of respondents said they distrusted developers and local authorities, respectively.

Alan Jones, RIBA President, responded by stating:

> 'We urgently need well-designed, mixed-use developments that provide long term value for their communities and residents, delivered by sufficiently resourced local authorities – not a race to the bottom. I call for urgent reconsideration of this legislation that fundamentally contradicts the Government's wider aim of revitalising town centres and developing better homes.'[42]

Jones identified the problem; namely, that despite the report stating that 'there is not enough focus on design', planning is not strategic enough and allows the private sector and the power of investment to influence and determine it. A more strategic plan is required, such as that for the 2012 London Olympics, which comes with a collective focus bringing people together. In order to more fully engage with planning, both strategic and detailed, architects should become more knowledgeable about the financial mechanisms and urban planning. Architects are involved in masterplans, single buildings and street design, and so are well placed to re-engage more widely and in a strategic way.

The tools of design

Until the mid-1980s, architects' design tools included a drawing board and parallel motion, pencils or fine-line ink pens, and tracing paper. Mistakes were erased by scratching the surface with a razor blade, and if the paper became fragile a new 'negative' was printed. All drawings were in 2D (plans, sections and elevations) and to specific scales. If 3D images were required to show the building in context, artists produced original watercolour renderings. Computer-aided design (CAD)[43] became ubiquitous by 2000. In 2020, 73%[44] of construction industry professionals were using building information modelling (BIM),[45] allowing design consultants to work simultaneously on a single computer model. Contractors can provide advice on building methodology and construction costs during the design process. The model becomes construction information and is issued to the contractor, and on completion of the building is handed to the client to facilitate better management of the completed building. Although 'just a tool' it has the capacity and offers the potential for architects to place themselves at the centre of the design process, leading and coordinating it. The complex geometry of the Bilbao Guggenheim[46] cladding would not have been possible without software such as CATIA.[47]

An architect is taught to think and solve problems in three dimensions. Students find working digitally becomes second nature, and from the beginning of their education they do this. A student designing on a computer and then making 3D robot-produced models is preparation for practice.

A report published by the RIBA, 'Client and architect',[48] gives clients' views on the profession, highlighting technical skills and collaboration as requirements for future practice. As each project becomes more collaborative, involving the design input of many parties, the question arises of authorship – who is the designer of the building? – and who has the associated responsibility and liability.

Over the past 50 years, construction methods have changed very little. Latham and Egan called for improvement in construction in the UK, citing examples that were standardised and mass produced. Precasting, prefabrication and offsite panellisation have been introduced, but this is hardly a sea-change. The motor industry has seen significant change both in terms of the vehicle itself as well as the process of manufacture, which is now less labour intensive and almost totally automated, thereby guaranteeing a high standard of assembly and finish. However, construction sites are muddy, dusty and still using techniques that are hundreds of years old. Housing in the UK, mostly built by large developers with no input from architects, uses outdated techniques and methods. The examples stated in the Egan Report are of little relevance, for they are retail sheds built using standardised products and construction with very little design input. Buildings are the result of an individual brief within the context and restrictions of site, budget and brief. They are each unique, and as such this doesn't lend itself to research for each project.

Early in their careers architects such as Rogers and Foster rejected labour-intensive, wet trades, for building components made offsite under factory conditions are of better quality and ease construction on site. They embraced new technologies and construction methods and found early opportunities on projects abroad.

New construction methods required reduced timelines and so 'top-down' became a preferred method of construction, whereby the basement was being dug while the upper floors were constructed. And while the main frame was being built the facade panels followed quickly afterwards, ensuring a weatherproof environment. Even neoclassical facades, formerly ashlar stone, were panellised.

The rise of sustainability

In the post-Second World War period there was a desire to use as much glass as possible to cast off the dark and gloomy past, representing a belief in a Modernist future. By the late 1970s buildings were relatively straightforward, with uncomplicated heating and cooling systems. The role of the M&E engineer was limited to specifying pipe and duct sizes, and was yet to develop into that of the environmental engineer of the 21st century.

An attitude to sustainability and energy conservation was unheard of in the ubiquitous box, clad in glass on all four elevations according to an ideal of platonic beauty, ignoring the sun's path with its associated implications of solar and heat gain, and condensation. Very few architects had an interest in environmental matters, and building regulations did not require particularly onerous standards. Sustainability and taking care of the world's natural resources were considered low priority by the developers commissioning buildings. Double-glazing was standard and enough to comply with regulations. Most office buildings were air-conditioned to cope with the additional heating load from all the glass, as well as computers.

The Building Research Establishment's Environmental Assessment Method (BREEAM) was launched in 1990 as the world's first method of helping clients understand and reduce the environmental impact of their projects. Along with Leadership in Energy and Environmental Design (LEED), its US equivalent launched in 1998, BREEAM is an international standard for appraising sustainability throughout design and construction and life-cycle monitoring. In the UK, BREEAM is not required by legislation or regulation other than being a requirement for most London planning authorities, as well as it being a condition of most publicly funded buildings to achieve a high BREEAM rating. Nevertheless, despite these limitations, the development of BREEAM and LEED presaged a change in attitude towards sustainable design.

Figure 8.7 Beddington Zero Energy Development [BedZED] designed for the Peabody Trust, Helios Road, Wallington, Sutton, London.

In the early part of the 21st century there was a shift in attitude towards sustainable design. Ecobuild, a construction exhibition popular with professionals and the public – later renamed Futurebuild – was launched in 2005. Organisations such as the UK Green Building Council (2007)[49] were formed. BedZED[50], one of the UK's first sustainable developments, was completed in 2002. Conceived in 1997 as a zero-carbon community, it was designed by architect Bill Dunster with Arup engineers in collaboration with project partner and developer the Peabody Trust. The Code for Sustainable Homes, a method of environmental assessment, was introduced in 2006:[51] initially voluntary, it was subsequently incorporated into the building regulations in 2015.

The Climate Change Act 2008 required emissions to be cut to 80% of 1990 levels by 2050, subsequently tightened in 2019 to 'net zero'. Mostly peripheral and considered 'nice to have' in the 1990s, sustainable design is now subject to regulation and essential. In the 1990s architects handed over their designs to be 'engineered'. That is a thing of the past: Arup's ambition of 'total architecture' is now a reality. Architects are at the centre of the design process, coordinating the concept, structure and environmental engineering into a cohesive whole.

Architectural practice is a less-than-ideal environment in which to test ideas, especially those of a technical nature. Invention requires fresh thinking unencumbered by the pressure of contracts and the restrictions of time, money and risk-averse practices (insurance may only allow minor variation of conventional construction methods).

Practices are often lazily differentiated as 'commercial' or 'design-led', as if the two are mutually exclusive. The former refers to those practices with a steady stream of work for developers, designing mostly office and retail developments, while the latter is associated with high-profile practices such as Foster + Partners. Developers realised that by commissioning architects who challenged standard design notions they could 'add value' and charge higher rents and sales. Although a hackneyed term, 'adding value' has become a byword along with 'award-winning' on many architects' websites.

After the Grenfell tragedy, the increase in risk and liability, and with it the cost of professional indemnity insurance (PII), more practices are choosing to focus on the early stages of design and are either declining to work on the later, technical stages and construction, or teaming up with specialist practices. The increased prevalence of D&B procurement has resulted in practices reviewing their business plans and they may decline to offer technical design on a design–bid–build project or – in the case of D&B – decline to be novated.

Hackitt and the golden thread

On 14 June 2017, an electrical fault on a kitchen appliance in a second-floor flat in Grenfell Tower in west London caught fire, and this fire quickly spread to the whole building. Seventy-two people lost their lives. A few weeks after the fire, an independent review was commissioned by the government, led by Dame Judith Hackitt and focusing on high-rise residential buildings, including:

- the regulatory system around design, construction and ongoing management
- compliance and enforcement issues
- international regulation and experience in this area.

The final *Building a Safer Future Report*[52] was published on 16 May 2018. It makes more than 50 recommendations for government as to how to deliver a more robust regulatory system. Previous reports have proved largely ineffectual in provoking significant change. However, it is certain that the Hackitt Report will prove otherwise, and the consequential changes in the design and procurement of buildings will be significant. If correctly interpreted, architects designing high-rise residential buildings will be required to retain PII run-off cover for 30 years. The limitation period for claims, currently six years, will extend to 15 years.

The Building Safety Act[53] received royal assent and became law in mid-2022. Hackitt refers to the 'golden thread of building information', ensuring that the original design intent is preserved and that all design decisions and changes can be managed through a formal review process.[54]

As a result, the role of the architect and all design professionals will undoubtedly change. The architect is best placed to lead this, as they are trained to link things together, and their skills and talent enable them to find design solutions in difficult circumstances.

But if the role of the architect continues to be further eroded, who will link the design process and the issues that arise? Egan and Latham highlighted how common issues of lack of leadership, collaboration and technical knowledge present challenges for the profession. All professionals involved in contemporary construction are confronted by a bewildering amount of legislation, ever-changing planning and building regulations, best-practice guides, various forms of procurement and complex construction methods.

In 2020, the UK had around 123,000 registered doctors, 146,000 lawyers and 380,000 accountants, and even around 110,000 estate agents. Very few would bemoan the number of healthcare professionals, but the figure of only 40,000 registered architects brings into question the value that society places on the built environment.

The challenge for the contemporary architect is not to reclaim former roles. Of more pressing importance is the need to define and explain their value, and in so doing regain public trust. In her 2002 Reith Lecture 'A question of trust',[55] Oona O'Neill, the philosopher and crossbench peer in the House of Lords, stated that it should be easier in an age of open communication to trust institutions and professions. She elaborated that new information technologies are abundant, and that this should enable more transparency and openness.

In the decade from 2010 a number of factors combined to facilitate a potential positive future. Internationally, UK architects are respected and held in high esteem for their design skills. The golden thread and tools such as BIM ensure that the architect plays the key role in a coordinated design process.

Arup's aim of 'total architecture' is as valid now as when first delivered. The architect is the generator of ideas and, as Bingham states, 'an architect is very, very good at designing buildings'.[56] Architects cannot solve society's problems alone, but the very least the profession can do is to become more knowledgeable, collaborative and courageous.

CHAPTER 9

Educating architects

The relationship between academia and practice in the UK is often considered to be disconnected and fractious. Academia often caricatures practice as the 'real world' as if it is unrelated; practice complains that students lack basic skills that should be taught in school.

The architecture schools contend that it is not their responsibility to create young people 'ready for practice' and that they educate students to be reflective practitioners able to make a lifelong contribution to society and the built environment. Young people, in turn, enter schools of architecture with enthusiasm and naivety in the belief that they can change the world. Yet, conversely, few practitioners are calling for the schools to produce students 'ready for work'. Rather, practices call for students to become reflective and develop the ability to make considered decisions based on the knowledge gained in schools. This sets them up best for a career in practice.

The Oxford Conference

The foundations of this uneasy relationship between practice and academia were laid in the Oxford Conference of 1958,[1] during which a group of prominent practitioners formulated a three-part system of qualification: Part 1, the three-year undergraduate degree; Part 2, the two-year Master's; and Part 3, the gateway qualification leading to registration as an architect. There is also a year out between Part 1 and 2 in practice, which is an integral part of the architecture student's journey. The proposed move away from the 19th- and early 20th-century apprenticeships and in-office and site-based training to a formal, prescribed education was designed to achieve parity of status with other professionals such as lawyers, doctors and accountants.

In so doing, architectural education became a form of restrictive practice and only those with A Levels,[2] introduced in 1951, were permitted to apply. Those with O Levels could pursue a career as a technologist.

Architecture departments became part of university faculties and equivalent to other academic subjects. The academic, tripartite structure of architectural education was conceived for its time and, since then, the construction industry and the role of an architect have changed significantly, particularly in the early part of the 21st century.

Architectural academia presents itself as radical and progressive, yet very little has changed in the format and structure since the late 1950s. During this time higher education practices and pedagogy have developed across many other university courses.

Doctors, for example, attend medical school for five years followed by two years' foundation training in hospital, during which they assimilate the theoretical knowledge learned at university. The relationship between academia and practice is recognised and continuous and, as the British Medical Association states, 'at the end of foundation training, you must demonstrate a high level of skill and competency in managing acutely ill patients, team work and communication'.[3] In medicine, academia and practice are interconnected; theoretical, knowledge-based learning is assimilated in the surgery and hospital. Junior doctors learn 'on the job' by accompanying a consultant surgeon on the ward, visiting hospital patients and directly observing and participating. William Osler (1849–1919),[4] a respected Canadian physician and academic, was the first to establish the medical residency programme, giving emphasis to practical experience over learning in the lecture hall. This can be contrasted with a traditional, formal architectural education where the degree is not set up in the same way, with continuous practice experience.

The vast majority of UK schools of architecture are prescribed and validated by the RIBA and ARB, allowing them to award Parts 1, 2 and 3 qualifications.[5] ARB/RIBA prescription and the associated general criteria mean that schools offer very similar programmes and are differentiated only by their interpretation, their geographical location and the university facilities. For example, those schools allied to art departments share workshop spaces and 'making' facilities.

The disconnect between education and practice is the impetus behind The Way Ahead, the RIBA educational and professional Development Framework, which sets out a single standard running through education and continuing professional development.

In September 2021, RIBA Procedures for Validation[6] was published setting out the revised criteria to be used by RIBA Visiting Boards against which schools of architecture are validated. Although not challenging the tripartite structure of education, the RIBA's new validation framework, Themes and Value for Education (T+V4AE), is a single framework which has arisen out of national building failures and international issues such as the climate emergency and connects formal education in school with continuing professional development in practice.

Schools of architecture are transitioning into the new RIBA validation procedures, and the new themes and values have come into being in September 2022. All courses are also at the behest of the Office for Students (OFS) and internal quality management and governance, restricting and discouraging deviations from the established standards.

In October 2021, ARB published a discussion paper on 'modernising initial education and training of architects'[7]. Respondents concurred with ARB's view that the Part 1, 2 and 3 structure is no longer appropriate for the education of the contemporary architect. The areas of competency under question are the need to have business skills, professionalism and ethics, climate and sustainability and health and safety, all broadly in line with the RIBA's T+V4AE framework.

Although the ARB and RIBA require schools to meet their criteria, they do not prescribe the teaching method for the course and modules, and they leave it to the schools to determine content and process.

Design studio is the primary focus of study, and commands at least half of the credits each year as required by the RIBA's validation procedures and criteria. Yet, having spent 50% of their time in design studio, some students begin their year of practical experience with little understanding of the process of designing a building.[8] Of further concern is that, having studied alone, some students believe that the architect is the sole generator of 'the concept'; they lack an appreciation that design is the result of collaborative endeavour.

Peter Buchanan, the urbanist and architect, said that:

> In Britain, and in most other countries too, architectural education is based upon an increasingly irrelevant role model, that of the architect as an elite professional independent of and superior to the building industry and each architect, if not actually principal in his own firm at least a job runner and designer aspiring to genius.'[9]

Aside from the outdated reference to male-owned business, the point is as relevant today as it was in 1989. In reaction to the 'sole genius' idea, the musician Brian Eno has come up with the idea of 'scenius' to question the 'Great Man' theory of history:

> Scenius stands for the intelligence and the intuition of a whole cultural scene. It is the communal form of the concept of the genius.'[10]

Eno proposed the concept to counter the myth of the lone genius and instead convey the view that 'geniuses' such as Picasso were born out of an environment of intense creativity involving many people with different skills and experiences.

It is no wonder that the architectural profession has become marginalised and the architect's role diminished when students undertake design as a solitary activity, often believing this also means working long hours, in the mistaken belief that their creativity might otherwise be frustrated.

A common complaint of clients[11] is that architects have difficulty engaging in teamwork. Clients want architects to be able to lead and be collaborative, and so it is questionable why the focus of five years' academic study is on autonomy, when this is so far from the reality of practice.

Group work and learning to collaborate

Few schools adopt group work other than for small, introductory projects early in the academic year, and they have an aversion to working in teams for two reasons. Firstly, the belief that a weak student can 'hide' and pass coursework without fully contributing to the team effort. Secondly, there is a fear that group work generates tensions between students who are unused to working together and unable to effectively organise themselves. A contrary view is that the experience of having to negotiate within the group is an essential skill to develop and carry into practice. Several schools, such as Liverpool, Sheffield and Bath, believe that peer-to-peer learning is fundamental.

Some university-based schools have other construction courses such as project management, engineering and construction law, and yet very few either encourage or facilitate group learning.

David Dunster, a well-respected academic, considered the inability to assess group work as a 'bureaucratic absurdity'[12] and set up collaborative programmes at UCL and the University of Liverpool[13] in the early 1980s and 1995, respectively.

Architects liaise with different parties in their professional life, including clients, design team consultants, regulatory authorities and contractors, and yet they are often criticised for an inability to communicate ideas in a straightforward way. The most important thing a school can teach is to listen and be receptive to others' comments: communication studies is often limited to abstract visual representation interpreted only by a small audience. Architectural students learn the esoteric language of the unit, and consequently many are unable to explain even the most straightforward ideas to a lay audience.

Flora Samuel, speaking at the RIBA Education Forum in 2015, articulated this by stating:

> 'I want students to say what they can do in layman's terms to be critical, address different audiences to get the message across.'[14]

All prescribed courses are required to include modules in support of design studio and include technical and environmental studies, history and theory, communication and management practice, and law. In some schools, each module is mapped against the RIBA and ARB general criteria, yet, curiously, taught and assessed separately from studio. This box-ticking exercise inevitably leads to an artificial separation, further reinforcing a student's notion that 'design' is of singular importance and other activities are secondary and need not be connected. Technical and environmental studies is also sometimes taught and assessed as a module separate from design studio, thereby furthering a student's misconception that an architect produces a concept and others will 'engineer' it. But no architect in practice divides their working life into distinct activities such that they design one day and manage on another. And, as we have seen, one of the core roles of an architect is to communicate ideas, yet the public has only a vague and narrow understanding of the architect's role.[15] Clients tell us that we struggle to explain ideas with clarity and that we are obsessed with imagery rather than process and technical performance.[16]

A module-based course structure ignores the fact that design is a complex, integrated and collaborative activity involving many people who bring their skills and experience to the process. It is inconceivable that medical students – for example – would be taught in a similar way separating knowledge from diagnosis and patient care.

Professional practice used to be afforded around 5% out of 240 credits awarded in a two-year postgraduate programme. In the new RIBA Validation procedures, however, professional practice is expected to cover 20% of the postgraduate programme. Schools are required to map where they cover all aspects of professional practice. All students are expected to understand the business of architecture and to act professionally and ethically, yet this is barely taught or properly discussed until Part 3, undertaken only by those wishing to register. In practice, all architects and particularly those running their own offices or in senior positions in practice will spend varying degrees of their time on non-design activities and management. Client feedback in an RIBA report of 2015 is unequivocal:

> ‘Architects need to be business analysts – you need to understand how the client's business works.’[17]

Although an architect is not expected to offer specialist advice on finance and investment, it is undoubted that in order to play a fuller role in the design of buildings they would benefit from greater knowledge of business and management processes. Finance and cost barely enter the education framework and yet these subjects embrace all aspects of practice, from the funding and construction cost of buildings, to financial management of an office, to fees and resources. It also encompasses risk, liability, intellectual property and licences, all of which should be of interest to an architect in order to protect their ideas. Entrepreneurial students with an interest in setting up their own business would benefit from a short course on the legal and financial implications of forms of practice and associated risks and rewards.

The RIBA founding charter of the 1830s advocates:

> '... the general advancement of Civil Architecture, and for promoting and facilitating the acquirement of the knowledge of the various arts and sciences connected therewith ...'[18]

If young architects are to have a positive influence, they need a well-rounded humanities-based architectural education, connected to include sociology and community studies. Ethics has not always featured highly in the curriculum. In contrast, lawyers, for example, are taught their ethical responsibilities and examined on this before registration. At present, the ARB criteria at Parts 1, 2 and 3 refer to ethics just once, and it only makes an appearance in Part 3 under PC1 (Professional ethics), further implying that ethics is not a requirement of the curriculum for the first five years of architectural studies. Ethics and Professional Practice is one of the key six Themes and Values in the new RIBA validation procedures, so in the future ethics should have a significantly higher value within the curriculum.

Design studio – the unit

Schools teach design as a single subject, typically in a unit comprising a group of students following themes led by tutors, their protagonists. The unit system encourages competition between tutors and their students, with the danger that it can lead to introspective isolation; it does not foster debate between units investigating different themes. Design is central to academic study, and it must be asked how studio can be fully engaged without the context of so called 'real-world' problems – specifically if the student is setting their own brief and site while also playing the role of client, designer and sole decision-maker without taking into account external factors such as cost or regulatory framework. Tutors counter this by saying that a lack of real-world constraints encourages creative freedom. The unit should be a laboratory in which a student is free to research and test ideas, positively and unafraid to fail. It should recognise that a design process is iterative and that it is rare, if not impossible, to arrive at a 'correct' project. The fixation with a right and correct 'answer' should be abandoned.

It is questionable how unit-based teaching has relevance and purpose if connected with neither practice nor research. Furthermore, the student is also effectively the client and sole designer – so who is challenging them and asking them to robustly defend and explain their 'concept'? Zaha Hadid expressed her 'boredom of the unit system and inflated self-promoting egos of the teachers',[19] and argued for a broader-based approach to teaching.

In response to 'concerns … of students and staff relating to the culture, [and] educational practices',[20] Howlett Brown was commissioned by UCL to carry out a study into the culture of the architecture programme at the Bartlett, culminating in a report published in June 2022. The unit system was heavily criticised, with the report stating that it is the 'catalyst for allowing poor conduct and culture to thrive … and a breeding ground for inequity and abuse of power'.[21]

It was not in Howlett Brown's remit to propose solutions and alternative teaching methods; nor should it be assumed that all schools suffer from the same issues. However, no student should have to endure such a negative experience, and it is evident that the unit-based model requires calibration.

Heads of school and tutors

A number of heads of school have very little practical experience and have neither engaged with clients and design collaborators nor built a building. The career of those such as this is mostly centred around academia, with its associated aversion to risk. They may have little engagement with practice and a general reluctance to adapt and change course.

In 2004, the Architectural Association (AA) held a series of talks on the search for a new director in which Zaha Hadid[22] encouraged the AA to consider a practitioner, asking, 'Why does the school appear to be disconnected from the real world?' Tutors hold their students' futures in their hands, but many immediately step into teaching after graduation with little experience of practice, design and construction.

Patrik Schumacher has said that education is 'mired in confusion about society and architecture's role within it … too many teachers without professional work or experience use design studios in schools of architecture as vehicles for their own, largely isolated pursuits with often highly idiosyncratic criteria of success'.[23]

The three-part course structure was intended to facilitate a more academic grounding for the profession. It is not without irony that practice and

Figure 9.1 Zaha Hadid at the Architectural Education Symposium, 2004.

academia have become so distant from each other. Academia seems to be biased neither towards the academic nor the practical. Is it truly academic when tutors and academics are not leading research programmes? Not enough architectural academic output is considered research led and, although this is understandable in the degree, the two-year postgraduate qualification is an opportunity for specialist research-led programmes.

Crit, jury, review and tables

The crit, jury and tables (now referred to in most schools as 'reviews') are, traditionally, typical methods of reviewing students' work. The student pins up their work and presents their project to a panel of tutors and students and sometimes other invited guests. Having previously never experienced this process, students (particularly those at the start of their journey) can be unprepared for such an intense experience. Being critiqued in such a forum is not common in other university courses. Historically, the power of judgement was held solely by the critic with students as bystanders, witnessing the posturing; this reinforced the false idea that tutors are the sole bearers of knowledge.

Figure 9.2 Fifth-year diploma tables, AA library.

However, this traditional form of crit process is, thankfully, much rarer than it used to be. Satwinder Samra, Director of Collaborative Practice at Sheffield University School of Architecture, inverts the conventional hierarchy and places critics at the back and students at the front, encouraging all to make a contribution. Similarly, the AA set up is to have 'tables' which, as the name implies, does not involve a pin-up. Rather, the student's work is laid out on tables and students and reviewers gather around, thereby subjugating the them-and-us relationship. There are many schools around the UK where the traditional crit is no longer employed.

This method of reviewing students' work has been defended in the past as 'character building' under the proviso that it helps prepare students for the world of work, in which architects must explain and defend their designs to clients, planners and others. But a value system such as this, inculcated from day one, is misguided and damaging for students.

Kenneth Frampton, the critic and architect, considers it as negative that a student is trained to give a sales pitch in a jury process. He believes that the student should first be silent and the jurors should understand the project in a Socratic way, asking questions and drawing out the underlying ideas and themes in the work.

This would be a more positive and enriching process for the student, allowing them to develop communication skills and articulate their ideas with fellow students and invited guests who participate in a positive, non-judgemental way.

Cost of study

The Higher Education Act 2004 replaced income-linked deferred fee payment and introduced upfront fees, allowing universities to charge students. Despite the loans system, which only defers the repayment of debt, the privatisation of education has effectively become a form of restrictive practice – for many wishing to study architecture, prohibitively so. On concluding five years' full-time study an architecture student will have incurred a total 'debt' of around £100,000,[24] made up of university tuition fees of £46,250 as well as equipment, trips, presentation materials and general living expenses.

Unit trips are an important part of education, and yet it is curious that when so many social and environmental problems exist within the immediate vicinity of any school, it is deemed necessary to travel to remote areas of the world. The associated cost is unjustifiable and discriminatory; some students are excluded, as they cannot afford the additional expense or may have visa limitations or other reasons.

Given that 39% of architecture students do not receive family financial support, it is not justifiable to ask students to spend so much money on travel, modelmaking and presentations. As one post-Part 1 student explains:

> 'I am from a working-class family … upon completing Part 1, I would not recommend the course to anyone unless they are from a middle/upper class background, no matter how talented they are. I will never pay off the ridiculous sums of money I have had to pay for my degree.'[25]

To add to their precarious financial situation, a young person concluding their studies with a such significant debt then enters the profession, after Part 2, on a salary of around £25,000.[26]

Practical experience

In the UK, 24 months' practical experience is required prior to sitting the Part 3 exam. For many students, this experience is far from the professional learning it is intended to be and is more a test of endurance and survival. It is unsurprising that having become so disillusioned some students decide not to return to architecture studies and follow different career paths.

In the UK, a student spends an average of 9.5 years in full-time study and professional practice before registration. Practitioners often contend that a young professional is 'not ready for Part 3' and should wait to gain further experience. Yet they do not offer that opportunity, thereby delaying and frustrating young people even more. However, time should not be the main concern, as understanding the complexity of designing a building is too important to be hurried.

In 1990, 2,125 students entered Part 1 and 705 passed Part 3 and registered with the ARB.

The Burton Report in 1992 'encouraged education to broaden the first three years thereby providing a springboard for students to move into other careers, rather than inevitably proceeding to Part 2'.[27]

In 2021, around 9,000 students completed Part 1 and, of those, 5,000 will continue with postgraduate studies and complete Part 2, and around 1,000 will complete Part 3 and register with the ARB. They all attend one of 56 schools in the UK validated by the RIBA and offering Part 1, 2 and 3 qualifications.

Rather than being a source of concern, the so-called 'dropout rate' should be properly understood, for many students continue in the profession, contributing through their research, writing and teaching as well as other forms of practice, and enhancing a broader definition of the role of the architect. Although a significant number forsake a career in conventional architectural practice many, having completed a degree, leave with 'transferable skills' and follow other paths. Of concern are those who leave the profession having become disillusioned and disaffected during their studies or, as is all too often the case, after a dispiriting experience in practice.

Many international students return to their country of origin to practise rather than registering in the UK. This is to be acknowledged as making a significant contribution to the UK knowledge economy.

Students' voices

Part 3 examination candidates submit a career appraisal in which they offer reflection and critical analysis of their time in academia and the early years in practice. Part 3 examiners attest that the appraisals, written with maturity and honesty, convey discontent centred on two main themes. Firstly, that the two years' postgraduate study is too similar to the undergraduate degree; secondly, that the schools did not prepare them for practice and that after five years' study they are unable to undertake simple, straightforward tasks, let alone command a significant role in practice. Although the number of students undertaking Part 3 is relatively small, at around 20% of those in postgraduate education, the views expressed are mostly consistent. Given the cost of formal education, the low entry salaries and the difficulties in transitioning to practice, it is surprising that both students and architects in practice are so passive and do not demand change.

It was not always the case. The Architectural Association (AA) in London, one of the earliest schools, originated as a student-centred collective in 1847 as 'a radical proposition to the Beaux-Arts training … [it] aimed to challenge the established ways in which architecture was taught, argued and … urged its members to reconsider the commonplace social and cultural responsibilities of the profession at large'.[28]

The AA continued this history of activism in 1935/36 when a group of students dismissed 'the prevalent training methods as being divorced from reality and unrelated to the social and technical conditions of their age'.[29] And in 1974, the Architects' Revolutionary Council (ARC), founded by AA tutor Brian Anson, was committed to a comprehensive overhaul of the profession for the good of society. The ARC questioned the profession and the role it had played in the planned destruction of Covent Garden. Its demands for institutional change and for architects to take responsibility for society and offer their skills and services for the local community are still relevant today.

Anson declared his opposition to 'the new breed of conceptualist architects', considering them 'blind to the fact that in Britain thousands are still forced to live in ugly and poverty-stricken environments'.[30]

More recently, in January 2021, the Future Architects Front (FAF) wrote an open letter[31] to the RIBA expressing their concerns about young professionals and the employment conditions they suffer in practice. To his credit, then RIBA President Alan Jones replied, saying that the RIBA is 'committed to driving out poor employment practice'.[32] While the focus was on the early years in practice, poor behaviour begins in academia. Architecture schools have a duty to help students find employment, and then engage and support them while in practice.

RIBA Education Review (RER), 2013 to 2015

In autumn 2013, the RIBA launched a review of architectural education in the UK, concluding the first substantive phase by defining five principal recommendations as scheduled below, debated and concluded at the RIBA Education Forum in March 2017.

The RIBA Education Review group, representing academia and practice, intends to catalyse relevant new models for architectural education, to be taken forward and established by schools of architecture and other course providers.[33]

In the *RIBA Journal*[34] then RIBA President Stephen Hodder wrote:

> 'I believe that 55 years later (after the 1958 Oxford Conference) we need a review of architectural education. "Partial qualification" is perceived as failure, there is a lack of consensus on the balance of theory and practice, profession is separated from education, and there is poor conversion of Part 2 graduates to registered architects. These problems are compounded by mounting student debt and the apparent privatisation of university education and are set in an increasingly complex construction industry.'

Hodder identified pivotal issues:

- 'integration of professional matters within course delivery restoring and enhancing synergistic relationships between practice and academia;
- structuring course delivery to allow a more diverse profession;
- above all, acknowledging, retaining, and enhancing traditions of innovation and invention which characterise UK architectural education.'

The RER set out with laudable intentions. Yet observers of the Education Forum held in March 2015 questioned why the majority of those presenting were male academics discussing the minutiae of credits with little reference to practice.

Ultimately it fell short of the radical review and shake-up of education as was promised. It resulted in very little change to the curriculum, and was a missed opportunity to conduct a full review of the structure of architectural education as well as defining a strategic response offering different pathways into practice, acknowledging that the profession is open to all who aspire to become architects, no matter their background. One practitioner, Jane Duncan, at the time RIBA President-elect, said, 'As practitioners we are not doing our job … we will die out unless we look after young people and nurture them.'

Future architectural education

Architectural education has been the subject of many symposia and essays, almost exclusively by academics, but with very little change in the established tripartite system. Entry is still restricted to those with academic qualifications and the finances to cover five years of study.

Reforming architectural education has been slow, and change barely discernible. Students, practitioners, clients and many in academia concur that architectural education needs to be redefined and, despite many conferences, essays and pleadings, little is achieved other than tinkering around the edges. Any future strategic review of education should begin with an understanding of the various ways architects practise and contribute to the built environment in related fields such as policy and management.

How, then, should young architects be educated and prepared for a world we hardly comprehend and that is in constant flux? How do we define the education of young people who come from many different backgrounds and who will practise in many different ways?

What are the core skills a future architect needs?

The undergraduate degree should retain the format of teaching a broad range of skills as a grounding for future careers. Postgraduate courses should offer more specialised, research-based programmes to suit students' particular interests and career development.

To become effective designers and problem-solvers, architects must apply their knowledge, generating evidence in a rigorous way, and then communicate their solutions such that the audience comprehends.

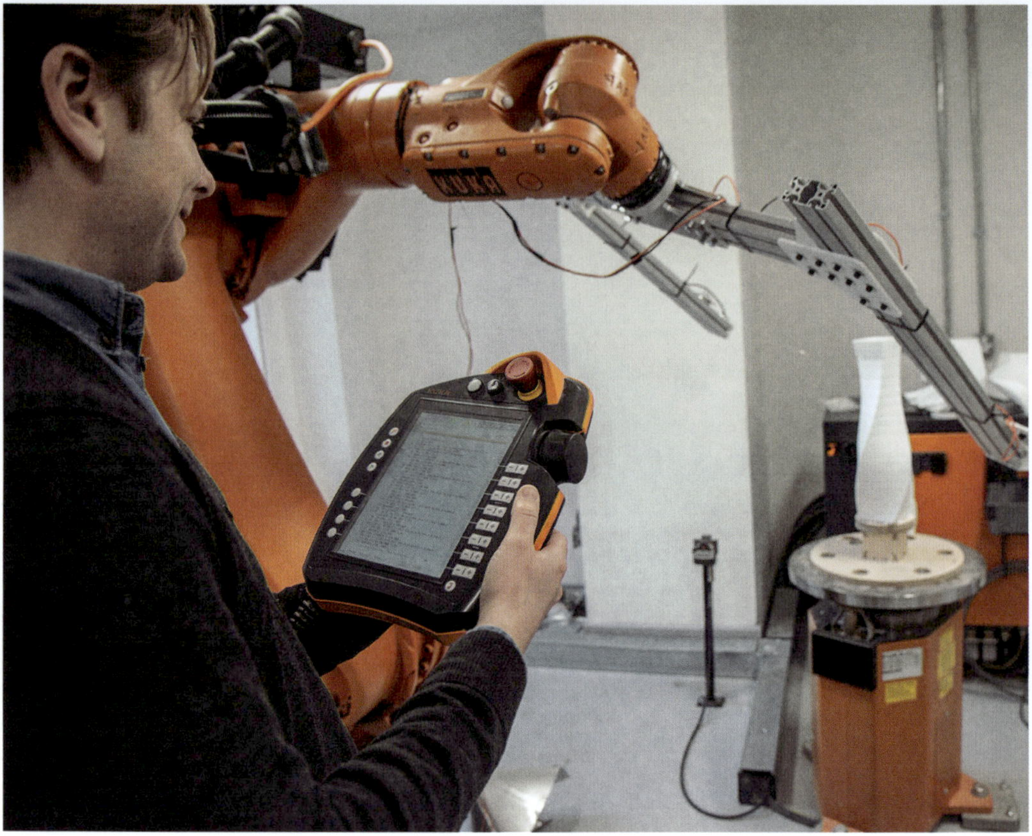

Figure 9.4 Robotic fabrication.

Schools should encourage students to develop a social, political and environmental awareness about the urban environment.

RIBA chartered status requires the practice to support students in their careers. The schools are reluctant and hesitant to acknowledge that curriculum change is required. Sitting in their hermetic bubbles, they are restricted by their reluctance to listen to the profession and students alike and strategically reflect on the issues.

The RIBA is best placed to implement significant change, and yet it has been unable to redefine the essence of architectural education, acknowledging that the pace of change is slow. In response to a question asking where are the new courses following the RER, David Gloster, then RIBA Director of Education, acknowledged that *'shifting the inertia around the existing system will take time'*.[35]

Nevertheless, the publishing of *The Way Ahead* by the RIBA in 2020 represents a change in the approach of the RIBA to education, even if not a fundamental change in direction.

In August 1973 50 people died as a result of a fire at Summerland Leisure Centre on the Isle of Man. The subsequent public inquiry concluded with a report in 1974 titled 'Summerland Fire Commission', in which it was recommended that:

> 'Architectural training should include a much-extended study of fire protection and precautions … An assessment of safety, particularly fire safety, appears so far to have been generally neglected in architectural education.'[36]

During the Grenfell inquiry Paul Hyett, the expert witness, was asked by the QC if he remembered the Summerland fire of 1973, and if 'the recommendations here … were ever put into practice, ever acted upon?'[37] The QC further asked, 'If an architect's training is predominantly project-based, how would that architect know what to do in relation to fire safety if the projects they have worked on throughout their career so far are low-rise buildings?'

Hyett responded by referring to his own education, stating that:

> 'I think all students … will have been involved in larger and more complicated buildings … I was involved in a very large scheme … I had to research what was required, but I was tutored to apply code to that building plan arrangement, and so I had to actually describe the building in terms of its construction. I remember going to structural engineers to have advice on how I would fire protect the building. So pretty heavy-duty stuff, actually.'[38]

Many students would not recognise Hyett's comments. Postgraduate education involving the design of a 'real' project is atypical, and rarely does a student have significant engagement with building codes. There is no guarantee that had the Summerland recommendations been acted on, lives would not have been lost in the Grenfell disaster. Worryingly, it is unclear why no formal action was taken by those responsible for education to address these basic recommendations.

Part 2 and research and knowledge – social value

There is little evidence that schools of architecture are contributing to contemporary debates, let alone leading them. Very few are at the forefront of research and policy, whereas postgraduate courses in the sciences and management have close links with their respective industries. The schools of architecture would do well by listening to students, academics and those involved in the built environment. Clients want us to have knowledge and an understanding of the regulatory environment such as planning and building regulations, and technical construction methodology and materials.

Whereas most university courses occasionally occupy a lecture hall and perhaps a seminar room a few times per week, architecture requires significantly more space per student and occupies large studios, self-study spaces, workshops and modelmaking facilities. In London alone, there are 12 schools of architecture,[39] and many cities have two within a short distance of each other, largely as a legacy of the former polytechnics achieving university status. Imagine a scenario where schools share facilities, and the opportunities for engagement and crossover that would provide.

Although short-lived, institutions such as Black Mountain College and the Bauhaus experimented with new pedagogic forms. Powerful images from the latter show Eva Hesse[40] and Josef Albers teaching in groups without hierarchy, with the impression that all are engaged and contributing.

> An alternative to sharing facilities might be to have no formal, fixed space at all, as proposed by Cedric Price in his project Thinkbelt, using redundant factories and other buildings in a temporary 'pop-up' mode: 'Thinkbelt was Price's response to the proliferation of new "glass-plate" universities … "more monuments to a medieval sense of learning" when they could be re-thinking the concept of education itself.'[41]

The London School of Architecture (LSA), a new school of architecture set up in 2011 with no formal teaching spaces, uses 'the city as the campus'[42] and comes closest to Price's model.

A return to apprenticeships[43] may be the path for some. In April 2022 two Oxford Brookes University graduates were the first in the UK to complete the Architect Level 7 Degree Apprenticeship Standard qualification.

The apprenticeship scheme combines part-time study and professional experience and gives those who do not want to study full-time the opportunity of becoming an architect.

The formal architectural education path is long – and rightly so, for there is much to learn in the formative years and knowledge to gain before a student enters practice. It requires redefining rather than reduction.

ARB consultations

In October 2021, the ARB launched its vision 'for modernising architectural education and training' and invited students, architects, academics and others to join a number of open consultations to discuss the themes.

The Royal Institute of Chartered Surveyors (RICS) has defined many routes to qualification and the associated pathways to suit individual preferences, circumstances and interests. The RICS has 22 sector pathways[44] leading to various careers in construction, such as project management, valuations and management consultancy. In any future review of the profession the ARB, in consultation with the RIBA, the academies, those in practice and students should construct courses reflecting the roles that architects play in improving the built environment. In a 2015 interview, Will Hunter, founder of the London School of Architecture said:

> The ARB is taking the lead where the RIBA prevaricates and has missed opportunities to conduct a full and proper review of education and implement recommendations. Architectural education needs a fundamental reset, and the ARB is listening to all those involved and giving them a voice, to "set out a new vision for the way in which architects are educated and trained which, if approved, could be the most significant changes to architectural education and training in 50 years" and leading to "fundamental reforms in architectural education."[45]

A new model of architectural education is required that is well-rounded and not restricted to a sequential, linear 1–2–3 pathway which implies a route towards so-called traditional practice. While the general criteria should underpin the curriculum, teaching should respect each individual student, acknowledging that not all are designers, or technically or managerially minded.

Figure 9.5 Design & Make, Sawmill Shelter, Hooke Park, Beaminster.

New postgraduate courses are being launched that embrace contemporary concerns with a necessary focus on environmental design and interdisciplinary studies. The Centre for Alternative Technology (CAT) offers a Master's in Sustainable Architecture, an ARB-prescribed Part 2 qualification. The Architects Climate Action Network (ACAN) believes that UK architecture students 'felt they were ill-equipped to mitigate the effects of the climate emergency in their future work'.[46] The ACAN's main aim is to 'reform education, actively seeking to increase levels of climate literacy in built environment courses across the UK'.

The primary purpose of architectural education should not be securing registration in the UK, but enabling young people to find their own path and interests unconfined by prescriptive models; and it should be available to all, and not just those who can afford it. One of the most important things to take from school is for students to never lose their ambition. The ARB's review of education is likely to result in a change of emphasis from courses having to meet rules and criteria to an outcomes-based approach. ARB states that 'the most important factor is what a newly qualified architect should be able to do – not how they got there'.[47] This, coupled with RIBA's T+V4AE, the growing appeal of apprenticeships and more courses with practice-based training will encourage young people previously without access to the profession to have the opportunity of becoming an architect.

CHAPTER 10
Conclusions

At the very beginning of this book an architect was defined as 'someone who imagines built space in response to a need, and guides the process that turns that idea into a built reality', and while this essential thread has remained constant across the centuries it is in the day-to-day practice of that essence that the interest and turmoil of the profession has come. As we write in 2022 it feels as if we might be at a precipice. Britain has left the EU and is in recovery from the global Covid-19 pandemic. Building material prices and labour costs have soared and the UK is facing its highest inflation rates in around 30 years. As we write these words Russia is invading Ukraine, and the global sanctions on its unprovoked attack are already beginning to bite on financial markets and energy costs.

More locally to architecture the inquiry into the tragic Grenfell Tower fire has not yet returned its conclusions, and the Building Safety Act promises unprecedented overhauls to competency, qualifications, the ARB's powers, construction information and even professional indemnity insurance cover. The widely recognised climate emergency is calling common building practice and materials into question, and architects are questioning their role within a rapidly evolving building industry as they become increasingly marginalised within the design and construction team. It would be easy to become overwhelmed and fatalistic.

There is no doubt that the contemporary British profession is facing significant challenges that question the status quo and seem likely to cause upheaval in the near future, perhaps even before this book is printed. However, very few are challenges that the profession has not faced before. Following the Second World War the profession weathered the storms of full employment and high labour costs, with the challenges to the accepted norms catalysing the use of innovative building forms and materials. The results have not always stood the test of time, but the challenges of this period ultimately led to the profession reaching heights of influence rarely seen in its history.

The recessions and forced privatisations of the early 1990s, when inflation was equally as high as it is today, forced the profession to rethink its reliance on public sector jobs and catalysed the growth of globally significant architectural practices based in Britain's largest cities. The individuals who began in this era have had such an impact on the public's understanding of architecture that even just the first names of some – Norman, Zaha – mean something to the non-architect.

Brexit may be complicating international relations, but Britain's architects have always had a complicated – albeit largely positive – relationship with international clients and projects. Even after the end of the British Empire many countries invited their ex-imperial master's architects back, commissioning work from them and sending their students on exchange trips and to study architecture in Britain's universities.

Growing legislative oversight has complicated daily life for British architects and altered workflows, but there is no reason to suppose that the effects of Building Safety Act will be overwhelmingly negative. Previous introductions of legislation have raised the minimum standards of architects and resulted in better outcomes for end users and higher competence within the profession.

And, while a globally recognised climate emergency is a new situation, previous shifts in understanding of context and climate have resulted in technological breakthroughs and provided the impetus needed to persuade the somewhat conservative construction industries to reform or change course.

In all 'adapt or die' challenges the profession has faced over the centuries it has adapted and survived. We cannot pretend to prophesy the specifics of how the modern British profession will weather the next decade, but there is no reason to think it is in the 2020s that architects will cease to be. It is not, however, that the matching of contemporary circumstances to isolated but superficially similar scenarios in history should leave us optimistic, but that the same debate that has been regularly had throughout history is working its way to its latest climax. This is the debate of whether architecture is a profession or an art. Is it intellectual or practical – a profession or a trade?

Architecture – a profession or an art?

We see something of this debate hinted at in the ancient world – when the Greeks praised the wide skills of architects applying knowledge in practical ways for the common good, but also celebrated more eccentrically artistic figures such as Dinocrates; or when the Roman architects drew from such a broad pool of talent – freed slaves, artists and ex-military personnel. It was in the Italian Renaissance, though, that this debate was had in real earnest, when Leon Alberti reframed architecture as an intellectual and learned pursuit, rather than the extension of a tangible construction skill. His reframing helped raise the social status of architecture as a career and challenged the construction industry to evolve. Until this point, the master masons of medieval Europe had developed their architectural styles slowly and iteratively, based on their 'by hand' knowledge of the construction materials. The intellectual architects of the early Renaissance did not know the materials by hand, instead conjuring feats of engineering and architecture limited only by their imaginations; using the force of their personality to drive through these designs, forcing the builders of the day to innovate.

Inevitably a backlash occurred, and by the later Renaissance we begin to see the debate swinging back to a definition of architect that retained the intellectual prowess of Alberti's visions, but with some of the more practical and technical knowledge of the masons. The profession developed rapidly in these decades, and the debate over the architect's position left us with a defined role for architects that sat alongside, but separate from, construction. The turmoil of this period also led to some feats of engineering and architecture that still astound us today.

The intellectualising of architecture also brought architects closer socially to their clients – often wealthy or powerful people who embraced architecture as a pursuit for aristocratic leisure. In Britain it was this that drove the tradition of the 'amateur architects' – the usually socially elevated designers with an interest in the principles of design, who leant heavily on the expertise of their construction teams to achieve anything built. We also begin to see the emergence of architects such as Robert Smythson, who began as an experienced builder aiding his clients in achieving their designs and slowly transitioned to designing himself. As in Italy's Renaissance, we see the balance between technical skill and intellectual pursuit worked out, drawing different types of people into the profession and enriching the architecture of the day as the mix of artistic imagination and 'by hand' knowledge combined and challenged each other.

The proximity and intertwined nature of architects and builders is a fact of the existence of both groups. In the same way that an architect cannot realise any of their designs without a construction team, a builder cannot build anything without someone designing it – even if it is a more architecturally inclined member of their own team. In the 18th and 19th centuries this interplay in Britain was essential to the lives of architects. They had emerged definitively as a separate profession to builders by this point, but many of them augmented the irregular income of an architect with an interest in quantity surveying, building or building products – using the more technical sides of their skillset to offer a broad range of services, thus safeguarding their incomes.

It is in the early 1830s that we see this change. The usual debate recurs – how technical are architects? In an environment in which fraud in the construction industry was rife, and other professions such as the law were gating and regulating themselves, architects chose to define themselves as a profession rather than a trade. In order to create professional reserve and impartiality, and in an attempt to engender public trust, they drew a clear divide between architects and builders for the first time. Architects were framed as educated professionals, the social superiors of the builders, and the arbiters of good taste and construction knowledge. They sought to ringfence all design aspects of the profession with long-lasting attempts to protect both the title and the function of the architect. Arguably this was the point where the profession began to fail, despite the good intentions they had at the time.

In the decades that immediately follow we begin to see the immediate results of these decisions. Building skills lose their prestige and build quality suffers as the skilled tradesmen struggle to attract apprentices to a career that has been socially devalued by its division from the intellectual, aristocratic-adjacent pursuit of architecture. Architects themselves become responsible entirely for their education, passing on their understanding of design and detailing to their trainees and encouraging a remove from site and from the builder. Drawings and specifications become ever more detailed as the architect becomes ever more remote from the process of construction.

However, building technology remains roughly as it had been over the preceding centuries, so there is no significant knowledge gap between the newly professionalised architects and the processes on site. As such there isn't an immediately noticeable negative impact of the physical and intellectual remove between the designer and the materials from which their building is built. It is when building technology begins to change though that we see problems beginning to emerge.

We cannot neglect to mention that it is also in these years immediately after the formation of the RIBA and the attempted closure of the profession that debates appear between architects more forcefully than they have been recorded before. When the architect was loosely defined there was space in the profession for the Smythsons – builders turned architects – to practise with impunity alongside the aristocratic amateur architect. When architects sought to define themselves more formally, the intricacies of the definition took on new importance – and spawned new disagreements. Perhaps the most notable was in the 1890s when Norman Shaw and Thomas Jackson published their collection of essays, and a heated letter in *The Times* arguing against the professionalisation of architecture. They argued for a more artistic definition of the profession and worried about defining an architect as someone able to pass the RIBA exams, which only tested for competence in understanding of technical details rather than artistic ability or talent. In the past this art versus technical debate had been had with the space of the whole construction industry to move in; now it was being fought in the closed confines of the committee rooms of a single professional society and spilling out into ugly public denunciations of other architects' positions. Rather than catalyse growth and development of architects and architecture it seemed to only engender bad feeling that lingered for decades; and because it happened within a profession that was formally defining itself there was not space for both definitions. Someone had to lose the fight.

In the years between and immediately post the two world wars we see other tensions growing in the uneasy truce that had been called. The 'professionals' had 'won' the debate and architectural education was being standardised, efforts to define architects legally looked as if they were beginning to bear fruit, and the likes of Shaw and Jackson had largely admitted defeat, confining themselves to grumbling from the sidelines. The two world wars, however, catalysed change that this more narrowly defined profession did not have the resilience to withstand. The nation's knowledge of building skills, already in decline, took a devastating blow in the loss of life during the two wars as thousands of young carpenters, builders and bricklayers were killed. Alongside this the technological advancements of war found an outlet in building technology and products post war. Construction technologies that had remained more or less similar for centuries began to be overhauled. This combination of reduction in skilled labour and influx of new products created a challenge to 'upskill' for the architects. However, the profession had been moving ever further away from the process of construction and few architects ever grasped a full technical knowledge of the new products – let alone getting close enough to know the materials by hand.

The problems became immediately obvious. Leaving aside anything dramatic, there were the everyday failures of rotten window frames and leaking wall/roof interfaces – caused by a de-skilled construction team, but also by architects not sufficiently aware of construction methodology to detail these interfaces competently, or check their construction on site. To compound this problem the architects of the late 1950s and 1960s sought to further cleave the profession from its construction roots with the architectural technologist role – seeking to define this as a lower form of architectural practice that was fit only for those who could not reach the increased entry requirements of architectural courses. This role, equally remote from the construction process as the architect, was to draw up the technical details. The intellectual and highly educated architects need therefore no longer bother with these 'boring bits', focusing instead on the 'design' and 'leadership'.

To return briefly to the essential definition of the architect we began with – 'someone who imagines built space in response to a need, and guides the process that turns that idea into a built reality' – it could be said that the architects of the 1960s who fully embraced this separation between architects and technologists could no longer be defined as architects in any historical sense.

The problem with the leadership offered by these architects was that they were both so removed from the process of construction and, by virtue of being significantly employed in the public sector, from the end users of the buildings, that the architecture they created has largely, albeit not universally, failed. There were brilliant and principled architects in this period, but the structure of the profession that had been defined by this point had failed them.

The government policies of the early 1990s sought to force a change in all professions – not just architecture. The deregulation, privatisation and flat refusal to consider protecting the function of architects forced them to adapt – and allowed the broader market to intervene. New forms of procurement began to force architects into closer proximity with contractors in the earlier stages of design, and the hallowed 'territory' that architects had been seeking to protect for the preceding century began to be invaded. The implications of this are what we are living now.

A technically incompetent profession?

I (Eleanor) trained in architecture at a university that demanded top A Level grades and I spent nine years in work and education before, following an interview with an architect more curious about the business practices of my employer than my personal competence, I was able to describe myself using the word 'architect'. This education touched very briefly on how to detail a load-bearing brick house with a timber-framed roof, and I was occasionally encouraged to glance at *Detail* magazine. Were it not for my decision to study a course that combined an architecture degree with an engineering one my technical knowledge would have been negligible.

My postgraduate Part 2 was enjoyable and intellectually stimulating but left me better prepared for a life of architectural academia than one in daily practice; Part 2 has never evolved into the technical specialisation course envisioned by the 1958 Oxford Conference. It is in practice that I have learned the most about being an architect, and I am distinctly aware that this leaves me open to the vagaries of my employer. Much like the problem of inconsistent apprenticeships in the early 1800s, today's architects are being professionally formed in their early years of practice – and are therefore liable to pick up all the bad habits of their employers. I (Paul) see technical and practice mismanagement in an all-too-high percentage of the Part 3 case studies, career appraisals and practice record sheets submitted by my students. The aim of the 1958 conference to raise the standards of architects by a more thorough and consistent education has not been realised.

To further compound the problem, we are splitting the profession again. Already we had architects and technologists; now architects are dividing themselves along the artificial lines of 'design' and 'delivery'. It distances a profession already too remote from the physical realisation of their designs still further from the process of construction, compounding poor design decisions as 'design' architects rarely acquire the knowledge of 'delivery' that would so enrich their work. Some architects now actively turn away work in the technical drawing and construction stages of design. Should such practices even call themselves architects?

Paul Morrell, former Chief Construction Adviser to the UK government, has warned that the value of the architectural profession is being challenged and that we are resistant to change.[1] It is undeniable that the role of the architect has diminished in the last 20 years, largely as a result of the growing distance between the profession and the process of construction and its procurement, but talk of reclaiming aspects of the architect's former role is facile; time, technology and construction have moved on. As should architecture.

In the large, complex and multifaceted projects many architects work on daily they work alongside vast teams of specialists. The legislation of the previous few decades has spawned an almost endless array of consultants and specialities – everything from structure and MEP engineers to fire engineers, CDM consultants and even 'retail enlivenment' consultants. The ever-narrowing definition of 'architect' that began in the 1830s has left a title so narrow in scope that many of the functions of an architect that could have sat under a broader definition of the term have established themselves separately, leading to a deeply complex and fractured design team, and to an architectural role as lead designer that is as much about coordinating information and egos as it is about design work. The definite and closely defined titles 'architect', 'engineer' and 'contractor' begin to seem increasingly loaded; perhaps they have had their day.

However, it is here in this 'loss of territory' that hope may lie. The Building Safety Act is pushing for architects to keep roles such as CDM Principal Designer in-house, and defining new roles which would demand a higher level of technical competence for those filling them. At the time of writing the secondary legislation around the Act is still to be confirmed. It calls for significantly higher technical ability for those working on some building typologies. Professional exclusivism, such as that centred on the foundation of the RIBA or the creation of the architectural technologist role, has had its moment. The challenge for architects now is to embrace the new environment of design and construction – and the wide team of co-authors each project represents. Technology such as BIM and new legislation offer architects the opportunity to be at the centre of coordinating fully considered, compliant and technically competent designs.

A self-congratulatory profession?

Open almost any UK architect's website and it will be filled with images of finished buildings; beautiful, perhaps award-winning. Very few offer information about the wider project team, method, collaborative process or social value. The beautiful coffee table monographs, often self-published by individual practices, also offer little substance on the briefing, designing or construction of the buildings they portray. They advertise form and material, but not the value of the architect. This sort of communication speaks architect to architect, reinforcing an echo chamber of architectural design, value and professional style.

Architectural awards similarly speak most potently to architects. Few professions have as many awards – with the RIBA, periodicals and trade bodies, architecture is saturated in highly specific award categories. Many are judged solely by architects, suggesting a profession uncomfortable with allowing their work to be judged by the wider public or indeed the end users of the buildings. It is a legacy of the early days of the RIBA, when the profession was seeking to establish itself as the only competent voice to speak on architectural value. Such arrogance should surely be a relic of our past?

The Stirling Prize, the highest award the RIBA offers, has been organised and awarded by the RIBA since 1999, and it seeks to find the best building of the year. The jury of five consists of just one layperson and compares a shortlisted six buildings of disparate typologies, forms, locations, budgets and uses that have been finished within the last year. As in most years, the 2021 People's Vote winner was awarded to a building other than the final winner overall.

An alternative award, more considerate of the vast team effort of a construction project, could permit only the entry of buildings in use for a minimum of five years, with entries including environmental performance data and narratives from clients and end users, as well as the design team and the contractor. Project citations could go beyond an architectural description to describe the almost living being that is a well-designed building functioning well for the people it was designed for. The jury for such an award could have no more than 50% architects on its panel. Such an award may be of interest and use to the world outside of the architectural profession; such an award may communicate the value of good architects.

A homogeneous profession?

The diversity of skills involved in modern architectural practice reflects a need for a diversity of people, and of experience. In 2018 the architectural profession was 74% male and 94% white. By 2021 it had barely diversified, to 71% male and 82% white. Both figures are taken from the annual reports of the ARB, which holds equality, diversity and inclusion data for less than 70% of the register of architects. The profession could be even less diverse than these figures suggest.

The profession's social background is also alarmingly monotonous. A report in 2021 identified 73% of those employed in the architectural and urban planning industry as coming from a high socioeconomic background compared with a 38% average across all industries.[2] The three-part educational system that came from the 1958 Oxford Conference has created a restrictive, expensive and elitist method of training a profession. It overturned centuries of diverse routes into the profession and effectively denied entry to all but a privileged few.

Furthermore, the university-based system enshrines a values system out of step with the professional reality. Students largely work on individual projects, working long hours on abstract design briefs, only to enter a profession in dire need of collaborative professionals who can respond to interlinked technical, legislative and design challenges. It is not what they trained for, and many find the culture shock difficult to traverse. An education system dictated by academia also places undue importance on university league tables and academic rankings – the mental stress placed on students to perform to these quantifiable metrics is unhealthy for them, and such a system does not nurture or celebrate the diversity of skills or approaches that enrich architecture, and make it such a rich profession to practise.

Where academic principles could bring value to the profession, though, they are failing. In medicine and the sciences, research and industry are constantly informing each other, generating new technologies and methodologies. Architecture by comparison has very little integration between academia and practice. Architects frequently conduct research through design, yet the data is not captured and measured in order to influence or improve future design or construction. Architectural academia has chosen its place in the 'profession or art; intellectual or practical' debate: it has all but turned its back on the 'profession' to focus on the 'art'.

Students and practice alike are calling for an overhaul of education, and the ARB, emboldened by new powers under the Building Safety Act, is beginning to consider what can be done. Whether the ARB and the universities will rise to the challenge is yet to be seen, but there is an opportunity here to broaden the definition of an architect's role, diversify routes into architecture, raise the technical competence of architects and increase the diversity of the profession. Central to this is the opportunity to redefine the art versus technician debate to bring us closer to the essence of an architect that we have seen so successfully adapt across the millennia of human history.

An unethical profession?

In January 2021 a student activist group called the Future Architects Front submitted an open letter to the RIBA, signed by over 200 architecture students, highlighting their experiences of unethical business conduct and asking the RIBA and the ARB to introduce mechanisms to hold practices to account and enable employees to 'demand justice in the face of exploitation and discrimination'.[3] The accounts in the letter included numerous instances of racial and gender-based discrimination, low pay, long hours, and poor management and employment practices. A survey conducted a few months later by the *Architects' Journal* found that 48% of the, admittedly self-selecting, sample of Part 1 architectural assistants were paid less than the Living Wage.[4]

All were employed by RIBA-chartered practices which, according to the terms under which they were chartered, must pay staff the Living Wage. No investigation seems to have been made by the RIBA, and no practices seem to have lost their chartered status. The nascent architects' union, the Section of Architectural Workers, has suggested that 'the culture of overwork … contributes to the already inaccessible nature … [and] makes inclusivity impossible. Working class, disabled, migrant and black and brown workers are affected the most.'[5]

Architects frequently complain that the profession is poorly regarded and poorly paid, but the way in which the modern profession is treating its trainees suggests that it does not respect or value itself. With so little self-respect, how can architects expect clients and collaborators to value them? However, not all practices engage in unethical employment practices, and many are making social and environmental values explicit in their founding principles, statements and daily practice. They sit within a wider societal movement as increasingly UK consumers are making informed decisions about ethically sourced groceries, clothing and technology. Architects should engage with this societal shift and seek to adopt ethical and sustainable business management; and encourage ethical and sustainable procurement and construction.

Architects' training, skills and expertise encourage them to act creatively, demonstrating originality for their clients. This duty to their clients, however, does not and should not limit their wider role. It is morally incumbent on them to make projects that deliver quantifiable social and environmental value. The Hippocratic Oath compels doctors to 'do no harm'. In architecture this is unachievable. Architects are complicit in the environmental and human damage inherent in the design and construction of buildings. The challenge for the profession is doing the least harm possible.

Architecture does not have to be defined by the decisions of a group of men in the early 1800s, nervous of the growth of the world around them, or constrained by an imagined postwar golden age. The profession can look back further and draw inspiration from its multifaceted ancestors. Few, or hopefully no, future architects will be freed slaves, but they will perhaps come from more diverse social and ethnic backgrounds. Few architects will ever have the opportunity to learn construction from a master mason constructing a Gothic cathedral, or from a Renaissance polymath, but perhaps they will get a more rounded, more technically competent education. Few future architects are likely to tune torsion-based artillery as their career unfolds, but perhaps they will get closer to the process of construction as they hone their craft; maybe one day they will even know the materials by hand.

They are likely to engage in the great debate, though: is architecture a profession or an art? We would, perhaps controversially, say it is not an art. Architects do not produce works individually to be exhibited or sold in a gallery. Architects are not sociologists, anthropologists, engineers or politicians. They cannot solve society's ills with a beautifully designed community building – but they can contribute. Architects are professionals; highly skilled and extensively trained people who have specialised in a historically rich role in a complex and multifaceted industry. They work in large teams and need to engage collaboratively with many other professions and trades. The weaknesses the profession currently faces, the failures in its professionalism, stem from an unwillingness to engage with the wider construction industry.

Is architecture a profession or an art? Intellectual or practical? A profession or a trade? The answer that has developed over the last two centuries – the intellectual profession – is failing. The construction industry needs a designer who both understands the art of architecture and grasps the technical details of construction. It needs a person who can balance the millennia-old artistic versus technical debate in the context they are operating within – and if the modern profession refuses to fill that role, someone else will.

References

Introduction

N Toth and K Schick, 'The first million years: The archaeology of protohuman culture', in M Schiffer, *Advances in Archaeological Method and Theory Vol. 9*, Academic Press Inc., 1986, p56.

'Behavioral influences, *Britannica*, https://www.britannica.com/topic/Homo-sapiens/Behavioral-influences#ref1268209 (accessed 7 March 2022).

Chapter 1

1 S Kostof, 'Architecture in the ancient world: Egypt and Greece', in S Kostof (ed), *Architect: Chapters in the History of the Profession*, University of California Press, 1977, p10.
2 J Breasted, *Ancient Records of Egypt Volume II*, University of Chicago Press, 1906, p242.
3 Kostof, p5.
4 Breasted, p161.
5 Ibid., p373.
6 Kostof, p7.
7 Breasted, p147.
8 S Clarke and R Engelbach, *Ancient Egyptian Construction and Architecture*, Cavier Corporation, 1990, p1.
9 F Ching, M Jarzombeck and V Prakash, *A Global History of Architecture*, Wiley, 2017, p38–9.
10 R Baker and C Baker, *Ancient Egyptians: People of the Pyramids*, Oxford University Press, 2001, p24.
11 Kostof, p7.
12 Ibid., pp7–8.
13 Ibid., p10.
14 Ibid., p5.
15 G Pont, 'The education of the classical architect', *Nexus Network Journal*, vol. 7, no. 1, 2005, pp77–8.
16 Kostof, p4.
17 Ibid., p4.
18 M Briggs, *The Architect in History*, Clarendon Press, 1927, p22.
19 H von Hesberd, 'Greek and Roman architects', in Marconi (ed), *The Oxford Handbook of Greek and Roman Art and Architecture*, Oxford University Press, 2015, pp141–3.
20 Briggs, p19.
21 Kostof, p21.
22 Ibid., p26.
23 Briggs, p22.
24 Kostof, p22.
25 Briggs, p17.
26 Ibid., p13.
27 Kostof, p17.
28 Briggs, pp23–4.
29 Ibid., p23.
30 Von Hesberd, p142.
31 Kostof, pp12–15.
32 A Smith, 'Building inscriptions at the Acropolis in Athens', *Architecture*, vol. 5, no. 20, 1926.
33 Briggs, p18.
34 Kostof, pp23–4.
35 Vitruvius, *Ten Books on Architecture*, Bibliolife, 2009, p267.
36 Smith, p20.
37 Vitruvius, p33.
38 Vitruvius, p33.
39 L Landrum, 'Before architecture: Archai, architects and architectonics in Plato and Aristotle', *Montreal Architectural Review*, vol. 2, 2016, pp5–25.
40 Vitruvius, p5.
41 Briggs, p44.
42 Ibid., p46.
43 Vitruvius, p7.
44 Briggs, p35.
45 W MacDonald, 'Roman architects' in S Kostof (ed), *Architect: Chapters in the History of the Profession*, University of California Press, 1977, p37.
46 Briggs, p35.
47 Briggs, p44.
48 MacDonald, p43.
49 Vitruvius, p12.
50 Ibid., p14.
51 MacDonald, p40.
52 Vitruvius, p267.
53 Vitruvius, p195.
54 Briggs, p42.
55 C Dio, *Roman History, Volume VIII: Books 61–70*, trans. E Cary and HB Foster, Loeb Classical Library 176, Harvard University Press, 1925, pp431–3.

Chapter 2

1 S Kostof, 'The architect in the Middle Ages, East and West', in S Kostof (ed), *Architect: Chapters in the History of the Profession*, University of California Press, 1977, p67.
2 Ibid., p65.
3 Ibid., p71.
4 M Hallissy, 'Writing a building: Chaucer's knowledge of the construction industry and the language of the "Knight's Tale"', *The Chaucer Review*, vol. 32, no. 3, 1998, pp239–59.
5 LR Shelby, 'The role of the master mason in mediaeval English building', *Speculum*, vol. 39, no. 3, July 1964, pp387–403.
6 M Briggs, *The Architect in History*, Clarendon Press, 1927, p61.
7 Shelby, pp387–403.
8 Briggs, p102.
9 Kostof, p76.
10 Briggs, p86.
11 J Gelder, *Specifying Architecture: A Guide to Professional Practice*, Construction Information Systems Australia, 2001, p6.
12 Shelby, pp387–403.
13 Kostof, p92.
14 Ibid., p93.
15 Briggs, p112.
16 Ibid., p104.
17 Briggs, pp88–9.
18 L Ettlinger, 'The emergence of the Italian architect during the fifteenth century', in Kostof, p96.
19 G Vasari, G DeVere (trans.), *Lives of the Most Eminent Painters, Sculptors and Architects*, Project Gutenberg, 2009.
20 Briggs, p137–42.
21 Ettlinger, p98.
22 LB Alberti, *The Ten Books of Architecture: The 1755 Leoni Edition*, Dover Publications, 1986.
23 Ettlinger, pp100–5.
24 Gelder, pp6–7.
25 M Carpo, *The Alphabet and The Algorithm*, The MIT Press, 2011, p23.
26 Briggs, pp161–2.
27 Carpo, p77.
28 Vasari, p221.
29 Briggs, p191.
30 Ibid., pp191–2.
31 MN Rosenfeld, 'The Royal Building Administration in France from Charles V to Louis XIV', in Kostof, p161.
32 Ibid., p162.
33 Gelder, p7.
34 Briggs, p212.
35 Ibid., pp212–13.
36 Rosenfeld, p177.
37 Briggs, p224.
38 Rosenfeld, p178.
39 Briggs, pp168–70.
40 Briggs, p179.
41 C Wilkinson, 'The new professionalism in the Renaissance', in Kostof, p127.
42 Ibid., pp126–30.
43 Briggs, p240.
44 Ibid.
45 S Foxell, *Professionalism for the Built Environment*, Routledge, 2019, p30.
46 F Jenkins, *Architect and Patron: A Survey of Professional Relations and Practice in England from the Sixteenth Century to the Present Day*, Oxford University Press, 1961, p6.
47 Jenkins, p7.
48 Ibid., p10.
49 Ibid., p45.
50 Briggs, p248.
51 Jenkins, p23.
52 J Wilton-Ely, 'The rise of the professional architect in England', in Kostof, p183.
53 Jenkins, p44.

54 Foxell, p32.
55 Briggs, pp264–8.
56 Ibid., p277.
57 J Heyman, 'The crossing space and the emergence of the modern professional architect and engineer', *Construction History*, vol. 31, no.1, 2016, pp25–60.
58 Foxell, p35.
59 Heyman, pp25–60.
60 Ibid.

Chapter 3

1 *RIBA Kalendar*, 1886 and 1887, RIBA Collections.
2 P Guillery and D Kroll, *Mobilising Housing Histories*, RIBA Publishing, 2017, p7.
3 F Jenkins, *Architect and Patron: A Survey of Professional Relations and Practice in England from the Sixteenth Century to the Present Day*, Oxford University Press, 1961, p200.
4 Jenkins, pp200–1.
5 B Kaye, *The Development of the Architectural Profession in Britain*, George Allen & Unwin Ltd., 1960, p56.
6 Jenkins pp128–9, 202.
7 Kaye, p58.
8 J Wilton-Ely, 'The rise of the professional architect in England', in S Kostof (ed), *Architect: Chapters in the History of the Profession*, University of California Press, 1977, p192.
9 Kaye, pp60–3.
10 Ibid., p76.
11 Ibid., pp76–7.
12 S Nenadic, 'Architect-builders in London and Edinburgh, c.1750–1800 and the market for expertise', *The Historical Journal*, vol. 55, 2012, pp597–617.
13 Ibid., p603.
14 Ibid., p604.
15 Kaye, pp78–80.
16 A Powers, *Architectural Education in Britain 1880–1914*, The University of Cambridge, 1983, p10.
17 Wilton-Ely, p198.
18 Briggs Martin, *The Architect in History*, Clarendon Press, 1927, pp355–6.
19 Powers, p10.
20 Jenkins, p169.
21 Ibid., p170.
22 J A Gotsch, *The Growth and Work of the Royal Institute of British Architects 1834–1934*, Simson & Co. Ltd., 1934, pp85–7.
23 Kaye, pp100–2.
24 RN Shaw and TJ Jackson, *Architecture: A Profession or an Art*, Murray, 1892, pp38–9.
25 RE Lotz and I Pegg, *Under the Imperial Carpet: Essays in Black History 1780–1905*, Rabbit Press, 1986, pp78–83.
26 RIBA Collections.
27 E Darling, 'An urban experiment in spiritual motherhood', in E Darling and N Robert Walker (eds), *Suffragette City: Women, Politics and the Built Environment*, Routledge, 2020, pp14–18.
28 Guillery and Kroll, pp62–3.
29 Briggs, p343.
30 Historic England, 'Royal Courts of Justice: The law courts, screen walls, gates, railings and lamps', https://historicengland.org.uk/listing/the-list/list-entry/1264258, accessed 27 April 2021.
31 J Gelder, *Specifying Architecture: A Guide to Professional Practice*, Construction Information Systems Australia, 2001, p9.
32 Ibid., p9.
33 D Maudlin, 'Beginnings, early colonial architecture', in GA Bremner, *Architecture and Urbanism in the British Empire*, Oxford University Press, 2020, p24.
34 C.Webster, 'The Architectural Profession in Leeds 1800-50: A case study in provincial practice', Architectural History, 1995, Vol 38 pp. 176–191
35 Jenkins, pp207–10.
36 Wilton-Ely, p196.
37 Briggs, p328.
38 Bremner, pp23–4.
39 Kaye, pp68–72.
40 Briggs, pp360–2.
41 Ibid., p364.
42 Gotsch, pp99–114.

Chapter 4

1 B Kaye, *The Development of the Architectural Profession in Britain*, George Allen & Unwin Ltd, 1960, p150.
2 JA Gotsch, *The Growth and Work of the Royal Institute of British Architects 1834–1934*, Simson & Co. Ltd, 1934, p48.
3 RIBA, 'Architects in the First World War', https://www.architecture.com/knowledge-and-resources/knowledge-landing-page/architects-and-the-first-world-war, accessed 17 July 2021.
4 Gotsch, pp161–2.
5 L Walker, 'An irresistible movement', in E Darling and L Walker, *AA Women in Architecture 1917–2012*, AA Publications, 2017, pp6–14.
6 Ibid., p14.
7 Ibid.
8 Ibid., pp6–14.
9 N Shasore, *Designs on Democracy: Architecture and the Public in Interwar London*, Oxford University Press, forthcoming, p21 of manuscript.
10 Ibid.
11 Ibid., pp20–1 (MS).
12 Kaye, p147.
13 Kaye, pp147–8.
14 Shasore, p21 (MS).
15 Ibid., p23 (MS).
16 Kaye, p147.
17 Shasore, pp23–4 (MS).
18 Kaye, pp152–3.
19 Ibid., p151.
20 Shasore, pp25–6 (MS).
21 Gotsch, pp78–9.
22 Hansard, Debate 8 April 1927, vol. 204, C2435.
23 Kaye, pp152–3.
24 Ibid., pp153–4.
25 Shasore, p23 (MS).
26 Kaye pp155–6.
27 Gotsch, p93.
28 Walker, p14.
29 Ibid., p23.
30 Walker, p134.
31 Kaye, pp160–1.
32 A Powers, *Architectural Education in Britain 1880–1914*, The University of Cambridge, 1983, p16.
33 Ibid., pp12–13.
34 Gotsch, pp49–50.
35 UK Parliament, 'Council housing', https://www.parliament.uk/about/living-heritage/transformingsociety/towncountry/towns/overview/councilhousing/, accessed 17 July 2021.
36 AJ Ley, 'Historical aspects of building control', Incorporated Association of Architects and Surveyors conference paper, October 1982.
37 Ibid.
38 Ibid.
39 EW Cooney, 'Innovation and contracts in the post war British building industry', *Construction History*, vol. 3, pp115–24, 1987.
40 JCT, 'Our history', https://corporate.jctltd.co.uk/about-us/our-history/, accessed 26 June 2021.
41 J Gelder, *Specifying Architecture: A Guide to Professional Practice*, Construction Information Systems Australia, 2001, p10.
42 BRE Group, 'Our history', https://www.bregroup.com/about-us/our-history/, accessed 18 July 2021.
43 Shasore, p56 (MS).
44 Ibid., p58 (MS).
45 E Darling, 'Becoming truly alive', in Darling and Walker, pp32–4.
46 Shasore, pp58–63 (MS).
47 Ibid., p63 (MS).
48 Ibid., p67 (MS).
49 Ibid., p68 (MS).
50 Ibid., pp72–8 (MS).
51 RIBA records, 'Analysis of the work of the public relations committee in the session 1936–1937', 1926.
52 Shasore, p55 (MS).
53 K Lloyd Thomas, 'This strange interloper: Building products and the emergence of the architect-shopper in 1930s Britain', in E Darling and N Robert Walker, *Suffragette City*, Routledge, 2020, pp110–23.
54 Lloyd Thomas, p121.
55 HB Creswell, *The Honeywood File*, Acadey Chicago Publishers, 2000, p175.
56 Ibid., p212.
57 Lloyd Thomas, p120.
58 Ibid., p125.
59 J Summerson, *Bread and Butter and Architecture*, Horizon, 1942, pp233–4.
60 Ibid, p233.
61 Kaye, pp163–4.
62 Summerson, p234.
63 Kaye, p164.
64 S Foxell, *Professionalism for the Built Environment*, Routledge, 2019, p144.
65 Kaye, p166.
66 Foxell, p144.
67 Ibid., p144.
68 Ibid., p146.
69 Ibid., pp146–7.
70 Shasore, pp26–7 (MS).

Chapter 5

1 Britannica, 'The Blitz', https://www.britannica.com/event/the-Blitz, accessed 16 October 2021.
2 The National Archives, 'The Cabinet Papers', https://www.nationalarchives.gov.uk/cabinetpapers/themes/wartime-housing.htm, accessed 16 October 2021.
3 Hansard, 'Building (Licensing) Termination', https://api.parliament.uk/historic-hansard/commons/1954/nov/02/building-licensing-termination, accessed 16 October 2021.
4 S Foxell, *Professionalism for the Built Environment*, Routledge, 2019, p149.
5 L Keay, *RIBA Journal*, 1946.
6 Ibid.
7 L Walker, 'Albery, Jessica Mary (1908–1990)', *Oxford Dictionary of National Biography*, https://doi.org/10.1093/odnb/9780198614128.013.112259, accessed July 2019.

8 R Spaven, 'Leverkus, Gertrude Wilhelmine Margaret (1898–1989)', *Oxford Dictionary of National Biography*, https://doi.org/10.1093/odnb/9780198614128.013.111927, accessed July 2019.
9 E Darling, 'Robertson [*née* Lewis], Doris Adeney, Lady Robertson (1899–1981), *Oxford Dictionary of National Biography*, https://doi.org/10.1093/odnb/9780198614128.013.369119, accessed July 2019.
10 L Walker, 'Albery, Jessica Mary (1908–1990)'.
11 R Spaven, 'Leverkus, Gertrude Wilhelmine Margaret (1898–1989)'.
12 L Walker, 'Aiton [*married name* Tollenaar], Norah (1903–1988), *Oxford Dictionary of National Biography*, https://doi.org/10.1093/odnb/9780198614128.013.112257, accessed July 2019.
13 Architects Registration Board, *Annual Report*, 2021.
14 E Darling, 'Drew, Dame Joyce Beverly [Jane] (1911–1996)', *Oxford Dictionary of National Biography*, https://doi.org/10.1093/ref:odnb/60171, accessed September 2014.
15 *RIBA Journal*, June 1945.
16 *RIBA Journal*, July 1947.
17 'The Architect's Dilemma', *The Economist*, 25 July 1953.
18 Ibid.
19 NM Day, 'The role of the architect in post-war state housing: A case study of the housing work of the London County Council, 1939–1956', The University of Warwick, 1988, pp119–21.
20 F Jenkins, *Architect and Patron: A Survey of Professional Relations and Practice in England from the Sixteenth Century to the Present Day*, Oxford University Press, 1961, p235.
21 *RIBA Journal*, October 1948.
22 M Floyd, *RIBA Journal*, December 1966.
23 Editorial, *RIBA Journal*, June 1945.
24 *RIBA Journal*: January 1949, December 1953, November 1959.
25 G Barry, 'The Festival of Britain: 1951', *Journal of the Royal Society of Arts*, vol. 100, no. 4880, August 1952, pp667–704.
26 Ibid., pp688–9.
27 Ibid., pp689–94.
28 *RIBA Journal*, September 1951.
29 Day, pp91–2.
30 E Harwood, 'White light/white heat: Rebuilding England's provincial towns and cities in the sixties', *Twentieth Century Architecture*, no. 6, 2002, pp56–70.
31 Ibid., pp58–9.
32 *RIBA Journal*, various 1945–8.
33 M Briggs, *RIBA Journal*, May 1951.
34 *RIBA Journal*, June 1958.
35 Ray Varrell, personal communication, 2021.
36 Ibid.
37 *RIBA Journal*, November 1959.
38 *RIBA Journal*, June 1958.
39 Foxell, p181.
40 *RIBA Journal*, February 1957.
41 *RIBA Journal*, June 1958.
42 M Austin-Smith, A Derbyshire, D Howard, J Madge and J Milne, 'The architect and his office', RIBA, 1962, p13.
43 Ibid., p63.
44 Ibid., p185.
45 Ibid., p16.
46 Ibid.
47 Ibid., p15.
48 Ibid.
49 Ibid., p63.
50 Ibid.
51 Ibid, pp63, 81.
52 Ibid., p147.
53 Ibid., p80.
54 RIBA Plan of Work, https://www.architecture.com/knowledge-and-resources/resources-landing-page/riba-plan-of-work, accessed 2 September 2022.
55 Foxell, pp156–7.
56 Ibid., pp157–8.
57 G Stamp, 'I was Lord Kitchener's valet or, how the Vic Soc saved London', *Twentieth Century Architecture*, no. 6, 2002, p142.
58 E Harwood and A Powers, 'From downturn to diversity, revisting the 1970s', *Twentieth Century Architecture*, no. 10, 2012, p14.
59 Stamp, pp130–44.
60 AJ Ley, 'Historical aspects of building control', Incorporated Association of Architects and Surveyors conference paper, Bournemouth, October 1982.
61 Ibid.
62 Simon Report, 1944.
63 Phillips Report, 1950.
64 J Masterman, *Introduction to Building Procurement*, Taylor and Francis, 2002, p31.
65 Ibid.
66 Emmerson Report, 1962.
67 Banwell Report, 1964.
68 Masterman, p32.
69 Ibid.
70 Ibid., p33.
71 Ibid., pp32–3.

Chapter 6

1 R Waite, 'RIBA to bin "outdated" fee scale graphs', *Architects' Journal*, 22 October 2009, https://www.architectsjournal.co.uk/archive/riba-to-bin-outdated-fee-scale-graphs, accessed 23 March 2022.
2 S Foxell, *Professionalism for the Built Environment*, Routledge, 2019, p216.
3 Architects Registration Board, Annual Report, 2015.
4 Foxell, p196.
5 Foxell, pp196–7.
6 F Samuel, *Why Architects Matter*, Routledge, 2018, pp14–16.
7 D Chappell and M Dunn, *The Architect in Practice*, Wiley Blackwell, 2016, p111.
8 Conversation with Bob Allies, 5 December 2021.
9 D Bennetts, in A Jones and R Hyde, *Defining Contemporary Professionalism*, RIBA Publishing, p18.
10 Ibid., pp18–19.
11 RIBA, 'Education statistics 2015/16', https://www.architecture.com/-/media/gathercontent/education-statistics/additional-documents/educationstatistics201516pdf.pdf, accessed 8 March 2022.
12 legislation.gov.uk, 'Sex Discrimination Act 1975', https://www.legislation.gov.uk/ukpga/1975/65/enacted, accessed 29 January 2022.
13 Foxell, pp189–90.
14 O Wainwright, 'Snubbed, cheated, denied, erased: The scandal of architecture's invisible women', Guardian, 16 October 2018, https://www.theguardian.com/artanddesign/2018/oct/16/the-scandal-of-architecture-invisible-women-denise-scott-brown, accessed 29 January 2022.
15 R Ainley, 'Tributaries, flow and an extraordinary alchemy', in E Darling and L Walker, *AA Women in Architecture 1917–2012*, AA Publications, 2017, p158.
16 Conversation with Graham Morrison, 15 February 2021.
17 Allies and Morrison, 'Joanna Bacon', https://www.alliesandmorrison.com/people/joanna-bacon, accessed 29 January 2022.
18 Reed Inauguration Speech, RIBA Archives, 2009.
19 Architects Registration Board, 'ARB publishes its latest annual report', 16 July 2020, https://arb.org.uk/arb-publishes-its-latest-annual-report-nr20/, accessed 29 January 2022.
20 UWE, 'Why do women leave architecture?, 3 July 2003, https://info.uwe.ac.uk/news/uwenews/news.aspx?id=371#:~:text=Carried%20out%20by%20the%20University,women%20to%20leave%20the%20profession, accessed 29 January 2022.
21 S Manley and A de Graft-Johnson, 'Women in architecture: Five years on', University of the West of England, 2008, p1.
22 ons.gov.uk, 'Population estimates by ethnic group and religion, England and Wales: 2019', https://www.ons.gov.uk/peoplepopulationandcommunity/populationandmigration/populationestimates/articles/populationestimatesbyethnicgroupandreligionenglandandwales/2019#:~:text=1.-,Main%20points,increased%20by%200.9%20percentage%20points, accessed 29 January 2022.
23 Ibid.
24 The National Archives, 'Black and minority ethnic representation in the built environment professions', June 2005, https://webarchive.nationalarchives.gov.uk/ukgwa/20110118095356/http:/www.cabe.org.uk/files/minority-ethnic-representation-in-the-built-environment-professions.pdf, accessed 4 December 2021.
25 Third Sector, 'Stephen Lawrence charity rebrands because family is no longer associated with it', 17 December 2020, https://www.thirdsector.co.uk/stephen-lawrence-charity-rebrands-family-no-longer-associated/communications/article/1703157, accessed 29 January 2022.
26 Penoyre & Prasad, 'Sunand Prasad: Principal', https://www.penoyreprasad.com/our-people/sunand-prasad/, accessed 29 January 2022.
27 J Masterman, *Introduction to Building Procurement*, Taylor and Francis, 2002, pp35–6.
28 Ibid., p36.
29 Ibid.
30 M Latham, 'Constructing the team', HMSO, 1994.
31 Ibid.
32 Constructing Excellence, 'About Constructing Excellence', https://constructingexcellence.

org.uk/about/, accessed 23 January 2022.
33 Considerate Constructors Scheme, 'History of the Considerate Constructors Scheme', https://www.ccscheme.org.uk/ccs-ltd/history-css-ltd/, accessed 23 January 2022.
34 Masterman, pp40, 232.
35 S Boudjabeur, 'Design and build defined', in P Stephenson (ed.), 13th Annual ARCOM Conference, 15–17 September 1997, Association of Researchers in Construction Management, vol. 1, p72.
36 Ibid., p78.
37 Ibid.
38 Report of the Independent Inquiry into the Construction of Edinburgh Schools, February 2017, p228.
39 Ibid., p241.
40 Conversation with Bob Allies and Graham Morrison, 15 December 2021.
41 S Akboy-Ilk, 'The nature of drawing in the changing culture of architectural documentation', *Journal of Architectural and Planning Research*, vol. 33, no. 1, pp33–4.
42 Ibid., p34.
43 Conversation with Paul Crosby, November 2021.
44 *RIBA Journal*, RIBA Publishing, June 1948.
45 Architects Registration Board, 'About ARB', https://arb.org.uk/about-arb/, accessed 29 January 2022.
46 E Jolliffe, 'A short history of protection of title', *Building Design*, https://www.bdonline.co.uk/opinion/a-short-history-of-protection-of-title/5101704.article, accessed 29 January 2022.

Chapter 7

1 M Hall, *The Burlington Magazine*, vol. 149, no. 1252, 'Italian art and architecture', July 2007.
2 F Duffy, *Architectural Knowledge: The Idea of a Profession*, FN Spon, 1998.
3 See Chapter 6.
4 See Chapter 6.
5 UK Parliament, 'Into Europe', https://www.parliament.uk/about/living-heritage/transformingsociety/trade industry/importexport/overview/europe/, accessed 27 June 2022.
6 OJEU, https://www.ojeu.eu/, accessed 5 September 2022.
7 The World Bank, 'The World Bank in China overview', www.worldbank.org/en/country/china/overview, accessed 28 June 2022.
8 Y Song, D Stead and M de Jong, 'New town development and sustainable transition under urban entrepreneurialism in China', *Sustainability*, vol. 12, 2020, p5179, . https://doi.org/10.3390/su12125179, accessed 6th July 2022.
9 W Shepard, *Ghost Cities of China: The Story of Cities Without People in the World's Most Populated Country*, Zed Books, 2015.
10 See Chapter 6.
11 'Architecture in progress: Internationale Bauausstellung Berlin 1984', *Architectural Design*, vol. 53, 1 January 1984.
12 British Library, 'Architecture and design of the British Library', https://www.bl.uk/about-us/our-story/explore-the-building/architecture-and-design-of-the-british-library, accessed 5 September 2022.
13 https://www.pritzkerprize.com, accessed 6 June 2022.
14 'The Bilbao Effect', *The Economist*, 14 August 2018, www.economist.com/special-report/2018/08/14/the-bilbao-effect, accessed 5 September 2022.
15 D Ponzini and M Nastasi, *Starchitecture: Scenes, Actors, and Spectacles in Contemporary Cities*, Umberto Allemandi & Co., 2012.
16 D Sudjic, 'Building a bolder future', Guardian, 20 August 2006, https://www.theguardian.com/artanddesign/2006/aug/20/architecture, accessed 29 June 2022.
17 O Arup, Inaugural Speech, Building Services Engineering Society, 26 October 1972.
18 O Wainwright, 'The Public: An inevitable end for the misguided arts centre', the *Guardian*, 14 August 2013, www.theguardian.com/artanddesign/architecture-design-blog/2013/aug/14/public-inevitable-end-arts-centre-architecture, accessed 5 September 2022.
19 Parliament.uk, 'Funding of the arts', https://publications.parliament.uk/pa/cm201011/cmselect/cmcumeds/464/46405.htm#a7, accessed 5 September 2022.
20 D Ward and K O'Hara, 'Bankruptcy threatens pop music centre', Guardian, 19 October 1999, www.theguardian.com/uk/1999/oct/19/davidward, accessed 5 September 2022.
21 E Heathcote, 'Turner Contemporary, Margate, Kent', *The Financial Times*, 5 April 2011, https://www.ft.com/content/3c4c54cc-5fab-11e0-a718-00144feab49a, accessed 6 June 2022.
22 Turner Contemporary, https://turnercontemporary.org, accessed 5 September 2022.
23 Heathcote, 2011.
24 RIBA, Plan of Work 2020.
25 D McNeill, *The Global Architect: Firms, Fame and Urban Form*, Routledge, 2009.
26 K Frampton, 'Towards a critical regionalism: Six points for an architecture of resistance', in H Foster (ed.), *The Anti-Aesthetic: Essays on Postmodern Culture*, Bay Press, 1983.
27 'Xi Jinping isn't a fan of weird architecture in China', *The Wall Street Journal*, 17 October 2014, www.wsj.com/articles/BL-CJB-24505, accessed 5 September 2022.
28 2020 Architects Council of Europe study.
29 L Monks and A Fourth (eds), *Global Talent, Global Reach*, RIBA, 2017.
30 The Danish Association of Architects, https://arkitektforeningen.dk/english/, accessed 5 September 2022.
31 RSHP, 'Centre Pompidou', https://rshp.com/projects/culture-and-leisure/centre-pompidou/, accessed 26 June 2022.
32 OMA, 'CCTV – Headquarters', https://www.oma.com/projects/cctv-headquarters, accessed 5 September 2022.
33 RIBA Business Benchmarking Report 2016.
34 ARB PII Guidance, https://arb.org.uk/architect-information/professional-indemnity-insurance/pii-guidance/, accessed 5 September 2022.
35 FIDIC, https://fidic.org, accessed 5 September 2022.
36 V Pitt, 'Austin-Smith:Lord reaches agreement with creditors to avoid insolvency', *Building*, 5 December 2011, accessed 5 September 2022.
37 VKH Platt, 'Copycat architects in China take aim at the stars', *Spiegel International*, 28 December 2012, https://www.spiegel.de/international/zeitgeist/pirated-copy-of-design-by-star-architect-hadid-being-built-in-china-a-874390.html, accessed 5 September 2022.
38 Companies House, Zaha Hadid Ltd Full Accounts made up to 30 April 2021.
39 J Riach, 'Zaha Hadid defends Qatar World Cup role following migrant worker deaths', *Guardian*, 25 February 2014, https://www.theguardian.com/world/2014/feb/25/zaha-hadid-qatar-world-cup-migrant-worker-deaths, accessed 5 September 2022.
40 H Cooper, 'Spielberg drops out as advisor to Beijing Olympics in dispute over Darfur conflict', *New York Times*, 13 February 2008.
41 T Dyckhoff, 'We can help change in China say architects Herzog and de Meuron', *The Times*, 12 March 2008.
42 J Duncan, FCDO Editorial, 13 February 2017.
43 The Architects Code: Standards of Professional Conduct and Practice, p16.
44 UIA, 'UIA on recommended international standards of professionalism in architectural practice', 2017, https://www.uia-architectes.org/wp-content/uploads/2022/03/uia_accord___updated_2017.pdf, accessed 5 September 2022.
45 UIA Accord on Recommended International Standards of Professionalism in Architectural Practice (amended September 2017)
46 R Venturi, Pritzker Prize Jury Citation, https://www.pritzkerprize.com/laureates/1991, accessed 5 September 2022.
47 Pritzker Letter, Lord Peter Palumbo Chair of the Jury, 2013.
48 Jury Citation Pritzker Prize 2020, https://www.pritzkerprize.com/laureates/2020, accessed 9 September 2022.
49 Jury Citation Pritzker Prize 2012, https://www.pritzkerprize.com/laureates/2012, accessed 9 September 2022.
50 Jury Citation Pritzker Prize 2022, https://www.pritzkerprize.com/laureates/diebedo-francis-kere, accessed 9 September 2022.
51 https://davidchipperfield.com/bibliography/essays/venise_canal_collectif_, accessed 9 September 2022
52 La Biennale di Venezia, 'Biennale Architettura 2016', https://www.labiennale.org/en/architecture/2016, accessed 5 September 2022.

53 R Waite, 'ARB figures reveal exodus of EU architects', *Architects' Journal*, 8 March 2022, https://www.architectsjournal.co.uk/news/a-third-of-all-architects-booted-off-arb-register-were-from-eu, accessed 5 September 2022.
54 Egan Report, Chapter 9.
55 Gov.uk, 'Brexit guidance', https://www.gov.uk/brexit, accessed 5 September 2022.
56 Monks and Fourth, 2017.

Chapter 8

1 J Cleese and G Chapman, 'The Architects Sketch' script, *Monty Python's Flying Circus*, www.mit.edu/afs.new/sipb/user/ayshames/Python/ARCHITEC.PYTHON, accessed 6 September 2022.
2 Grenfell Tower Inquiry, https://www.grenfelltowerinquiry.org.uk/, accessed 9 September 2022.
3 Arup, 'Ove Arup Key Speech', 9 July 1970, https://www.arup.com/perspectives/publications/speeches-and-lectures/section/ove-arup-key-speech, accessed 6 September 2022.
4 See Chapter 5.
5 *The Times*, 12 February 1974.
6 See Chapter 6.
7 R Moore, 'Architects do matter, Mr Gove', Guardian, 6 March 2011, www.theguardian.com/artanddesign/2011/mar/06/michael-gove-architecture-in-schools, accessed 6 September 2022.
8 UK Practical Law: Luton Borough Council and others v Secretary of State for Education [2011] EWHC 217, accessed 6 September 2022.
9 HRH The Prince of Wales, 'A speech by HRH The Prince of Wales at the 150th anniversary of the Royal Institute of British Architects (RIBA), Royal Gala Evening at Hampton Court Palace', https://www.princeofwales.gov.uk/speech/speech-hrh-prince-wales-150th-anniversary-royal-institute-british-architects-riba-royal-gala, accessed 6 September 2022.
10 HRH The Prince of Wales, *A Vision of Britain: A Personal View of Architecture*, Doubleday, 1989.
11 S Bayley, 'I'll show you a real carbuncle, Charles', *Guardian*, 7 December 2008, https://www.theguardian.com/commentisfree/2008/dec/07/poundbury-prince-charles-communities, accessed 6 September 2022.
12 J Self, 'Mies's Mansion House Square: The best building London never had?', *Guardian*, 11 February 2017, https://www.theguardian.com/cities/2017/feb/11/mies-van-der-rohe-mansion-house-square-best-building-london-never-had, accessed 9 September 2022.
13 S Creigh-Tyte and J Gallimore, 'The UK National Lottery and the arts: Reflections on the Lottery's impact and development', *International Journal of Arts Management*, vol 3, no. 1, 2000, pp19–31, https://www.jstor.org/stable/41064709?seq=1#metadata_info_tab_contents, accessed 6 September 2022.
14 Heritage Fund, 'About', https://www.heritagefund.org.uk/about, accessed 6 September 2022.
15 I West-Knights, 'Was the Millennium Dome really that bad? The inside story of a (not so) total disaster', *Guardian*, 12 March 2020, https://www.theguardian.com/uk-news/2020/mar/12/millennium-dome-experience-disaster-inside-story-new-labour, accessed 6 September 2022.
16 *Construction Reports 1944–98*, Wiley-Blackwell, 2003.
17 Constructing the Team: The Latham Report, 1994, p62, para. 6.45.
18 CIC, https://www.cic.org.uk, accessed 6 September 2022.
19 Rethinking Construction: The Egan Report, clause 61, p28.
20 Rethinking Construction: The Report of the Construction Task Force, https://constructingexcellence.org.uk/wp-content/uploads/2014/10/rethinking_construction_report.pdf, accessed 6 September 2022.
21 Constructing Excellence, https://constructingexcellence.org.uk/, accessed 6 September 2022.
22 HSE, The Construction (Design and Management) Regulations 2015, https://www.hse.gov.uk/construction/cdm/2015/index.htm, accessed 6 September 2022.
23 BDP, '60 years of design', https://www.bdp.com/en/about/history/, accessed 6 September 2022.
24 issuu, 'Building on our values', https://issuu.com/bdp_com/docs/annual-review-2021/s/12702366, accessed 6 September 2022.
25 issuu, 'The YRM Partnership', https://issuu.com/tecnospa/docs/edition, accessed 6 September 2022.
26 O Arup, 'The Maitland Lecture', Institution of Structural Engineers, 14 November 1968, *Arup Journal*, vol. 20, no. 1, Spring 1985.
27 Constructing the Team: The Latham Report, 1994, Chapter 5, paragraph 5.30, p42.
28 T Bingham, The JCT Povey Lecture, 13 November 2014.
29 NBS, 'National construction contracts and law survey 2015', https://www.thenbs.com/knowledge/national-construction-contracts-and-law-survey-2015, accessed 6 September 2022.
30 R Booth, 'Revealed: bitter row over BBC's £800m revamp that left architect out of a job', *Guardian*, 23 June 2008, https://www.theguardian.com/media/2008/jun/23/bbc.television, accessed 6 September 2022.
31 Constructing the Team.
32 Constructing the Team, Chapter 6, paragraph 6.18.
33 *Norman Foster Sketchbooks 1975–2020*, Norman Foster Foundation, 2021.
34 CDM 2105.
35 Gov.uk, 'Guidance: Planning obligations', https://www.gov.uk/guidance/planning-obligations, accessed 6 September 2022.
36 The London Plan, https://www.london.gov.uk/what-we-do/planning/london-plan, accessed 6 September 2022.
37 Gov.uk, 'Living with beauty: Report of the Building Better, Building Beautiful Commission', https://www.gov.uk/government/publications/living-with-beauty-report-of-the-building-better-building-beautiful-commission, accessed 6 September 2022.
38 RIBA, 'Design matters: Promoting good design through the planning system', https://www.architecture.com/knowledge-and-resources/resources-landing-page/design-matters-promoting-good-design-through-the-planning-system, accessed 6 September 2022.
39 www.architecture.com/education-cpd-and-careers/riba-validation/riba-validated-schools-uk, accessed 6 September 2022.
40 Hampstead and Highgate planning permission Athlone House, https://www.highgatesociety.com/media/news/Athlone%20House%2035.33-34%20for%20Ham-High.pdf
41 Gov.uk, 'Planning for the future', www.gov.uk/government/consultations/planning-for-the-future, accessed 6 September 2022.
42 https://www.architecture.com/knowledge-and-resources/knowledge-landing-page/riba-expresses-serious-concern-about-new-planning-laws, accessed 1 September 2022
43 See Chapter 6.
44 Statista, 'Share of construction industry professionals using building information modelling (BIM) in the United Kingdom (UK) from 2011 to 2020', https://www.statista.com/statistics/1019177/construction-industry-bim-adoption-rate-uk/, accessed 6 September 2022.
45 See Chapter 6.
46 See Chapter 7.
47 CATIA, https://www.3ds.com/products-services/catia/, accessed 6 September 2022.
48 RIBA, 'Client and architect – developing the essential relationship', 2015, https://www.architecture.com/knowledge-and-resources/resources-landing-page/client-and-architect-developing-the-essential-relationship, accessed 6 September 2022.
49 UK Green Building Council, https://www.ukgbc.org/our-mission, accessed 9 September 2022.
50 Bedzed, www.zedfactory.com/bedzed
51 The Code for Sustainable Homes, 2007, https://assets.publishing.service.gov.uk/government/uploads/system/uploads/attachment_data/file/7787/1161997.pdf, accessed 9 September 2022.
52 Building a Safer Future: The Hackitt Report, 2018, https://assets.publishing.service.gov.uk/government/uploads/system/uploads/attachment_data/file/707785/Building_a_Safer_Future_-_web.pdf, accessed 6 September 2022.
53 Gov.uk, The Building Safety Act, https://www.gov.uk/government/collections/

building-safety-bill, accessed 6 September 2022.
54 Building a Safer Future: The Hackitt Report, 2018.
55 O O'Neill, 'Reith Lecture 2002: A question of trust', www.bbc.co.uk/sounds/play/p00gpzc5, accessed 6 September 2022.
56 Bingham, 2014.

Chapter 9

1 A Bairstow and S Roaf (eds), *The Oxford Conference A Re-evaluation of Education in Architecture*, WIT Press, 2008.
2 UCAS, 'A Levels', https://www.ucas.com/further-education/post-16-qualifications/qualifications-you-can-take/levels, accessed 6 September 2022.
3 BMA, https://www.bma.org.uk, accessed 6 September 2022.
4 Johns Hopkins Medicine, 'The founding physicians', https://www.hopkinsmedicine.org/about/history/history-of-jhh/founding-physicians.html, accessed 6 September 2022.
5 ARB, 'ARB criteria', https://arb.org.uk/information-for-schools-of-architecture/arb-criteria, accessed 6 September 2022.
6 RIBA Procedures for Validation, 1 September 2021.
7 'Modernising architectural education and training'. Analysis report on ARB's IET survey, 2 October 2021 to 10 January 2022, https://arb.org.uk/modernising-architectural-education-and-training/, accessed 20 September 2022
8 F Samuel, RIBA Education Forum & Council, 'Context – architectural education and research', 14 April 2015, https://www.youtube.com/watch?v=uzOEBRFhNRE, accessed 6 September 2022.
9 P Buchanan, 'What is wrong with architectural education? Almost everything', *Architectural Review*, 1989, pp24–6.
10 The Creative Life, 'Scenius: why creatives are stronger together', https://thecreativelife.net/scenius/, accessed 6 September 2022.
11 RIBA, 'Client and architect – developing the essential relationship', 2015, https://www.architecture.com/knowledge-and-resources/resources-landing-page/client-and-architect-developing-the-essential-relationship, accessed 6 September 2022.
12 S Allford, David Dunster 1945–2019', *RIBA Journal*, 13 February 2019, https://www.ribaj.com/buildings/david-dunster-1945-2019-simon-allford, accessed 6 September 2022.
13 University of Liverpool, 'David Dunster 1945–2019', https://www.liverpool.ac.uk/architecture/news/stories/title,1102750,en.html, accessed 6 September 2022.
14 Flora Samuel, RIBA Education Forum and Council, 2015, accessed 9 September 2022.
15 P Morrell, *Collaboration for Change – The Edge Commission Report on the Future of Professionalism*, 2015.
16 RIBA, 'Client and architect – developing the essential relationship', 2015
17 Ibid.
18 RIBA, 'Our history, Charter and Byelaws', https://www.architecture.com/about/history-charter-and-byelaws, accessed 6 September 2022.
19 'Ideal practice: Architecture and education – Zaha Hadid, Dalibor Vesely, Peter Wilson', 7 May 2015, https://www.youtube.com/watch?v=Bpyw-IB3B3k, accessed 6 September 2022.
20 Howlett Brown Report, 2022.
21 Ibid., Clause 101.
22 'Architectural Education Symposium: Closing lecture', 5 November 2004, https://www.youtube.com/watch?v=AEiWlxY8z3I, accessed 6 September 2022.
23 P Schumacher, World Architecture Lecture, 10 July 2019.
24 RIBA, *Study Architecture Well*, https://www.architecture.com/knowledge-and-resources/resources-landing-page/support-guides-for-students-and-early-career-architects, accessed 6 September 2022.
25 RIBA Education Department, RIBA 2015 Student Finances Survey, April 2016.
26 RIBA Salary Guide 2022, https://jobs.architecture.com/staticpages/10290/salary-guide-2022-architects-and-architecture/, accessed 11 September 2022.
27 L Milliner, 'Delight in transgression', in D Nicol and S Pilling (eds), *Changing Architectural Education: Towards a New Professionalism*, E & FN Spon, 2000, pp192–9.
28 Architectural Association, 'History of the AA', https://www.aaschool.ac.uk/about/history, accessed 6 September 2022.
29 P Zamarian, 'The origins of the Oxford Conference within the networks of 1930s student activism', *The Journal of Architecture*, vol. 24, no. 4, 2019, pp571–92.
30 AA Prospectus 1997.
31 RIBA, 'RIBA President's initial response to the Future Architects Front open letter from students and architectural assistants', 11 February 2021, www.architecture.com/knowledge-and-resources/knowledge-landing-page/riba-responds-to-future-architects-front-open-letter, accessed 6 September 2022.
32 A Jones, RIBA initial response to FAF letter, https://www.architecture.com/knowledge-and-resources/knowledge-landing-page/riba-responds-to-future-architects-front-open-letter, accessed 9 September 2022.
33 'RER', www.architecture.com/knowledge-and-resources/resources-landing-page/riba-education-review
34 S Hodder, 'Common purpose', *RIBA Journal*, 1 January 2014.
35 D Gloster, quoted in 'How long can architecture schools resist reform?', *Building Design*, 29 August 2019.
36 The National Archives, 'Inquiry into a fire at Summerland Leisure Centre, Douglas, Isle of Man, 2 August 1973', https://discovery.nationalarchives.gov.uk/details/r/C90254, accessed 6 September 2022.
37 Grenfell Tower Inquiry, 'Day 63 transcript', https://www.grenfelltowerinquiry.org.uk/hearings?witnesses%5B927%5D=927, accessed 6 September 2022.
38 Ibid.
39 RIBA, 'RIBA validated schools in the UK', https://www.architecture.com/education-cpd-and-careers/riba-validation/riba-validated-schools-uk, accessed 6 September 2022.
40 AHTR, '"Learning and unlearning" Using Bauhaus exercises in art history classes', https://arthistoryteachingresources.org/2018/03/learning-and-unlearning-using-hands-on-bauhaus-exercises-in-art-history-classes/, accessed 6 September 2022.
41 St John's College, University of Cambridge, '"Anti-building" for the future: The world of Cedric Price', https://www.joh.cam.ac.uk/anti-building-future-world-cedric-price, accessed 6 September 2022.
42 L Mark, 'Interview: Will Hunter, founder of the London School of Architecture', *Architects' Journal*, 24 July 2015, accessed 26 June 2022.
43 RIBA, 'Architecture apprenticeships', https://www.architecture.com/education-cpd-and-careers/apprenticeships, accessed 6 September 2022.
44 RICS, 'Sector pathways', https://www.rics.org/uk/surveying-profession/join-rics/sector-pathways/, accessed 6 September 2022.
45 ARB, 'ARB announces fundamental reforms to architectural education', 7 October 2021, https://arb.org.uk/arb-announces-fundamental-reforms-to-architectural-education-2/, accessed 6 September 2022.
46 Architects Climate Action Network, https://www.architectscan.org/stucan, accessed 28 July 2022.
47 ARB Analysis Report - Modernising Initial Education and Training – ARB's IET survey 2 October 2021 to 10 January 2022

Chapter 10

1 P Morrell, *Collaboration for Change*, The Edge, 2015.
2 H Carey, D O Brien and O Gamble, *Social Mobility in the Creative Economy: Rebuilding and Levelling Up*, Creative Industries Policy and Evidence Centre, September 2021, https://cdn2.assets-servd.host/creative-pec/production/assets/publications/PEC-report-Social-mobility-in-the-Creative-Economy-Sept-2021.pdf, accessed 11 June 2022.
3 Open letter to the RIBA, 30 January 2021.
4 E Jessel, 'AJ investigation: Architectural assistants break silence on poor working practices', *Architects' Journal*, 24 March 2021, https://www.architectsjournal.co.uk/news/aj-investigation-architectural-assistants-break-silence-on-poor-working-practices, accessed 7 September 2022.
5 SAW presentation to AA Part 3 candidates, 12 March 2022.

Index

C

D

J

K

L

M

N

O

P

T

U

V

W

Y

Z

Image credits

pp5, 6, 7 (*top and bottom*) © Metropolitan Museum of Art
p10 Wellcome Collection. Attribution 4.0 International
p13 © Metropolitan Museum of Art
p16 Wellcome Collection. Attribution 4.0 International
p18 © Metropolitan Museum of Art
p23 Art Institute Chicago 1979.350
p26 © J Paul Getty Museum
p29 © RIBA Collections
p32 National Gallery of Art 1957.14.125
p22 © RIBA Collections
p36 Würzburg Residenz, Martin von Wagner Museum Photo: Birgit Wörz.
P37 © Royal Collection
P38 © RIBA Collections
P41 © RIBA Collections
P43 © RIBA Collections
P44 © RIBA Collections
P46 © RIBA Collections
p50 *top* and *bottom* © RIBA Collections
p51 © RIBA Collections
p52 *top* and *bottom* © RIBA Collections
p53 © RIBA Collections
p54 © RIBA Collections
p57 © RIBA Collections
p58 © RIBA Collections
p59 © RIBA Collections
p62 *both* © RIBA Collections
p65 © RIBA Collections
p66 © RIBA Collections
p67 © RIBA Collections
p69 © RIBA Collections
p70 © RIBA Collections
pp70–71 © RIBA Collections
p74 © RIBA Collections
p75 © AA Archive
P80 © RIBA Collections
P82 © AA Archive
P85 © RIBA Collections
P86 © Tony Ray-Jones / RIBA Collections
pp88–9 © Architectural Press Archive / RIBA Collections
p91 *top and bottom* © Architectural Press Archive / RIBA Collections
p93 © Architectural Press Archive / RIBA Collections
p102 © Architectural Press Archive / RIBA Collections
p103 © Architectural Press Archive / RIBA Collections
p104 © RIBA Collections
p107 © AA Archive
p108 © RIBA Collections
p109 © RIBA Collections
p114 © Jean Symons / RIBA Collections
p115 © Architectural Press Archive / RIBA Collections
p116 © Architectural Press Archive / RIBA Collections
p117 © Colin Westwood / RIBA Collections
p119 © John Maltby / RIBA Collections
p124 *top and bottom* © John McCann / RIBA Collections
p125 © John McCann / RIBA Collections
p126 © John McCann / RIBA Collections
pp130–1 © Tony Ray-Jones / RIBA Collections
p132 © Architectural Press Archive / RIBA Collections
p133 © RIBA Collections
p143 © Morley von Sternberg / RIBA Collections
p144 © Dominic Harris / RIBA Collections
p146 © Dominic Harris / RIBA Collections
p151 © Crispin Boyle / RIBA Collections
pp152–3 © RIBA Collections
p158 © RIBA Collections
p159 © Henk Snoek / RIBA Collections
p163 © Jeremy Harrison / RIBA Collections
p166 © Nicola Jackson / RIBA Collections
p167 © JZA Photography / RIBA Collections
p170 © Emmanuel Thirard / RIBA Collections
p178 © Eric Firley / RIBA Collections
p182 © Anne-Katrin Purkiss / RIBA Collections
p186 © RIBA Collections
p187 *top* © Christopher Hope-Fitch / RIBA Collections; *bottom* © Tony Ray-Jones / RIBA Collections
p190 © Jon May / RIBA Collections
p193 © Martin Charles / RIBA Collections
p197 © Martin Charles / RIBA Collections
pp204–5 © Christopher Hope-Fitch / RIBA Collections
p217 © AA Archive
P218 © AA Archive
P224 © AA Archive
P228 © AA Archive